"The Strokes! The best band o̶
was there. In fact, I think I nea̶
been around the winter of 1999'. I was in NYC at that time
and was advised by Geoff Travis to go and see this new
band that he was involved with called The Strokes. I, of
course, paid no attention to this and decided to stay home
and play scrabble."

Jim Reid
The Jesus And Mary Chain

"There was an excitement in us when we arrived for our
first show. We were gonna play two new songs,
"Modern Age" and "Last Nite".
The room was so beautifully lit. Looking back, it was
probably a very small room, but at the time Luna looked
like a masterpiece, a square in the middle of the room,
orange walls, and a thing that was starting to happen, fans!"

Albert Hammond Jr.
The Strokes

"Without Luna Lounge, the history of rock would have
changed. I may never have met The Strokes. And, the
number one album of the decade may never have
existed at all."

Gordon Raphael
Record Producer

Wake Me When It's Over

My Life As A New York Rock Club Owner And The Story Of Luna Lounge

Rob Sacher

April 4, 2012

John,
Thank you for being a part of the story of my life!
Best wishes,
Rob

Selena Press
Brooklyn, New York
United States Of America

Copyright © 2012 by Rob Sacher

All rights reserved
Printed In the United States of America
First Edition

For information about permission to reproduce selections from this book, for bulk purchases, and for promotional issues, contact the author at rob@lunalounge.com.

Front and back cover by Jeff Sheinkopf

Library Of Congress Cataloging-In-Publication Data

Sacher, Rob
Wake Me When It's Over: My Life As A New York Rock Club Owner And The Story Of Luna Lounge
Rob Sacher -- 1st edition

ISBN 978-0-61554-045-0
1. Sacher, Rob – Luna Lounge – New York City
2. Rock music – Social aspects - Autobiography
3. Musical groups - Social customs late 20th century

Selena Press
143 Havemeyer Street
Brooklyn, NY 11211
SelenaPress.com

For Gus,
   A candle lit my way, but only for a moment,
but in that time the light that shown
showed me the way of love,
for it was my friend
   who gave me the light within his heart,
   and showed me his way
as we walked together through this world.

Photo Credits

Harry Chapin, photo by Steve Stout	36
Ray Davies on stage – 1977, photo by Leahtwosaints	46
Ray Davies, photo by Leahtwosaints	46
Rick Danko, photo by Bob Sanderson	54
Richard Manuel, photo by Heinrich Klaffs	71
Levon Helm, photo by David Gans	71
Big Pink, photo by Johndan	71
Elliott Lloyd, photo by Justine Paioff	74
East Village buildings, photo by Sueann Harkey	78
William Tucker, photo by Chris Connelly	84
Bjork, photo by Masao Nakagami	92
Al Jourgensen, photo by Planetclairbear	106
Joey Ramone, photo by Dawkeye	116
Sarah Silverman, photo by Joan Garvin	180
Elliott Smith, photo by Constintina Trainwreck	198
Marty Willson-Piper, photo by John Stephen Coe	248

Above photos used by permission; photo credit requested.

Front cover, from left to right, top to bottom:
Steve Schiltz, Joey Ramone, Jody Porter, Ray Davies, Matt Long, Marty Willson-Piper, Marc Maron, Carlos D.
Back cover: Carla Capretto

Marty Willson-Piper, cover photo by John Stephen Coe

Acknowledgments

There are so many people who have shared in the story of Sanctuary, Mission, and Luna Lounge, I couldn't list everyone here so please accept my sincere apology if you do not see your name in this book. You know what your connection is and your memories are part of the collective consciousness of the clubs. I know that, you know that, and we know that we shared in it together. So, thank you from my heart.

For the folks who contributed in the writing of this book, my heartfelt thanks go out to Steve Schiltz, Gordon Raphael, Albert Hammond Jr., Kerri Black, Rob Lorenzo, Dave Kendall, Michael Hilf, Harold Kramer, Jonathan Daniel, Joe McGinty, Chris Connelly, Greg Fitzsimmons, Marc Maron, Amanda Schatz, Tabitha Tindale, Yanni Naslas, Carla Capretto, Shannon Ferguson, Shawn Christensen, Ed Rogers, Phil Schuster, Keith Hopkin, Adam Lippman, John Tirado, Kim Youngberg, Larry May, Lizzy Lee Vincent, Jack Rabid, andee blacksugar, Glenn Schloss, Brendan B. Brown, Dylan Nirvana, David Oromaner, Rebecca Moore, Rob Carlyle, Tyson Lewis, Chris Brocco, Christian Edwards, Joel Blecher, Brandon Wild, Christy Davis, Dave Ellis, Jodi Jett, Eric Butler, Jim Connolly, John Vitelli, Greg Welch, Daniel Stampfel, Wade Settle, Mauro Vegas, Greg Di Gesu, Jared Nissim, Jim Reid, Tony Lee, Bob O'Gureck, and a Pakistani deli cashier.

For the folks who gave me inspiration and encouragement; who listened to me as I fleshed out the stories, I extend my thanks to Stephan Cherkashin, Lance Rautzhan, David Fransen, Josh Gaffin, and Rich Diehl.

Special thanks to my friend, Steve Schiltz, songwriter and vocalist in Hurricane Bells, for the use of his song lyrics, "This Year".

Special thanks to the songwriter and poet, Steve Kilbey, vocalist and bass player in The Church, for the use of his song lyrics, "Field Of Mars".

Special thanks go out to Jeff Sheinkopf for his brilliant front and back cover design, and to my editors, Wendy Oneida and Robin Dark.

Last, I extend my gratitude to my very supportive family, Sue Posner (my mother), Paul Sacher (my father), Donna Hurd (my sister), her husband, Dan, and to my most awesome brother, Tommy, my sister-in-law Bridget, my nephew, Danny and his wife Christina and their children, my nephews Andrew, David, Julian and Brandon, my niece Taylor, and to my very special friends Sacha Lucas, Marty Willson-Piper, Mickey Leigh, Sean Schertell, Matt Sumrow, Matt Long, Jason Oliva, Jeffrey Szalkowski, Jody Porter, Dianne Galliano, Andy Inglis, Paul Dillon, Basil Scaperdas, Marc Philppe Eskenazi, Dana Distortion, Jaye Moore, Jeff Moore, Diva DEE, Aaron Minter, Mayumi Nashida, Robin Danar, Justin Mroz, J.C., Tony Zajkowski, Eric Altesleben, Michael Jurin, Helen Llewelyn, James Bray, and Cal Rifkin. You folks help me to believe in my own story and I will always appreciate your support. You ROCK!

Content

Introduction (With A Little Help From My Friends)   13
The Beginning – 1956
(Help Me Make It Through The Night)   17
Teenage Years (Break On Through To The Other Side)   31
Harry Chapin (Can't You Hear Me Knocking)   34
My Short Lived Publishing Deal (Blinded By The Light)   39
Ray Davies (Dedicated Follower Of Fashion)   43
The Pretenders and Johnny Depp (I'll Stand By You)   47
Debbie Harry
(I'm Always Touched By Your Presence, Dear)   49
Rick Danko (It Makes No Difference)   52
The Sanctuary (Do You Wanna Dance)   55
Simone Lester (I Will Take You Forever)   61
In The City (I Just Want To Have Something To Do)   65
Dianne (part one) (Anything, Anything, I'll Give You)   67
The Band (Knockin' On Heaven's Door)   69
Elliott Lloyd (Play That Funky Music)   73
The East Village (Walk On The Wild Side)   77
Mission: A Cast Of Characters (First, Last, And Always)   82
Psychedelic Furs (Into You Like A Train)   89
The Sugarcubes (Party Out Of Bounds)   93
John Moore (There's Something About You Girl)   95
Jerry Jaffe (People Are Strange)   99
The Jesus And Mary Chain
and Nine Inch Nails Party (A Hard Day's Night)   100
Ministry – The Industrial Music Scene
(You Know What You Are)   107
The Ancients (Touch The Fire)   110
Joey Ramone (I Remember You)   114

Joe McGinty (Take It As It Comes)	130
The Mentors (My Erection Is Over)	134
David Rockefeller (Down In It)	137
Sister Machine Gun/Warren Haynes (Riders On The Storm)	142
Elliott And The End Of His Life (The Long And Winding Road)	144
Selling Mission (Rehab)	146
London (All Day And All Of The Night)	148
Phillip Boa And The Voodoo Club (Satellite Man)	151
In Between Days (Halfway To Crazy)	153
Johnny Lydon (God Save The Queen)	155
The Lower East Side (Fairytale Of New York)	156
Luna Lounge (We're A Happy Family)	159
Lotion (First We Take Manhattan)	163
Sun Studio (That's All Right)	164
Valentino (The Lion Sleeps Tonight)	166
Adam Green (My Shadow Tags On Behind)	167
Jim Thirlwell And William Tucker (Steal Your Life Away)	169
Lydia Lunch (Are You Glad To Be In America)	174
Club Concept (Add Some Music To Your Day)	175
Eating It (What's So Funny 'Bout Peace, Love, And Understanding)	176
Jon Stewart (Mr. Big Stuff)	186
Eviction Proceedings (Breakin' The Law)	187
Dianne (part two) (When A Man Loves A Woman)	191
Elliott Smith (Somebody That I Used To Know – Bled White)	195
Sound Engineers (I Can Hear Music)	209
Jody Porter (Life Is Good)	214
The Basement (Yellow Submarine)	217
Sean Lennon (All You Need Is Love)	218
Disaster In The Basement (Sink To The Bottom With You)	220
Camper Van Beethoven (That Gum You Like Is Back In Style)	221

Jon Spencer (Blowing My Mind)	225
LunaSea Records	
(I Know It's Only Rock-n-Roll But I Like It)	226
Longwave (Make Me A Believer)	231
Marty Willson-Piper (Let Me Tell You A Secret)	241
The Strokes (part one) (Last Nite)	251
Gordon Raphael	
(Two Thousand Light Years From Home)	261
The Strokes (part two) (Is This It)	269
Our Bartenders And J. Mascis, Stephen Malkmus,	
Kevin Shields (Freak Scene)	272
Interpol (Turn On The Bright Lights)	274
Brian Wilson (You Still Believe In Me)	277
Totally Blind Drunk Drivers (We Are The Men)	280
Radio-Indie-Pop	
(Do You Remember Rock-n-Roll Radio)	282
Real Estate Killed The Video Star	
(Money Changes Everything)	285
Meeting The Girl That I Married	
(Baby's Got Her Own Ideas)	289
Luna Lounge In Williamsburg (Starting Over)	292
The Debacle Of Rob (Damn This Foolish Heart)	294
"This Year" lyrics	301
You Have To Take Care Of Yourself	
(Won't Get Fooled Again)	302
"Field Of Mars" lyrics	307
A New Beginning (Hanging On A Star)	309
Postcards From Paradise (Wish You Were Here)	315

Introduction
(With A Little Help From My Friends)

I must confess that the title for this book is not mine, it's borrowed from my good friend, Steve Schiltz, when he and the other members of his band, Longwave, wrote a song of the same title when they were on their first major tour in support of The Strokes' debut tour in the United Kingdom. I've always liked the evocative nature of the song's title, and the possibility that it could imply that one's time may, or may not, be going well. It's your own perspective; you may choose whatever meaning you may hear loudest. Or, you may, as I often do, feel both ways at the same time. I asked Steve to provide a bit of background,

"We wrote that song together, at a rehearsal hall in London called The Depot. This was right before a show in Glasgow, right before we did the UK dates with The Strokes. I was upstairs in the cafeteria of the place, and I ran into two guys from The Libertines. They were unknown then, just nice guys that wanted to talk to an American band that was going out with The Strokes. I heard this incredible music coming from below, and I couldn't focus on what Carl, The Libertines guy, was saying to me. I remember abruptly excusing myself and saying, listen to that, that's my band. I gotta go see what it is that they are playing. So, I walked in and the other three guys were playing the beginning of "Wake Me When It's Over". They were just fooling around. I had a little melody in my head that I began to sing, and they knew to keep playing until I got it right. We had the song arranged pretty quickly, and I turned over the words in my mind over the next couple of weeks in the UK, until I was happy with them.

    I remember singing it in soundcheck at the last show on our tour, in Dublin, at the Olympia Theater. I already knew that I loved that song. I was singing "Wake Me When It's Over" to an empty hall and it just felt like a perfect encapsulation of my feelings at that time. Longwave had already toured so much in our tiny van. We were finishing weeks of touring with The Strokes. We had some recording coming up, and more touring. I felt two things, very strongly. One, was just how lucky we were to be doing this, doing these tours and meeting people. The other was how tired I was, and how I missed my girlfriend and my friends back in New York. Sometimes, it definitely felt like, please, wake me when it's over."

    This book is about my time with friends, mostly musicians, and the music they created to which in my life I have connected. There are some places in my book where I cannot help but end some lines in rhyme. It's the musician and songwriter in me, always open and willing to connect and complete a musical idea. Feedback, distortion, reverb, chorusing and delay are all metaphors of musical articulation denoting impression about what I was feeling and what I am now feeling as I recover the mood of each moment written about on these pages. You will find those words written in one or two parts of my story. There are song lyrics on a few pages too. They are the soundtrack of my life like a movie in which the background music sets an important mood for the scene.

I worked with several thousand musicians and a few thousand bands including The Strokes, Interpol, The National, Longwave, stellastarr*, The Hold Steady, The Bravery, Nada Surf, French Kicks, Rainer Maria, Olivia Tremor Control, The Moony Suzuki, The Meat Puppets, and Elliott Smith. I am also fortunate to have or have had professional and friendly relationships with Joey Ramone, Marty Willson-Piper, John Moore of The Jesus And Mary Chain and Black Box Recorder, William Tucker, Ministry, The Sugarcubes, Nine Inch Nails, Killing Joke, Warren Haynes, Jim Thirlwell, Lotion, Camper Van Beethoven, Railroad Jerk, Jon Spencer, Joe McGinty, and The Psychedelic Furs. I also spent some time with my friend, Jody Porter, of Fountains Of Wayne and The Belltower, who introduced me to Brian Wilson, Oasis, and Sean Lennon.

This is my story. I am a musician and entrepreneur who created and ran nightclubs, a short lived record label, and an internet radio station; all now part of the history of music and nightlife in New York City. More than what I have done, this is the story of what I have learned about my life over these fifty plus years. I hope that I can adequately convey something of its meaning to you.

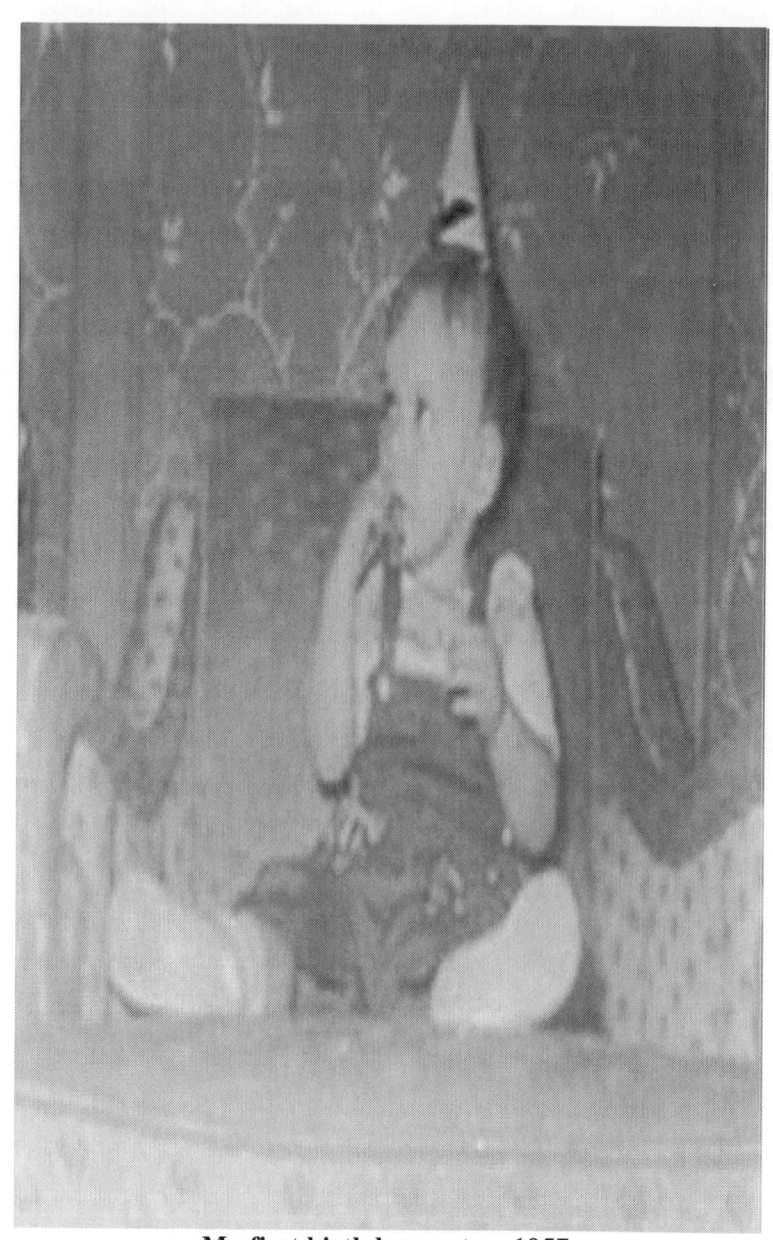

My first birthday party – 1957

The Beginning - 1956
(Help Me Make It Through The Night)

When I was a very small child, still in my crib, I used to be terrified of the shadows that would appear on my wall at night. I would scream out loud for my mother who would come into my room but could not understand what was happening. I would cry that something was moving and point to the wall. I was only two and a half years old and we had just moved into our new house. My bedroom window still had no shade and no curtain. I had no idea that the shadows were formed from city buses that passed underneath the overhanging streetlights on the block where I now lived. The moving images would vanish by the time my mother would get to my room and she had no idea to what I was referring. In order to help me relax and ease me into a sleep, my mother began to leave a radio by my crib. Eventually, my fear of the moving black shadows subsided, but my interest in the music coming from that radio would last for the rest of my life.

My father had been a United States Air Force airman trained to go and fight in Korea. But, not being of warrior mind and spirit and having spent some time at a New York City college working towards a degree in culinary arts, his superior officers decreed The Air Force would be best served if he rise up early each day and prepare breakfast for the hungry young men.
Having completed their basic training, his unit was sent down to MacDill Air Force Base near Tampa, Florida

Mom and dad in front of the new house in Brooklyn – 1958

awaiting dispatch to the Korean peninsula. But, this being the final year of the war, The Air Force no longer had a need for those drafted young men. Content to call it a victory, both sides had agreed to an armistice. While the war was not technically over, the shooting had ended for good.

My father awaited his orders and while The Air Force decided his fate, he got a job serving sodas in Tampa, behind the Madison Drug Store counter. He was a good looking man and with an Air Force tan he must have cut quite a dashing presence among the young ladies of that city. My mother being one, and both being young; they met behind that counter and fell quickly in love with each other.

His eventual discharge from the military meant his return to New York City; now married, they began to raise a family. They got jobs working in the same restaurant, he as a cook in the kitchen, and she as a waitress out on the floor. Soon, they had saved enough money so that my father could purchase a Checker Cab and start life as a self-employed taxi cab driver in New York. It was quite an improvement in the quality of his life to escape the hard life of a cook in front of the hot ovens and stove.

Raised in The Depression and having lived as adolescents through The Second World War, my parents were among the generation of young adults in their twenties just setting out in the fifties. They had most of their lives still to be lived and passion and youth on their side.

My mother had eagerly left Tampa, anticipating an exciting life beyond the restricted cultural confines of small town southern culture. This was a new time in America and for her generation opportunities for social and cultural gain were abundant. However, they would come at a cost. Authority was about to be challenged, but the old guard would never go silently into the night. They would rail against change and take steps to inhibit freethinking adults from challenging rule in their lives.

George Wallace, the popular four time elected governor of Alabama, led the southern wing of The Democratic Party, expounding the idea that "separate but equal" meant that in his own words, "segregation today, segregation tomorrow, segregation forever" in America was fair and honorable and should remain as the law of the land. There was Joseph McCarthy who fueled fear of a communist subversion, producing a bogus paper which he claimed had the names of Americans who worked in The State Department but whose allegiance was sworn to The Communist Party. There was the American terrorist Ku Klux Klan who advocated white supremacy and white nationalism while raging against Catholics, Semites, and Negroes. Even the Central Intelligence Agency orchestrated the overthrow of the democratically elected socialist government of Guatemala. They, among others, would serve notice on the nation that the 1950s would be a battleground where those seeking redress would be opposed at the gates of reform.

Rail all they might; soon within sight, the nation was going to change. Music is always a reflection of what people define as their culture and change is the cultural revolution of youth. And there was plenty of youth in the fifties.

The first iconic rock'n'roll album cover, a photo of Elvis Presley in the midst of a live performance on his first full length album, was the embodiment of the face of his generation; it was an expression of freedom, passion, and social gratification. Through the power and presence of music as formed through his body and soul, Elvis Presley did more to change American culture in the fifties than anyone else in control. And, while he may have offended older Americans by breaking down cultural norms; his electrification of the American youth would kick start the changes to come.

His first album, simply entitled *Elvis Presley*, was released on March 23rd, 1956, exactly five weeks before the day I was born and it was the biggest selling album of the year. That album spent ten weeks at number one in 1956; the first rock'n'roll album to ever make it to the top of the pop charts. It was also the first rock'n'roll album to sell more than a million records. Six days after I was born, on May 3rd, 1956, Elvis Presley had his very first number one single, "Heartbreak Hotel", and it sold over five hundred thousand copies. It was the very first rock'n'roll single to ever reach the top of the chart.

This was the face of change American youth would embrace and that new direction would first lead to white participation in the integration of black rhythm and blues with white country, gospel and pop. It meant more to America than a new style of music; it was a new style of culture. An open door beckoning towards a new awareness; American youth embraced new cultural values leading directly to white participation in the civil rights movement.

Across the nation in this decade, starting with rock 'n'roll music, continuing steps were being taken towards the fulfillment of The American Dream, leading to a new American awareness not only of our civil rights, but of our place as a nation among nations, our species as a species among species, and our relationship with the planet on which we live.

One day, having worked for his wages, my father came home with a package that a rider had left in the back of his cab. He knew it was a long-playing album and he hoped that it was something new in the classical world, a style of music my father held in high regard. Perhaps, it was Schoenberg, Copeland, Beethoven or Bach. Instead, it was rock; my dad who was into Pergolesi had brought home the first record from Elvis Presley.

Mom loved the record and played it all of the time, never knowing that the photo on the cover was taken back in her hometown of Tampa, at The Armory, and not far from where she grew up. As she cooked and made ready for dinner and whenever she cleaned our home, "Don't Step On My Blue

Suede Shoes" was the song she would play; the first song on side number one.

Some people, like Elvis, are born to rock and take their life to the edge of the stage. Not me, I was born with a secluded old soul; with a feeling that I've been here before, but not in any specific sense, more so in an obscure manner of having lived and lost, and now I was living again.

As I got older, at four years of age, when most children have their special blanket or a favorite stuffed toy, I had that radio that my mother had placed next to my bed. When I was alone in the night; the radio by my side, I would go to a place where my young heart could yearn and turn towards the blues and the grey. You see, I have had a sadness inside with which I have lived my life, almost as if I knew the end that would be coming and that it would not be good.

There was a song which for me expressed the plaintive feeling with which I was living, and may have foretold events as they would unfold in my life. It was called "Will You Love Me Tomorrow" and it is the first song that I can remember for waiting at night; hoping to hear it played. The first song that I could actually sing, if not out loud, clearly within my heart; I found a voice in Shirley Owens, of The Shirelles. I wanted her to be with me and to comfort me, not actually in life, but through her voice and the beauty of the song she sang. There would be other songs from The Shirelles and I would love some of them too. But, every time I hear this song, I am taken back to the time I spent in the night as a child. I can never get over that feeling of loss or go beyond that first moment of discovery.

A couple of years later, I was moved into the room with my older brother. Perhaps, my parents worried that I was a child too much alone in his inner world. My brother was outgoing and energetic. He had a bicycle and would ride to far away destinations beyond the end of our block. He would come back and tell me tales of what he and his friends had discovered.

Tommy was born in 1950, just over two weeks after my mother's nineteenth birthday. His father had been a hunter, a fisherman, an outdoorsman of Southern character; a young local with whom my mother would explore her first adult relationship and to whom she would first marry.

But, that marriage would not last long; my mother would file for divorce and move back to her parent's home with Tommy, just before she met the man who would become my father. He, along with my mother, raised both of us, including our younger sister, Donna, who would come fourteen years after my brother and eight years after me.

My brother was an action figure; always on the go chasing down one adventure or another while I was a boy at home in his mind, his music, and in the solitude of reading his books.

We had been given a portable used record player. It had a wood top with two metal hinges that slid out in order to remove the cover. The wood base held the motor, speaker, turntable, and turntable arm. It had a metal spindle that was not interchangeable. It could accommodate only one long-playing record or one seven-inch 45RPM single at a time. The records could not be stacked. An adaptor had to be inserted into the hole in the middle of the record in order to play a 45RPM single. Then, it could be attached to the spindle. The adaptors had more than one shape, but the most common adapters were yellow and had a very distinctive design.

The record player was about a third of my own body weight. I couldn't lift it, but I would drag it across the floor to connect it to the nearest electric outlet. I would usually find a location in a corner on the floor in the dining room closest to the opening in the wall that led to the kitchen. My mother would often be in that kitchen when I would be playing my records.

She was a lunchtime waitress in a neighborhood restaurant called Cooky's; one of the iconic Brooklyn restaurants of the 1950s and 60s. Cooky's was a large and happening place filled to capacity most afternoons with a lively lunchtime trade.

The NBC Brooklyn Studio was only two blocks away where *The Perry Como Variety Show*, *Sing A-Long With Mitch Miller*, and *Hullabaloo*, the mid 1960s music program featuring bands of the British invasion, were filmed for later broadcast on the television network. Crews, staff, and talent from those shows would often come by to eat and it would not be unusual to see well-known stars in a booth with their associates.

Cooky's had a long lunch counter just opposite the front door where the cashier would sit and collect payment from customers. Thirty or forty tables ran all the way through to the back of the building.

Unable to find a sitter for me on occasional Saturday afternoons, my mother would bring me into the restaurant. I would be given a seat and a job at a table in the back where the staff would take their meals. From a big metal bucket with big metal tongs, I would fill paper cup after cup with cole slaw for plate after plate that made their way out from the kitchen.

Cooky was a big man who smoked big cigars as he directed the lunchtime action. He'd check in on my table and make sure I was able to keep up with the plates that were coming. After an hour or so, I'd get tired and he'd let me retire from working. If I wasn't filling the paper cups, I had crayons to fill in my coloring book, or I would pass my time engaged with my first grade reader.

All the other waitresses would eventually come over and make a big fuss over me.

"Oh, what a handsome boy you are," and

"My, you have such beautiful eyes," I would often hear throughout the afternoon. It made me feel very special.

There was a small neighborhood record store on the

other side of Avenue J, directly across from Cooky's. On certain random days, my mother would cross that street and buy me a few records. Those 45s were the start of my singles collection and included "Puff The Magic Dragon", by Peter, Paul, and Mary, "Soldier Boy", by The Shirelles, and "My Boyfriend's Back" by The Angels. I would study the labels and look at them over and over again; thrilled to put them on for the very first time and hear the music that came through that monophonic speaker.

    My parents had sent me to a Montessori school for a couple of years where I attended kindergarten and first grade classes. Afterward, I was allowed to start second grade at New York City public school, PS 208, at six years of age.   Maria Montessori had died four years before I was born but her method of creating an environment where children would learn by experimentation and self-discovery would help shape me into an adult stimulated by continuing change and creation.
    Like most public schools in the city, the school in which I received my elementary education was a building filled with children whose parents or grandparents had immigrated to America. They had come from some faraway places and spoke different languages and shared a different cultural history.
    One of the groups who had come to America and had settled in New York City was the Jews of central and eastern Europe. They brought with them a cultural recognition of the value and importance of obtaining a good education. They also brought with them a knowledge and history of persecution and of having been forced to live as outcasts on the outside of society. While not all of the teachers were of Jewish descent, many of the teachers at PS 208 in the 1960s had last names like Rabinowitz, Edelson, and Reich; predominantly Jewish surnames.
    I am not sure who was the mind behind this idea, but every Wednesday was called Assembly Day. We had to

wear a collared white shirt and red tie. The student classes were brought into the auditorium and we would often be taught to sing protest songs of the era. I learned "Blowin' In The Wind", by Bob Dylan, "This Land Is Your Land", by Woody Guthrie, and "Where Have All The Flowers Gone", by Pete Seeger.

I have never met another person who obtained this as part of their elementary school education and I have to assume that the idea came from one of the progressive minded teachers who taught at the school. For whoever was in charge of such matters, I am eternally in their debt, for he or she taught me to be aware, not only of the value of music for social change, but the value of music as social change. And, that change was not just about the noble protest movements of the 1960s. It could manifest itself as protest music of any era; including songs whose protest power would come from the aggressive style of the music itself, and whose lyrics would send out a message of defiance, not necessarily overt, but expressed covertly more in the manner of songs like "God Save The Queen", by the Sex Pistols, "Blitzkrieg Bop", by The Ramones, and "White Riot" on the first album by The Clash.

But, it would be many years in the future before I would come to understand that the seed of protest had been planted within me by some unknown teacher who was in charge of the music we sang on Assembly Day. For the moment, a more immediate observation came quickly on a cold day in December at the end of 1963.

I was a year younger than my classmates in third grade. I was a bit smaller and I was a shy boy. There was a small luncheonette near my public school and at lunch most of the kids would go there to buy candy. It was called Penny's. There was another luncheonette that was a block further away and it was called Millie's. While most of the kids went to Penny's, I found myself going to Millie's. They had a radio that sat on the counter directly behind the candy display case. On that cold winter day in December, standing in front of that counter debating the merit of the cherry wax lips, revolution would come in an instant on the first day I first heard The Beatles.

The song was "I Want To Hold Your Hand" and I stood there not knowing what to make of it for a moment. It certainly was unlike anything that I had ever heard before and I am sure that it was the first song that I had ever heard from a band that came from outside of the United States. I had been raised on some pretty good American rock'n'roll and singles from Roy Orbison, The Coasters, and Elvis, were among favorites in my collection. Hearing The Beatles meant that I was hearing something new.
By the time I got back from lunch, it seemed like everyone else in school had heard of The Beatles too. Of course, I'm exaggerating, but it really only took a few weeks before every kid in Brooklyn was excited about the new band who hailed from a place called England. And the girls; the girls went crazy. The Beatles were so cute! The Beatles were so new! Which one do you love? I love Ringo! No, I love Paul! No, George is the cute one! It went on everyday for months. I was bearing witness to the first sexual urges of my female elementary school classmates although I could not have known it at the time. Still, I knew something was getting them very excited and it both scared and titillated me too.

There were many Beatles singles that followed including "She Loves You", "Eight Days A Week", and "Ticket To Ride". I loved all of those songs but was put off by the hysteria associated with Beatlemania. I refused to become a rabid fan of the band, until, one day I had an epiphany in a barber's chair sometime in the following year.
I was sent out with a dollar and instructions to get a haircut and tip the barber a quarter; the standard in my neighborhood at that time. The barbershop was only a block

away from my home. As was the case at Millie's and so many other local stores, the radio was on and tuned to WMCA-AM. I was in the chair with the barber's apron wrapped around me and while he cut my hair, I heard the deejay tell us that this was a brand new tune from The Beatles. By this time, I had heard all of the Beatles singles but had refrained from buying a record.

First, there was a weird sound that before I had never heard. It could not be described and it sounded like a mistake. But, these were The Beatles, so there could not possibly be a mistake on the record. Then, after about seven seconds of this weird sound, an incredible rhythmic guitar introduction and the opening verse to "I Feel Fine" catapulted me out of the barber's chair. Not really out of the chair, but inside my little head I was soaring. It was the first time on a record that The Beatles had used something called feedback and it was the first time that I had ever heard that amazing sound.

I went home and collected some change that I kept in a draw and took a long walk to the far side of my neighborhood where I knew of a small record store that had recently opened. I had to cross Ralph Avenue; a pretty wide street for a nine-year old boy. I crossed at the green and not in between; reciting that poem over and over many times, and returning with pride in the quest I had tried, and with my copy of "I Feel Fine".

About this same time, I came across a trio of teenage girls who were singing in the park that was just a couple of short blocks away from my home. Actually, although that's what we called it, this really wasn't a park. It was a playground and ballfield; both built on solid concrete.

The playground was for younger children and had swings, monkey bars, seesaws, and a sandbox. The ball field had a softball court with painted boxes on the ground to represent the bases and home plate. A batter knew a fly ball was a long out to right or right center, and there was a short fence to left. On the other side of that fence were the handball courts.

It was on one of these handball courts where I first heard those girls singing music out loud. It was angelic; without instruments, it was just them and their a capella sound. It was the first time that I realized that music was made by real human beings; that what I had heard on the radio and what came aloud on my records was made by people like me. They were alive and shared with me a passion for music.

It would be more than forty-five years later, during the writing of this book, that I would discover that one of the girls who was singing went on to become a back up singer of great repute.

Susan Collins grew up in an apartment in The Glenwood Housing Projects directly across the street from where my family had lived. The handball courts were about right in between our two homes. My older brother, Tommy, was in her elementary school class but I had no idea of that at the time. They knew each other well. What I knew well was that Susan and the other girls were singing a song that I loved, and I even wondered if they might have a record out of their own.

Susan Collins went on to work with Todd Rundgren, singing on his biggest hit, "Hello It's Me", Brian Wilson, Neil Diamond, Ace Frehley, of Kiss, singing on "New York Groove", Richie Havens, with whom she shared a helicopter as they flew into Woodstock, John Lennon, Joe Cocker, New Riders Of The Purple Sage, and the Electric Light Orchestra, singing background vocals on "Evil Woman" and "Strange Magic".

Years later, we would meet when I went to a concert she gave in Manhattan, and afterward, surprised my brother by telephoning him on my cell phone and putting Susan on the line. While they spoke on the phone, I stood there thinking that while it took more than forty-five years to meet, for me as a nine-year old boy, Susan Collins was the older girl of my dreams; showing me the way that music was made in the streets.

A couple of years later, I had a second epiphany in the summer of 1967. My parents had rented a bungalow for the summer at Ritzer's Bungalow Colony, upstate in Loch Sheldrake, New York. It was the kind of place where families from Brooklyn would go to escape the hot, humid city. My dad would drive his taxicab all week and then come up on Friday nights and spend the weekend with us.

I got my first kiss in the swimming pool, under the water, by a very cute fourteen-year old girl whose younger twelve-year old sister was the girl that I really liked. I was only eleven so a fourteen-year old girl was a much older woman and a bit too fast for my style. Still, a first kiss is not to be forgotten and is always appreciated for the rest of one's life. As good as that kiss was, that was not my second epiphany. That came on a Saturday in the early afternoon on a hot summer day when I decided to take a walk from our rented bungalow over to the recreation room where there was a jukebox, stage, card tables and a television.

It was the only place on the grounds where I could watch a baseball game or tune into *American Bandstand*. It was years before cable TV. Folks who lived in the country had to get a very big antenna and hope they could pick up broadcast signals from the closest city. It worked, more or less, but at Ritzer's you had to share that one television set with anyone else who wanted to watch a show. As I approached the recreation room, I heard live electric rock music for the very first time in my life. There was a band going to perform for the teenagers that night and they were tuning their guitars and running through songs. My excitement abounded as I took those last few steps cautiously approaching the door. There was no one else around except for these teenage rockers and me.

I stood in the doorway on the side of the stage. They were playing "Turn, Turn, Turn", a Byrds song that I absolutely adored. I had bought that record and now I was hearing a band perform that very same song, except that they were much louder than the sound that came from my record player. They were even louder than the jukebox, much, much louder.

They had that mid 1960s twelve-string chiming guitar sound and sang folk rock songs, including "I Got You Babe", from Sonny and Cher, and "Happy Together", by The Turtles. They called themselves The Lonely Souls and years later I heard that they were from my neighborhood in Brooklyn although I never saw them again. I heard a rumor that the singer had died in Vietnam, but I hope that wasn't true.

They changed my life. Something profound spoke to me through that twelve-string electric guitar and I've never been touched by anything else like I was touched by that sound on that day. Seeing and hearing them rehearse made me want to play an instrument, be in a band, and make a life for myself around rock'n'roll music.

Teenage Years
(Break On Through To The Other Side)

I had spent my last year in elementary school leading up to that magnificent summer of 1967 when in sixth grade I developed my first crush on a girl named Lori.

A shy girl, quiet and reserved and not one to run around and scream her words to the world; Lori was a mystery to me. She was not part of my social scene, and apparently not part of any social scene of her own. Everyone knew who Lori was but no one seemed to know her well. She was an intrigue, and like me, she moved through her days just slightly apart from the world.

Lori had lots of freckles and very long black or dark brown hair. Most of all about her that made my young heart flutter; she had the deepest and darkest big brown eyes. I wanted to look into them and imagine all the places to where we could go if only she knew my name. But, I could never find the courage to approach Lori and I sadly worshipped her from afar. Although I could never enter her world; still, very slowly I began to emerge from those misty years of my youth. Perhaps, it had something to do with the increasing level of testosterone in my body as I began to enter adolescence; while my inner world could still be like the last scene in Casablanca, in the outer world I was gradually becoming somewhat more outflowing, outgoing and confident.

Earlier on, even my fifth and sixth grade teachers had noticed the change in me happening. In those days, elementary school classes were ranked in order of the supposed intelligence of the students. The smartest kids were in the 'one' class and the slowest were in the 'five' rooms. Possibly because of my shyness and being a year younger than most of the kids, I had been placed in the 'four' category in second, third, fourth, and fifth grades. By the end of my fifth grade class I moved up to the 'three' level'; a fortunate turn of event as my sixth grade teacher was the first adult to begin to understand what was going on inside me. She helped me to find my inner confidence and to learn to appreciate my having a somewhat different connection with the world. At the end of sixth grade, I was told that I was being placed into a 'SP' class in junior high school and would now, officially, be considered intelligent and gifted. I'm not sure if any of that was truly relevant but it did help me to feel less removed. Mrs. Edelson may have known more about me than the family in which I lived.

My parent's relationship began to flounder in my early teenage years and they split up when I was sixteen. They had been drifting apart for three or four years and even the birth of my younger sister could not change the course on which they themselves had set. Gone were the loving days of their youth.

My older brother had left the house three years earlier, in 1969, when he and three of his friends volunteered to serve in the army in Vietnam. Upon his return, he married and moved into an apartment with his young wife, Bridget.

My mother had only recently entered middle age and she wanted to find a new life for herself. By this time, Cooky had redeveloped his restaurant into a steak house where my mom continued to waitress. The limited menu insured greater profits but there was no longer a significant lunchtime trade. Instead, she chose to work the dinner shift. She would leave the house just before 4PM and not return home until it was nearly midnight. Sometimes, she would go out after work and enjoy being in the company of her friends at night. She made good money; very important for her wellbeing and sense of independence. However, my sister and I were left to eat our dinner meals alone without a mother or father at the head of our table. It was a sad and forlorn time for us in that big house in Brooklyn. My sister was still a little girl and she especially suffered a deep and lonely heartache. Donna only got to see our father on Sundays and she would cry at the end of every weekend upon having to return to our sullen home.

I was a teenager and was handed the job of babysitting my sister most nights of the week. I did care for my younger sister and I tried to be a good big brother. However, I resented that my parents had cast off their responsibility and had placed it upon my shoulders. It was more than a young man who was nearly ready to go out into the world and start a life for himself should be required to handle.

My father was very good at paying child support and alimony; as well as taking care of the mortgage and other household expenses. However, he was not very good at paying attention to our needs in regard to what was good for our heart and soul. Self absorbed in his business and in meeting the requirements set out by his new wife and her family; Donna and I were left somewhere in a twilight zone between the unified loving family I had known when I was a small child and the house of despair within whose walls we were now living.

My father has a good heart, as does my mother. But, at this time in my life, my parents were focused on their own needs; leaving my sister and I unattended for a great many hours and left to find our own way in the world.

Harry Chapin
(Can't You Hear Me Knocking)

I had started playing a clarinet in my junior high school band class but it wasn't until I met Neil Walters, a professional musician who lived on my block, that I decided to start taking private lessons. Neil was an accomplished keyboard player and was an equally talented teacher. He played in wedding bands to make a living but he could play keyboards in any rock or jazz group too. He had a thorough knowledge in the theory of music and could explain the technical fundamentals. I started taking lessons from Neil at fifteen and consumed everything I could learn from him during my high school years.

By the time I was seventeen, I was playing in my first band; covering songs you could hear on the radio, and writing my first songs which led me to an encounter with Harry Chapin, a singer songwriter whose song, "Cats In The Cradle", went to the top of the Billboard charts in 1974.

It was particularly interesting that I met the man who co-wrote this song, along with his wife, as it was a song that deeply and profoundly touched my sister and me. "Cats In The Cradle" tells the story of a father who has neglected to connect with the heart and soul of his child. It is only near the end of the father's life that the father understands what he has done; realizing that his son had learned to be a father just like him.

My first girlfriend, Beth, had heard on the radio that Harry was going to perform at his home on Long Island in order to raise money for the local library in his town. She was able to secure two tickets as a gift for my eighteenth birthday and we made the trip out to see him.

When we arrived, Harry was sitting cross-legged on the lawn on the side of his home; around him were a group of thirty-five fans. With an acoustic guitar, he was playing some new songs he had not yet recorded. People were enthralled by his presence. He was an earthy man; honest, direct and relaxed. After awhile, he played a song that he said was not yet complete, but to which he had wanted to get some reaction. After playing it, I could see why it was not finished. I suggested to him that he invert the first line of a verse with the last. This would open up the verse and leave more room for development of his story. Harry looked at me, and in front of the people who had just heard him sing this unfinished song, he simply said, "You're right." He immediately understood the implication of what I was suggesting. I thought that that was the end of our moment, but after we all got up to walk around his property, Harry approached me and asked me if I was a songwriter. I told him that I had just started but I hoped to keep working at it. He then asked me if I would be interested in joining him and some of his friends in a songwriting workshop that he was planning to start at his home. I replied that I would be very interested in being a part of the meetings. We exchanged phone numbers and in a few weeks I got a call from Harry Chapin; asking if I would join him in a songwriter's session.

I drove out to Long Island and met his lovely wife, Sandy, and two-year old son, Josh. Sandy served us tea and cookies while Josh crawled around on the floor. The songwriting workshops met on and off for a couple of years.

Harry Chapin – c. 1976

They were very important to me. Harry was the first famous creative person I had met and he took an interest in my writing. The only problem was that, at that time, I was not yet playing guitar.

Harry had a stand up piano against a wall in the room in which we played our songs but it was dreadfully out of tune. Living only a few hundred feet from Long Island Sound; the salt water was eroding the strings inside his old piano. I couldn't use it so I had to record my songs in advance and play the tapes for Harry and the other writers who were present. It worked well enough but it did make me want to play a guitar and soon after I bought my first acoustic guitar and started taking some lessons.

I only saw Harry one more time after the last songwriting workshop, about five years later, when I was going to state college and was a member of the college concert committee. I had lobbied my fellow students into having Harry perform at the school. The show was booked and Harry played in front of more than a thousand people on campus. The only time that I ever saw him play in front of a large audience, I feel fortunate to have seen him perform on that night.

A great human being and a very great talent, Harry's interest in me helped me to believe that I was someone unique while taking my first steps into adulthood. We spoke briefly after the show and then parted company never to see each other again. He died shortly thereafter from a heart attack sustained before and during an automobile accident on the Long Island Expressway on a summer afternoon in 1981. My friend, Harry, was only thirty-eight years old.

I had been thinking about it for several months and finally made the decision in August of 1975 to move out of my parent's home. It was a very difficult decision for me. It was the only home I had ever known and my memories were long and deep going all the way back to the first nights that I would lie awake in my room worried about the moving images on my wall.

The home; symbolic refuge of the heart where my parents had once loved each other and where on a Saturday morning in October of 1972, after a particularly loud fight at the kitchen table, my father came back upstairs to their bedroom, pulled out his suitcase from their closet, packed it with his clothes, and moving past the woman that he had once loved so dearly, walked out through the kitchen door; forever severing the bonds that had made my mother his lover, and his children, the family to which he would return from labor at the end of his working days.

Leaving the house meant leaving my little sister to the will of my parents who were completely absorbed in their own fear and desire to move on and find new lives for themselves at any cost. Still, I was nineteen and the beckoning world could not be denied. I had to go out and start adult life for myself.

In addition, I had made the decision to break up with Beth. We had met two and a half years earlier, just before my seventeenth birthday and with each other we had truly fallen in love. We had shared our first teenage sensual and sexual experience, both leaving childhood behind on an autumn Sunday night in my Volkswagen van parked several blocks away on a quiet dead end street. Beth, the first love of my life also came from a home where the love between her parents had died, and for whom we were each a lonely port in the storm.

In the house from which I was departing with my little sister inside; I would leave them behind and set out on the cusp of a new adult life filled with hope for adventure and new experience to come.

My Short Lived Publishing Deal
(Blinded By The Light)

During the time I was attending songwriting workshops at Harry Chapin's home, I was taking a recording engineering class at Ultrasonic Sound Studios, the premier studio on Long Island and one of the best studios in the New York area at the time. Many artists cut important records there in the 1960s, including Iron Butterfly's, "In-A-Gadda-Da-Vida", The Shangri-Las', "Remember Walking In The Sand", and Vanilla Fudge's, "You Keep Me Hangin' On". Along with Jimi Hendrix's, Electric Lady Studios, it was one of the first two sixteen track studios in the New York area in the early 1970s, and many prominent artists continued to record at Ultrasonic well into the 1980s.

I had the good fortune to be there at the time when the studio was doing a series of live performance recordings that were aired on WLIR-FM, an important Long Island radio station. Among the artists from that time, these recordings included performances from Big Star, Jackson Browne, Taj Mahal, and Little Feat. I was offered an internship after my engineering class was completed and I got to set up and move around microphones in the performance room of the studio on some of these nights.

When the studio was available, I was allowed to go in and use the facilities as long as a studio engineer was present. The first music that I ever recorded and produced was with a band called Green Apple Quick Step who performed two of my songs. At those sessions it was a great thrill for me to play on the same Hammond organ that was so incredibly important to the arrangements used on those classic tracks from those iconic bands of the sixties.

Later on, I started hanging out with a band called Timberlake who performed at clubs on Long Island. They were an alt country band predominately performing cover versions of songs by recording acts from Southern California, as well as some artists who played Southern rock. They were very good but were not known for original music. I offered to record and produce the band if they would perform my songs when we recorded in the studio. We hit it off well and we recorded three or four tunes. They seemed to enjoy playing my songs and would introduce me from the stage at nightclubs where they played,

"Hey everyone, the next song is an original tune we're gonna play for you. It was written by our friend, Rob, standing over there at the bar," and all eyes would turn towards me in the room. It gave me my first taste of attention from the general public.

The best of these recordings was a song called "Let Me Sing You A Love Song", which led to a publishing contract for me with Dick James Music, the publishing company Dick James originally co-owned with The Beatles. Unfortunately, by the time I arrived on the scene, Dick James had sold the company to a third party without offering The Beatles an opportunity to buy control of the company which ultimately led to Michael Jackson owning the publishing rights to The Beatles catalog.

The A & R guy who signed me at Dick James Music had first heard one of the songs that I had previously recorded with Green Apple Quick Step when I pressed up some copies and sent them to a few small radio stations around the country. He was a music director at one of those stations.

When he received his copy, he called me to find out something about the band. We spoke for quite awhile and he told me that he really liked the song. He gave it some airplay and that was the last I had heard of him until a couple of years later when I received a phone call when I was up at state college.

By then, I was a freshman living in a dorm on campus. I had decided that while music was still a priority, I did not want to miss out on the opportunity to have a college education. I was now a few years older that the average incoming student and it was, now or never, if I was to have this experience. Also important to me was that I take part in the social involvement of going away to school and living on and off campus.

We only had one pay phone in the hall. There were no cell phones yet. I came home from a class and there was a message written on a piece of paper taped to my door that had been taken by one of the other students who happened to be walking by the phone when it rang. It said that Dick James Music had called and that I should call them back about my songs. I didn't know who or what was Dick James Music.

I called the number and it turned out to be the guy from the radio station. He told me that he had moved to New York and was doing A & R for the publishing company that handled music from The Beatles. He remembered my record and wanted to have me come up to the office and see if I had any other songs. At that meeting, he heard "Let Me Sing You A Love Song" and felt that it would be a perfect follow up single for The Bellamy Brothers who had just scored a huge number one Billboard crossover hit the year before, in 1976, with a tune called "Let Your Love Flow".

I took the next semester off from college and while my friends at school were now in their sophomore classes, I was back in another recording studio on Long Island recording a group of new songs for possible interest at Dick James Music.

The owner of this studio, Steve Young, had been a touring musician in The Grass Roots, a California folk rock group with soul and British influences, whose highly charted singles, "Where Were You When I Needed You",

"Midnight Confessions", "Let's Live For Today", and "Sooner Or Later", paved the way for sales in the tens of millions of records for the group.

At the time that I was at the studio, Steve was also working with Johnny Maestro, who had sung the lead vocal on "Sixteen Candles" while with The Crests in 1958, and as the vocalist in The Brooklyn Bridge, had sung "The Worst That Could Happen", a huge hit in 1968.

One day, while Steve and I were laying down tracks with a couple of musicians who Steve had lined up to play on my songs, Johnny came by the studio to pick up a tape that he had recently recorded with Steve. Steve asked Johnny if he had time to play his music for me. He did, and Steve cued up his tape while Johnny and I made small talk in the control room. Honestly, I cannot recall what I thought of that tune but I do remember being in awe of this extremely pleasant, unpretentious man who had a voice that had made him a legend of his generation. Whenever I happen to hear his songs on the radio, I think back to the day we shared some time together; both of us making music.

Several weeks later, I met with my A & R guy again up at the publishing company. Unfortunately, he had been moved to an office down the hall, next to the elevators; so small, only he could fit in the room. I had to stand in the doorway while he sat behind his desk.

I'm not sure why things were not going well for him, but my supporter, my A & R guy, wasn't cutting it at Dick James Music and there was no one there who had any interest in working with me when he left the company. All that effort working with Steve Young, and the musicians we chose to best represent the vibe and sound for each tune and recording, was wasted and lost with his exit. It was a revelation for me to learn that an artist's career could only be as successful as the business people with whom he or she worked. If your A & R guy was gone, so was your opportunity to get your song heard by The Bellamy Brothers.

It didn't seem to matter how good the song might be, no one else at Dick James Music had any interest in even giving it a listen. They had their own agendas and they did not include me. It had nothing to do with art, nothing to do with music, and nothing to do with the song. It did have everything to do with their corporate political alliances and how they would be best served in advancing their careers. It's no wonder that Michael Jackson ended up with the company and it's no wonder that so much bad music is released through these types of music business relationships.

So much for my short lived music publishing opportunity. It had been interesting and I might someday return to seeking a publisher for the songs I have written, but on this day I returned to my college classes at the State University of New York, upstate at the College at New Paltz.

Ray Davies
(Dedicated Follower Of Fashion)

Several months earlier, I had previously spent one semester at Brooklyn College, a New York City school, before transferring to The State University Of New York. I was a member of the college committee that was in charge of presenting concerts at the school. We arranged for The Kinks to perform on the night before Thanksgiving, Wednesday, November 23rd, 1977.

My job was to be at the venue when the band arrived and get them anything they might need before the show. I eagerly awaited meeting one of the original bands of the British invasion. I thought back to the nights that I would lie awake as a child, a dozen years earlier, hoping to hear "Tired Of Waiting For You" or "You Really Got Me" on the radio next to my bed.

It was in the early part of the afternoon when Ray Davies and the rest of the band walked in through the backstage door. He was chugging a bottle of Jose Cuervo tequila. It was full when he walked in. It was empty by the start of the show.

Their crew had arrived earlier and had set up their gear, even their guitars were tuned and were sitting in their stands on the stage. The band started to jam around 2PM. They instrumentally played through little bits of a lot of tunes but I didn't hear a Kinks song performed on the stage. I heard what sounded like guitar riffs from The Beatles, The Who and the Rolling Stones.

The soundcheck eventually began in earnest. At this point, the sound engineer had one musician at a time play his instrument with the drummer going first by repeatedly hitting one drum or cymbal at a time. The rest of the band left the stage for awhile. Then, the bass player returned and completed his soundcheck. The engineer got sound levels from the guitarists, and then the vocalist. I was on the stage for the entire jam and soundcheck.

When the soundcheck was completed and the band's stage monitors were up and running, the band continued to play for another hour and a half. They only left the stage when the support band arrived for their soundcheck around 6PM. The Kinks had been on stage for four hours and had been playing music for almost the whole of the time. I never saw a band do that before or after that day. This was only the second show of their American tour and I believe that the band had previously been in the studio for months recording their new album, *Misfits*, which would be released later, in 1978. *Misfits* would contain one of the biggest hits, "Rock'n'Roll Fantasy", that the band would ever have in America. It would resurrect their career in the states, bring their music to a new younger audience and enable them to move from college size venues to arenas in big major cities. It was the first of a short series of additional successful big rock singles. But, that was just up the road, several months later. On this particular day, The Kinks were knocking the rust off the hinges while they tightened up on that stage.

The members of the concert committee had tee shirts especially made up for this show. They were yellow shirts with a black image of King Kong holding a Flying V guitar over his head as he straddled the top of The Empire State Building. They were made in celebration of The Kinks' song, "Ape Man", a current tune at the time. I was wearing one of these tee shirts that day. When the band finished playing, before the support act took the stage, Ray approached me and said,
"I like your shirt." I replied,
"I like your suit." He did look very sharp in his mod British clothes. He smiled at my reply and then asked if there was another shirt that he could have for himself. I said that I would go upstairs to the student government office and see if I could find one for him and he waited on the side of the stage for me to return.
 I ran upstairs and looked through the office but could only find a girl's small tee shirt that had been left behind in a box. I brought it downstairs and gave it to him. He reached into his suit trouser pocket and pulled out a large printed button he gave to me with an odd smile on his face. It was the kind of button that a fan would pin to one's lapel. It was a replica of the cover of The Kinks album, *Schoolboys In Disgrace*. The album cover is an illustration of a little boy bending over with his pants pulled down and his rear end exposed in the air. I'm not really sure, but Ray's smile along with that button, gave me the impression that Ray was interested in me in some ways other than making music. I had never before been approached by a man. I had never even thought about it. It's one of those moments in a young person's life when they learn something about who they are, or perhaps, who they are not. I suppose, had I more

Ray Davies on stage – 1977

Ray Davies - 1977

experience, I might have handled the moment better, but I was truly surprised and caught off guard. My response was instinctual and I smiled back but retreated to a spot further away on the stage.

The Pretenders And Johnny Depp
(I'll Stand By You)

The following year, now a student at the state college at New Paltz, I joined the college concert committee. We were just several students who were in charge of spending a part of the student budget to bring entertainment to campus. While I was very much in tune with new music and the new groups coming out of New York and the UK, my fellow committee members were not quite as connected to music. In January of 1980, I tried desperately to bring a brand new band called the Pretenders to the school.

At this time, their first album had not yet been released in America but I had heard the entire record over the Christmas break when a short lived New York City alternative rock radio station, WPIX-FM, played the entire album as part of a show called *The PIX Penthouse Party*. It might have been the very first time that the Pretenders were played on commercial radio in America. At this point in my life, I was listening to some pretty aggressive music and I was floored by the record. It had so much attitude, every song was a journey through a pissed off poet's miserable life. The album simply rocked in a way that I had never before had heard. Every band has influences and I think that I am pretty good at picking them out. But, when I heard the Pretenders for the very first time, I could not know from exactly where they were coming. They were punk, but with an original approach and with a singer who seemed to have no fear in taking her life to the edge of the stage.

No one on the concert committee had yet heard of the

Pretenders. The head of the committee called the local commercial rock station, WPDH-FM, in Poughkeepsie, and asked the music director there if he had yet heard of the band. He said that he had not heard of the Pretenders and the committee decided to decline my request to book them at our school. It's a shame because they were only a two thousand dollar act and we could easily have afforded to have them perform on campus. What a thrill it would have been to have produced that show and have presented such a world-class band at the start of their career. But I suppose, this is an example of why there are no statues of committees anywhere found in the world.

A few months later, a couple of friends and I went down to Fort Lauderdale, Florida, to spend a week in the warm Southern sun along with tens of thousands of other northern students who went south for the Spring Break vacation.

The Pretenders first single, "Brass In Pocket", was now all over the radio down there and they were going to perform in front of two thousand fans of the band. My friends and I bought tickets for the following night, just moments before the show had sold out. So psyched that we were seeing the band in concert, I knew that it would be a show we would not soon forget.

Later that night, we were in a nightclub on the strip called Art Stock's Playpen. The giant Florida club held wet tee shirt contests whose contestants were local strippers from topless bars around town; so popular among the beer drinking students who came down from the North. They also had a deejay and a stage where a local Florida band called The Kids, performed their original new wave tunes. That band was the best thing about the club. Their music was similar to The Knack, Cheap Trick or The Romantics. They had great energy and a cool new wave look. I approached one of the musicians after their set and introduced myself. He told me that his name was Johnny.

I told him that I was a member of a concert committee at

a college in upstate New York and that I would like to have their band come up and play a show at the school. I was sure that we could get a few hundred people to come out and see them perform. My thought was to have them play for our Spring Weekend celebration when we booked several bands and presented free outdoor shows.

Johnny seemed very interested in my offer and we exchanged telephone numbers. He told me that he was only sixteen, still in high school, and still living at home with his mom. He said that he would talk with the other members of the band. The following night, I saw The Kids open for the Pretenders on stage in front of two thousand people. I knew I was on to something special.

When I returned from vacation, the committee started to plan for the upcoming Spring Weekend shows. I called Johnny to see if we could make The Kids concert happen in New Paltz. His mom answered the phone. I introduced myself and she told me that Johnny had told her about my offer. I can still remember her words as I held the phone to my ear. She told me,

"Johnny isn't leaving the state until he turns eighteen!" There wasn't much I could say in return, but to tell her that her son was a very talented musician, and that I understood her feelings. After all, he was underage, and she was his mother. I had no idea at the time that the Johnny I had met, was Johnny Depp. I wonder if Johnny remembers my offer. I think I would bet that he does.

Debbie Harry
(I'm Always Touched By Your Presence, Dear)

I had a girlfriend who went to school at a different upstate college; we would get together between semesters. Eventually, she transferred to an out of state college. More than a year had passed since we had last seen each other when I decided to give her a call around Christmas, assuming that she would be back home on Long Island with her family for the holiday. My assumption was correct and we decided to get together at her parent's Manhattan apartment which they kept as a retreat in the city. There was always a unique physical bond between us, and even though we had not seen each other in quite awhile, we had great fun in being together again that evening. Afterward, we decided to go out to a club called Hurrah.

Originally designed as a disco, after the opening of rival Studio 54, Hurrah became a bastion for the post punk and new wave scene in New York. Although the club was only open for a few years, The Brains, Bush Tetras, Magazine, PYLON, Liquid Liquid, Teardrop Explodes, Polyrock, The Fleshtones, Our Daughter's Wedding, Waitresses, The Cure, Gang Of Four, Speedies, and The Go Gos were among the many bands that had performed at Hurrah.

It was near eleven o'clock when we arrived at the club. We ascended a flight of steps to the second floor and entered directly into a room with a bar on the opposite wall from the door. My girlfriend told me that she had to use the bathroom to our left in another, much larger room where the stage was located. She told me to get her a beer. The bar, which was directly in front of me, was packed with people trying to buy their drinks. I was dressed in my post punk new wave clothes which probably consisted of straight black jeans with black leather boots, a red shirt with narrow collar, skinny dayglow green and black angular striped tie, and black leather motorcycle jacket.

I hadn't noticed the person standing to my right when the bartender took the order for both of our drinks. It was Debbie Harry and she was at the pinnacle of her stardom and beauty with platinum blonde hair and wearing a small white cocktail dress. She turned to face me and gave me a definite look over. Debbie smiled that big wide smile of hers and said with her slightly nasal New Jersey accent,

"I like the way you look." I replied,

"I like the way YOU look," letting the sweet but slightly lecherous Jack Nicholson side of my personality emerge. She continued to smile at me and then after a short pause, she asked,

"Do I know you?" with a slight accent on the word 'know'. I said that I had seen her a few times at CBs but that we had never been introduced. At that, she put her hand out to shake mine in a quick energetic up and down motion and said,

"I'm Debbie," as if I didn't already know who she was. God, she was cute! I said,

"I'm Rob." At that moment, the bartender brought our drinks. I had two beers. Debbie only had one. She looked at me and then down at the two beers that I was holding, and after a slight pause, she said,

"I've got to go see some friends backstage." And then added, in a somewhat playful tone,

"Maybe I'll see you later." I replied,

"Maybe," confident and hopeful; leaving our fate open to possibility. She started to move past me and then paused, turned back to me and added,

"If I don't see you, I'll catch you down at CBs." She was looking directly into my eyes. I replied with honesty, confidence, and with a bit of a tug on my young heart,

"I hope so," and I looked directly back into her eyes. Debbie had a wonderful smile. She was a superstar and she was totally present with me. She was adorable and I was certainly smitten that night.

As she walked past me and went into the main room, my girlfriend had just returned from the bathroom. She looked at me and then looked at Debbie as she walked by, and then looked back at me. She asked in a somewhat surprised and whispered tone,

"Is that who I think it is?" I replied,

"Yeah." Then, becoming more incredulous and in a somewhat louder tone, she asked,

"Do you know her?" I said,
"We just met." Then after a brief pause, I added,
"Just now, at the bar." We walked into the main room where I noticed Debbie walking along the far wall across the width of the room and enter a backstage door.

My girlfriend and I stayed for the show and then I drove her back to her parent's home on Long Island. She soon returned to her out of state college and I never saw her again. In addition, I never did see Debbie at CBs again until more than twenty years later when we were both there to attend a memorial service for Joey Ramone. I did not approach her but I still think she's beautiful, I'm still smitten, and she still rocks my world!

Rick Danko
(It Makes No Difference)

I love the music from The Band. Even in my punk rock, new wave days and beyond, I would still put on any of their albums when I needed a spiritual lift. Among the members of that group, I was touched most deeply by Rick Danko. There was something in that gentle man's voice that allowed me to connect with the pain and sorrow I had once had in my life. Yet, his voice and the songs that he sang had never made me feel down or depressed. The effect had been the opposite. His presence made me feel uplifted, like I had been touched by someone whose well ran deeper than my own.

Somewhere, I heard someone say that we die in the way that we live. If that is true, then Rick Danko lived a peaceful life because he died quietly at home, in his bed, in his sleep, near his family, on the night at the end of his birthday. But, that was in 1999. Twenty years earlier, we booked Rick

Danko, vocalist and bass player from The Band, to perform on campus for our Spring Weekend celebration in New Paltz. Rick lived just up the road, near Woodstock. It was an easy local gig for him and we students were fortunate that we were members of the same community.

Rick had been in one of the most important American bands that had ever recorded music. Originally, known as the backing band for Bob Dylan, they had gone on to create music in their own right, among the creators of the genre now known as alt country music. Only three or four years had passed since The Band had broken up and Rick's voice was still strong and soulful.

It was mid afternoon when he arrived with his new band, which to my surprise included Blondie Chaplin, who I had first seen when he was a member of The Beach Boys in the early 1970s. Blondie has a voice somewhere between Sam Cooke and Marvin Gaye. You might know it. He sang the Beach Boys classic, "Sail On Sailor". He is also greatly appreciated by many musicians and is considered to be a highly regarded guitar player. Blondie has gone on to perform with Paul Butterfield, The Byrds, The Band, Keith Richards, David Johansen, Charlie Watts, Bonnie Raitt, Mick Taylor, and The Rolling Stones.

At the time that we met, I had lost track of him and it had been four or five years since I last saw him perform. I was quite surprised to see Blondie walk in with Rick Danko. I introduced myself and started talking with Blondie about having seen him play with The Beach Boys. He told me that those years had been very good to him and he was still in touch with them occasionally. We spoke about Ricky Fataar, Blondie's friend and former band mate in the Beach Boys, and in an earlier South African band called The Flames.

Rick seemed happy to have my focus of attention be on Blondie and he smiled as Blondie and I made small talk. He

Rick Danko - 1977

never mentioned that Blondie and he were working together on Rick's solo album. I think Rick appreciated that the conversation never got around to him. He seemed like a shy individual. Rick did have a bottle of Jack Daniels and he and Blondie passed it around as we sat in the backstage room before eventually making our way down to the stage.

The Sanctuary
(Do You Wanna Dance)

The following year, early one winter evening while walking down the hill that leads towards town from campus, I noticed that there was a new bar opening in a building that had been vacant for quite awhile. It was called Sanctuary. I walked in, curious to know something about it.

Sanctuary was big enough to hold one hundred college kids and it was mostly a large dance floor with a long bar which ran along one wall. It had a giant deejay booth built on top of a four-foot riser that towered over the dance floor. The turntables were mounted on wooden platforms that were suspended from plastic wire shock absorbers that were attached to the ceiling to prevent the turntable arms from bouncing all over the record when people really got moving.

I met the owner, Vinny, and asked him what type of music he was going to play at Sanctuary. He told me it would be a disco. Disco was still popular in most dance clubs across America in 1980 and it was no different in New Paltz. The only problem was that New Paltz already had an even larger disco called Joe's, so successful, Playboy magazine named it the best club in the country in which to pick up girls. It would be impossible to compete with Joe's.

I was not interested in disco music but I convinced Vinny to let me promote one night each week at the bar. He asked me what type of music I would play if I would not spin disco. Vinny was not the type of fellow who seemed to make music a priority in his life. Not wanting to lose the gig, I told him that I would play music that was new and was influenced by Elvis Presley. I didn't want to tell him that it was called punk rock. Most people at that time had not yet heard of punk rock. Vinny probably knew nothing about punk rock but the term would have made him uncomfortable.

I really wanted this gig and so my life in the bar business began on a Thursday night in the winter of 1980 when my friends and I pooled our records together and had our first punk rock night at Sanctuary.

It was a big success and word spread quickly around campus. By the middle of the semester there was a line to get into the club on the nights that we promoted, and many kids from college along with some very hip locals were dancing to the Ramones, Sex Pistols and The Clash.

Around the end of that school year in 1980, a friend and I got together for drinks down in the city. He told me about a new music magazine that he and another friend were starting and he asked me if I would like to partner with them in their endeavor. The magazine was called, *Concert*, and it was to be given out free at rock concerts, in the vain of *Playbill*, as it's given out at plays on and off Broadway.

Concert was to have interviews specific to each venue with an emphasis on the upcoming shows at that venue. It was provided free to the patrons, free to the concert venue promoter, and free for the bands. We planned to sell national advertising that would pay for the printing and make us a profit.

At one point, we were making issues of *Concert* magazine for more than a dozen venues scattered around New York City. The only problem was that no matter how hard we tried, there was no way that we could secure the national advertising. We were just three young guys with no business track record and no financing for our project. In the end, it was a noble idea but it died in a year and a half's time. When *Concert* magazine came to an end, I made arrangements to go back to school. It was time to return to New Paltz.

I called Vinny while I was packing my car for the trip upstate. I had not spoken to him since I had left New Paltz. Before I could ask him for a job, he told me that Sanctuary was closed and that he owed a lot of money to his landlord. He asked me if I was interested in taking over the bar and keeping him from going into bankruptcy. My older brother, Tommy, and a friend of his, agreed to invest some money in helping me to get the bar reopened.

When I turned off the thruway at New Paltz, instead of making that left hand turn that would take me back up to campus, I continued downtown and turned into the Sanctuary parking lot where Vinny gave me the keys to the bar. I now owned Sanctuary and would never be a college student again.

Sanctuary had been closed for months and it was nearing the end of January. Fortunately, the plumbing was still in good shape despite the cold weather. I had to quickly turn on the heat and turn this room into a club that would accommodate punk and new wave music.

An artistic friend of mine painted a ten-foot high dayglow mural under ultra violet black light of four of our favorite idols: Johnny Rotten, Chrissie Hynde, Joe Strummer, and Joey Ramone. That painting always reminded me of our punk rock version of Mount Rushmore.

On the night that I reopened Sanctuary there was a line to get into the club. I overheard someone saying that they did not know what Rob did when he had left school, but he's back in town and he now owns the bar.

Our reputation began to grow. A local radio station in Woodstock, WDST-FM, approached me with an idea that I do a radio show each week called *The Sanctuary Hour*. It would be the first time in the Hudson Valley, in upstate New York, that people would hear punk and new wave music on a commercial radio station.

WDST had been *Billboard* magazine's small radio station of the year. I was interested in the idea and recorded the music in the club. A person from the station would pick up the tape and a few days later punk rock and new wave music would be coming through car radio speakers up to fifty miles away. The first song that I played was "Radio Clash", by The Clash.

I did the show for several months until I quit over a disagreement with the station owner who censored one of the songs from a show because she thought it was offensive to people in the community. It was called "Johnny Are You Queer", a simple new wave song about a girl who can't get a guy to pay attention to her. I was a very independent young man. Censoring me was not an option over so trivial a tune.

Then, there was a bit of a local scandal when I was arrested for endangering the welfare of a minor.

A storeowner in town had asked me if he and his wife could use the Sanctuary for a place to hold a sweet sixteen party for his wife's daughter. It was to be on a Sunday afternoon. I consented to the request but told them that I would have one of my bartenders on duty to serve sodas and that no beer or liquor would be served to anyone; even if they were of legal drinking age. Also, I was assured that parents would be there at the party. My bartender would keep an eye on the guests and make sure that all went well in the room.

A couple of times during the afternoon, I went over from my apartment, checking on the party and all seemed fine. They had lots of colorful balloons and streamers and the kids were having fun. The parents were there and all seemed well. My bartender said that there were no problems. The party ended around dinnertime.

A few days later, I got a call from the town police telling me that I was under arrest and that I had to come into the police station the following morning for mug shots, finger prints, and to be formally charged. I asked the sergeant what it was all about and he told me that it was on orders from the county district attorney. He told me that one of the girls at the party had said that the bartender repeatedly served her alcohol. When she went home, her parents were outraged to find her intoxicated. That girl said that everyone at the party was drinking.

I knew this wasn't true but could not understand why she had lied, until the police eventually interviewed the other guests who had also attended the party. I was told that the other kids had said that there was no alcohol served to them in the room. As it turned out, the girl had left the party and met a couple of older guys she knew and finished a bottle of alcohol with them out in the fields behind campus. When she went home and her parents confronted her, she made up this story to deflect attention away from her illicit behavior. The charges were eventually dropped against me, but not before a daily newspaper in the nearby city of Kingston ran a headline in the Sunday edition on the front page, "Sweet Sixteen Goes Bust".

That district attorney ran as a Republican candidate for governor later that year and I believe that he was looking for cheap headlines. He should have waited until the police completed their investigation before charging me with a crime. Today, he sits on the Supreme Court Of The State Of New York. I never received an apology from him and I do not believe that the newspaper ever bothered to follow up on the story.

Later on, someone got an idea to have a beach party at the Sanctuary. We set up a volleyball net and my doorman, Jody, who was born and raised in New Paltz, told me that he knew where he could get a few hundred pounds of sand which we could spread out on the dance floor. It sounded like a good idea and I went about creating and printing flyers and distributed them around the college campus and dorms.

When the night came for the party, Jody pulled up in his flatbed truck and brought in four fifty-five gallon containers of sand. As we poured it out on the floor, I noticed that the color was brown. I was used to sand being more of a light tan or cream. No bother though, I figured that sand could certainly come in more than one color.

The girls started to arrive and dressed down to their bikinis while making good use of the open bar set up for their pleasure that evening. Soon, the dance floor filled in the room with the girls who were filled at the bar.

I noticed a slight haze in the air. Quickly, the haze grew thicker and thicker, so dense that we could not see from one end of the room to the other. But, we were committed to the night and once the party had begun, there was no way to remove the sand we had earlier set out on the floor. The girls were covered from head to toe and all you could see were their eyes peering directly out through the haze. We tried to wet down the floor with a few buckets of water sprinkled lightly around the room. All that did was successfully make some mud. Now, we had a very thick dust filled haze in the air and gallons of mud on the floor. There's a part in the B52s song, "Rock Lobster", when the vocalist cries out and tells the Rock Lobster to get down, down, and the dancers lie down on the floor. We played that song a hundred times before, but on that night when the music came back and everyone rose up in the dance, it looked like a scene from the movie, *Dawn of the Dead*, with people having just risen from their graves in the earth. The air was so filled with haze that people would have to retreat though the front door and stand outside for a bit. Then, like heroic soldiers, they would reenter the club and grope their way back through the mist. Our vinyl 45s and LP records were covered with a film that took months to properly clean.

Later, I took a short walk through town and met some of my customers who were now sitting in some of the other bars, covered with the remains of the party. Like a badge of honor, when asked by their friends who had not been at the party what had happened to them that night, I heard the simple reply,

"I was at the Sanctuary."

Afterward, I asked Jody from where he had obtained his sand. He told me that he had gone down to the Wallkill River that runs just outside of town and had found a spot on its bank where he had decided to dig up the sand. I said,

"Jody, that wasn't sand. That was dirt." Jody replied,

"Sand, dirt, I'm from upstate. It's all the same to me."

It was logic, like from the mall in that movie, *Dawn Of The Dead*, from which there was no escape.

Simone Lester
(I Will Take You Forever)

Simone Lester was a very close friend. We met while I was still a student and we dated for a bit; going down to the city to see The Ramones, hanging out together and talking on the phone. Simone was one of the people who had donated her records for play on the first night at Sanctuary, back when Vinny was still the owner. She and I were not boyfriend and girlfriend; we were still too free spirited for that at that time. Still, we had a deep affection for each other and she said that she recognized in me something unique and magical. She used to call me, "Rob-Bee", and her voice and her warm embrace are still with me today.

Simone was a senior at New Paltz when I took over the Sanctuary. I gave her a job as a bartender while she completed her last semester of school. After finishing her courses, we hugged and said goodbye. She was going back down to her parent's house in Queens for the summer and going to start looking for work in the city.

Summer was a very slow time of the year in New Paltz.

The Sanctuary was very quiet and I barely eked out a living in those months. But, there were plenty of free swimming holes and a lot of hiking trails and I made great use of them all summer. The bartenders around town became a sort of fraternal association. Charlie Papaceno, Jeff Zimmerman, and the entire Mazzetti family were among my favorites. A five-dollar bill might make the rounds between each of us, insuring a few rounds of cold beer for all. One night, we might be in Bachus or Coochie's and on another, we could be in P&Gs, Snug Harbor or Thesis, some of the many bars in town. These were the lazy days of my summer of 1982. I had rented an apartment on an apple orchard several miles away in the neighboring hamlet of Highland. I didn't have much in those days: a bed, some clothes, and a telephone answering machine.

While I regularly commuted from that apartment in early January, by the middle of that following summer I was content to sleep on a couch in the bar a few nights every week. When I awoke, there was a great place to have breakfast right in the middle of town. Afterward, I would drive out to Split Rock, a swimming hole with a small waterfall I would dive into for my morning bath and shower. Then, I might hike down to Smitty's and find a sunny spot on one of the many rock outcrops and lie there for a good part of the day. After awhile, I would hike back to my car, drive further west out to Lake Minnewaska or Lake Awosting where there were good hiking trails to explore. Eventually, I would make the drive back into town, meet up with friends and split open a few beers before dinner.

One weekend, I decided to leave the bar in Jody's hands and go down to Pennsylvania and visit a girl I had recently met in town. While I was away and unknown to me, Simone had made arrangements with a guy she knew in the city to come up and see me that weekend. He had a motorcycle and she would take the ride on the back of his machine.

I'm not really sure of what happened but two days after I

returned from my trip, I received a call on the pay phone in the bar. It was from Nancy, another bartender at Sanctuary, and a close friend of Simone. In tears and in a desperate voice, Nancy cried out in her call,

"Where have you been? I've been trying to call you for days." I replied that I had been out of town. She said,

"I don't know how to tell you this, Simone is dead."

I made no reply as the shock slowly set in. It was the last thing that I had expected to hear. Nancy was in emotional free fall on the other end of the line; crying for the loss of a part of her soul. Finally, after a moment forever seared in my heart, I started, stopped, and then stuttered,

"How, how did it happen?" Nancy cried out,

"She was coming to see you." The dam had now burst and Nancy was nearly over the edge. But, through her tears and her broken heart, she found inner strength to continue,

"She was on the back of a motorcycle with a guy that she knew, and something happened, and she fell off on the thruway. They took her to the hospital in Poughkeepsie. She had a broken neck. She died on Sunday." I was silent on my end of the line. Nancy continued,

"I've been calling and calling you. The funeral was today." Barely keeping myself together, I asked Nancy for the name and address of the cemetery. Then, I thanked her for calling me and giving me the news. When I hung up the phone on that quiet afternoon, I knew nothing would ever be the same in my life again. Later that evening, I went back to my apartment in Highland. I had not been home since Friday before the start of the previous weekend. When I walked through the front door, I noticed that I had a message on my telephone answering machine. It was Simone; calling to ask where I was, and to let me know that she was coming up to see me this weekend.

A few days later, I went down to my parent's house in Brooklyn and then made the trip out to New Jersey; to the cemetery where her family had buried my friend. I looked around for quite sometime but could not find her place in the earth. Then, with some help from an attendant, I was directed to where I belonged.

I saw a piece of a sign partially sticking out from underneath the dirt which was piled high, a few feet above the ground. I instinctively pulled it out and then saw her name written upon the sign. No pile of bricks, no earthquake of any magnitude, no mountain of any size could rain down more heavily upon my soul than the two simple words written upon that sign: Simone Lester. I was crushed. It was as ever a final moment as I will ever have in my life.

I had no flowers, no gift; not a remembrance of any kind. But, in my mother's car I had used to make this visit, I remembered that there was a floral scented printed cardboard rainbow attached to her sun visor. I went back to the car, removed it and made my way back from where I came and attached that little rainbow where the sign beheld her name.

With tears, and with bittersweet joy for the beauty she brought to me in this world, I spoke of my heart and my love for her. I apologized for not being home when she had called and having missed her final message. I thought of her voice and how filled with life and vitality it had always been to me. I told her goodbye, but only for a moment, as I hoped that somewhere, somehow, we would meet again. All these years later, I can still hear her voice. She has never faded; never faded with time.

In The City
(I Just Want To Have Something To Do)

The five years that I spent at the Sanctuary were my first five years in the business. I had no idea that Sanctuary was just the first part of my life but I do remember growing bored of being upstate and wishing for a way to open a bar in the East Village down in Manhattan.

The East Village was where the action was; the place where I bought my records and the place where new bands were making new music. It was the holy grail for me at that time. I went to live shows at CBGBs, Max's Kansas City, and at the Ritz. I hung out at the bars on Avenue A and took meals at the many Greek and Polish diners in the neighborhood. I stayed on the couch of a close friend, Rob Lorenzo, who lived on East 7th Street and celebrated New Year's Eve in punk rock style at the opening night of The World. That nightclub had no working toilets in the men's room but the Ramones rocked The World down that night.

Rob is the friend you meet at college, who, no matter how far away you may live from each other after all the continuing years; whenever you do speak on the long distance phone, it's like you are always still sharing that dorm life together you knew when you first met over thirty years earlier. We are still close friends and we both still endeavor to stay connected to modern new music.

We both majored in communications and were in many of the same classes as students in college at New Paltz.. Our emphasis was in radio and television; sometimes we would work together on class projects involved with creating student productions using the various studios on campus.

We had great fun in writing scripts, operating video cameras, directing talent, and producing and recording student radio and television shows.

Rob graduated the year before Simone; the year that I too would have graduated with him had I not taken a semester off to record those demos with Steve Young, and had I not taken a whole year and a half off to co-publish *Concert* magazine. I have no regret about recording my songs or about co-publishing that music magazine. Both experiences were great fun and brought something into my life of lasting value.

After his graduation, Rob eventually found himself an apartment in the East Village. In Rob's own words,

"I moved into the East Village in late summer, 1983. The playlist on the radio went something like this: Stray Cats' "Stray Cat Strut", Madonna's "Borderline" and the Eurythmics "Sweet Dreams (Are Made of This). When I hear those songs, it reminds me of my first apartment on East 7th Street, between First Avenue and Avenue A. The East Village was just beginning to transform from an old world tired and dirty state into a new, vibrant, young art and music scene. Gentrification was the buzzword. And all around the neighborhood, you could find stark juxtapositions: elderly Ukranian people walking the sidewalks in drab woolen garb next to young punks with electric blue hair in tight black leather.

You could walk down a couple of steps into the Holiday Bar and Grill, a decades old hole-in-the-wall with arguably the best punk rock jukebox in the entire city at that time. Or, you could eat cheese blintzes at Leshko's after a sweaty evening at the Pyramid Club.

Change was happening all around and music enveloped it all. I like to think that I was a big part of the inspiration for a new neighborhood club. On their ever more frequent visits to the East Village, and my apartment, Rob and Dianne began to have a vision for a nightspot in the neighborhood."

Rob's apartment was the starting point, and although it took three or four years to eventually open the Mission, Rob faithfully provided a base from where we could make our entry into the East Village scene. Without his friendship and hospitality this story might never have been written.

New Paltz was only an hour and a half away from the East Village by car, but New Paltz was a world away each time we had to return to that little bucolic college town after spending our time in the city. Fortunately, or unfortunately, depending upon how you look at it, the opportunity presented itself at the end of 1985 when the legal drinking age was raised from eighteen, then nineteen, and then to twenty-one in the state of New York.

Almost everyone at college is under twenty-one. I struggled through one last semester but I knew that I would soon be out of business. Of course, the kids were still drinking alcohol at parties in their off campus apartments. The Sanctuary dance floor had been replaced by the keg in the bathroom tub.

Dianne (part one)
(Anything, Anything, I'll Give You)

I had a girlfriend, Dianne Galliano, through most of the years at the Sanctuary, Mission and through the opening of Luna Lounge.

When we were young there were inevitable moments of restlessness, but for the most part, we were great support for each other and she became my business partner when I opened Mission and Luna Lounge. Dianne and I were a team. She was the most important person in the world to me. We never had a legal document between us, but we shared our hearts with an unspoken understanding for thirteen years. I met her at the Sanctuary in September of 1982.

I had contracted with a local video projectionist to have a video event at the bar. In those days, rock video was a new art form. This fellow had a large screen, rock videos on Beta video cassette tapes, and a video projector he brought into the bar. We advertised the event and people showed up to see what he had to present. It's hard to believe, but I've read that the motion picture industry started in much the same way before the development of the movie theatre.

I did this event twice. The first time he projected a variety of rock videos and that's where I first discovered a band called, The Church. They would become one of my favorite groups over the years. The second time, the projectionist brought a live-to-video tape concert of The Rolling Stones. I'm not sure if Dianne came for the concert video, but we did meet at the Sanctuary afterwards on that night.

We dated throughout that semester and she moved in with me in the following year. Dianne and I shared an interest in similar music and she would often accompany me to concerts and clubs down in the city. We would both bartend and deejay at the Sanctuary.

There would be much that we would share together within the time between those years. Sometimes, these days, I think about how fragile relationships can be, and how little time we really have together. I thought we would have an entire lifetime, but as it turned out we had only thirteen years. If you're young; in your teens or twenties, thirteen years may seem like a lot, but when you reach your fifties, thirteen years is not very long and it seems to grow shorter as more time passes us by. This year, an anniversary of sorts, was the fifteenth year that Dianne and I have parted, and now she and her boyfriend, Dan, are in their relationship longer than the time that she and I had had together.

Dianne has an honest, creative, and compassionate approach to life. But, she could be distant and her emotions were not always something she was willing to share with me. That left me feeling separated and out in the cold sometimes. And, I still wonder if that was in some way my fault. But, I don't think so as I feel that that had more to do with her nature, her family, and the way she was raised. In any event, I was the entrepreneur and she was the artist. It was to her that I would bounce off my ideas and I always greatly appreciated her thoughts. And, in moments when I was feeling insecure or unsure of my path, she would be there to help guide me through some of those difficult times.

The Band
(Knockin' On Heaven's Door)

Sometimes, it takes a bit of time for a plan or a path to materialize. My income had dried up. I was feeling depressed and worried over my future and concerned that my money would run out before I could find a place to open a club down in the city.

Several weeks after the legal drinking age was raised, I heard that The Band was performing in a bar just outside of Woodstock, only a handful of miles up the road from where I lived. The Band had broken up almost ten years earlier and their final concert is gloriously documented in the film, *The Last Waltz*. Now, the reforming group, minus one member, Robbie Robertson, was going to play a show for their friends and nearby fans.

I arrived to find that the place was not a live music venue; it was a restaurant with a bar at one end of the room. There was no stage. The Band had set up their gear in the middle of the room against one wall. A really intimate show, it was amazing to hear them perform in such a small space. Their music communicated something of comfort to me that night. Everything was going to be all right. My life and my problems would work itself out. Stay near music and I would be on the right path.

The members of The Band thanked their audience and invited us all to join them at the bar for a drink. Everyone went over to the bar, except for Richard Manuel, Dianne, and myself. Richard played keyboards and sang on several songs on The Band albums, including Bob Dylan's 'I Shall Be Released", and "Tears Of Rage", which he co-wrote with Bob Dylan.

While everyone was having a joyous good time at the bar, I observed Richard sitting alone at his electric piano, lost in his thoughts and very slowly packing up his equipment. I really wanted to approach him and tell him that I was so grateful for their performance; tell him that my life was going through a rough time, but after hearing them perform I knew that everything was going to work out fine. I wanted to tell him that what they were doing was important. I was not alone. There must be others in the world feeling the same way, and that performing again was a wonderful thing. I wanted to say all this but I ended up saying nothing. He was so far into his own thoughts; he seemed so fragile, and I didn't want to disturb him.

That was a moment that I shall always regret. I should have told him how I felt. Something was pushing me to do it but I held back and did not approach him. Instead, I looked back towards the happy drinkers at the bar. The room was filled with joyous goodwill and when Dianne and I left the restaurant and drove back down to New Paltz, I was content to know that I had found a new, revived energy on that cold winter night.

A few months later, possibly despondent over the lack of respect and attention that the reformed group was receiving, Richard Manuel hung himself in a motel room while on tour with The Band. I always wonder if my words would have made any difference every time I hear him sing, "I Shall Be Released".

Richard Manuel – c. 1976

Levon Helm, drummer and vocalist in The Band - 1976

Big Pink, the house where the band lived, near Woodstock

Elliott Lloyd
(Play That Funky Music)

He was a blues musician and singer with a few different names. Elliott Lloyd could also be known as Little Elliott, Little Elliott Lloyd, or my favorite, Ellis Dee.

He lived in his late 1960s pink Cadillac for awhile in the Sanctuary parking lot until the weather got cold and some back pay came in. Then, he moved into the apartment next door to us in New Paltz. Elliott played the blues circuit in the Deep South and all the way up to Montreal. He made a living and released a few recordings. He was even The Honor Harmonica Player Of The Month on the Honor Harmonica calendar one year.

We spent many days and nights discussing life over whisky and beer in the bars around town. One summer afternoon, my front door was open but the screen door was closed when a man came knocking. I went to the door and he asked me if Elliott Lloyd was here. I pointed to the door next door and he thanked me for the direction. There was something very intense about this guy, very sweet, and I knew that he was a special player. Later that night, I asked Elliott what was the name of that man. He told me that he was Pee Wee Ellis, the man who arranged and co-wrote James Brown's late 1960s albums including the songs "Cold Sweat" and "Say It Loud, I'm Black And I'm Proud".

Pee Wee is one of the unsung founding fathers of soul music. Everyone should know his name. His rhythm structures formed the underlying foundations of modern funk on which today's hip hop and rap records are based.

Sometimes, Elliott and I would compare multiple versions of certain songs by different artists and look for

Elliott Lloyd, rockin'out the blues – c. 1981

issues we would debate in regard to the qualities of each recording. He once pulled out three different versions of "When A Man Loves A Woman", all of them recorded by Percy Sledge. I had no idea that he had rerecorded the song so many times. Elliott told me that he knew of seven different versions of the song; all sung by Percy Sledge.

One version that I had heard that night was the original and we both agreed that it was the best. A second slower version seemed to be in a different key. The third version that Elliott played for me was about the same tempo as the original but the mix was quite different and the vocal was not quite as good. I asked Elliott why Percy had recorded the song so many times. He explained to me that every time you hear a late night advertisement for those old hits from the past done by the original artists, those original artists would often record the song over again for each new marketing package. They had to because they did not own the rights to their original recordings. They had often given those up way back in the past in exchange for some quick cash and a new car. I received a music education hanging out with him.

Elliott and I did not always share the same taste in music. He hated the Depeche Mode cover of the Charles Brown classic, "Route 66". He felt that it had no swing and that the Depeche Mode version had no soul in its approach.

One day, Elliott and I were sitting on his couch when he asked me what would make me feel successful. It was the type of question he would often throw out which would lead to my answer and a discussion in which he would provide some earthy wisdom. We were watching MTV. He used to get a kick out of those 1980s new wave big hair band videos. He wasn't always sure if the artists were talented but he certainly enjoyed their silly fashion sense. I pointed to the television and said I'd feel successful if I ever see her hanging out in the new bar that I was hoping to open down in the city. We were watching The Sugarcubes and I was pointing to Bjork. We both agreed that that girl had pipes.

Elliott Lloyd at the Sanctuary in New Paltz, N.Y – 1985

I had started looking for a storefront location and made the run several times down to the city when promising advertisements in the New York Times real estate section caught my attention. It took quite awhile but I finally found an affordable spot. It was in a pretty dodgy section, although most of the neighborhood was really wild in those days. We would make our stand at 531 East 5th Street, between Avenue A and Avenue B, in Manhattan's East Village. We would call the bar, Mission.

Elliott came down to Manhattan with me while Dianne stayed up in New Paltz bartending at The Chance, a live music venue in Poughkeepsie. We still had rent to pay and other expenses on our apartment up there.

I slept in my street clothes on a futon in the middle of the space that we were building. Elliott slept on a couch we found at the Salvation Army. It went this way for a few months in the late winter and spring of 1989 while we were creating the new club.

After we opened, Elliott gave up his apartment in New Paltz and lived on that couch in the bar for months before eventually returning upstate. I think he wanted to make sure that Dianne and I were safe and doing well in the neighborhood. He was originally from Brooklyn, as was I, and we both knew that the East Village, at that time, could be a dangerous place to live.

The East Village
(Walk On The Wild Side)

New York City had gone broke in the late 1970s. A decade later, landlords were still burning down their empty apartment buildings in desperate attempts to collect insurance money. Hardly a week would go by without a fire

East Village abandoned buildings, c. late 1980s

somewhere in the East Village; sometimes set by squatters living in the abandoned buildings. Almost every block had at least one squat, as they were called. Some blocks had two, three, or more abandoned buildings.

The good thing about this time was that the rents were relatively cheap and musicians could afford to live in the city. It seemed like everyone I knew was in a band and you would see them walking up and down Avenue A with their guitar case in hand. Some musicians were in really good bands. Seeing them come down the block was always a bit of news that you would relay to one of your friends,

"Hey, I saw Thurston Moore at Odessa," or

"Iggy Pop was standing at the bus stop when I walked by yesterday," meant that we were living in the same place as our heroes. At the same time, you had to beware of the Puerto Rican gangs that were roaming around the neighborhood looking for white kids to beat up. The drug dealers were everywhere but they were not out to hurt people. They were trying to make a living in the best way to them that made sense.

There were little stores that had bulletproof glass windows that separated the cashier from the customer. You had to give them your money through a sliding glass door that provided the cashier with some sense of security. These little stores were called bodegas. Many bodegas sold drugs, although most of the drug that was sold was marijuana. People would go in and buy nickel and dime bags for five or ten dollars a piece. You usually had to buy a can of soda too. The cashier didn't want his customer walking out without something to be seen in his customer's hand.

The East Village was a place for all kinds of people. Some of them were crazy. There was a guy who killed his female roommate and then boiled her skin in pots for days as he tried to get rid of her body. The cops found his plumbing filled with her remains. He railed against the press when they called him the cannibal killer. Just because he kept her body parts in his refrigerator and he boiled her skin in a pot, that didn't mean he was having her for dinner.

Gordon Raphael, the record producer who recorded the first two albums from The Strokes, arrived in the East Village right about the same time. Our apartments were only four or five blocks away from each other although we did not know it at that time and had not yet knowingly crossed paths. Gordon's impressions of the East Village,

"I was born in the Bronx in the late 1950's, and after moving to Seattle at age eight, went back periodically in the sixties and seventies to visit relatives and catch up with my cousin, Scott, who introduced me to the art of cinema and the pleasures of three movies a day on weekends, at an early age.

My best friends from Seattle all took turns moving to the East Village in 1983, becoming part of what I saw as an ecstatic and exotic subculture of glamour, punk, drugs and alcohol, based on way out rock and roll. They were called The Berserkers and The Fags, and when I visited them, it seemed that they had the key to the city, the VIP rooms and the killer discos. On the street, you could practically tell someone's interests and record collection by the way they dressed, and the make-up job they had. The downside was that this was the generation that was kind of the tail end of the new pioneers of reckless irresponsible lifestyles that culminated in almost total drug casualties, death disease insanity and the beginning of the AIDS epidemic. Some of these patterns were quite universal among my friends, and when I moved to Manhattan in 1988, I was kind of the last of my crew to go down the same roads, in almost all the same ways.

1988 Manhattan /East Village bore a lot of similarities to the scene my pals had brewed in four years earlier, but much had changed, and soon almost everything would be altered, cleaned up, modified and transformed in the Greenwich Village area. While I lived there for two years, I was selling basically street-found thrown away items on a table on St Marks along with an almost twenty four hour flea market that took place there and in front of my apartment on Second Avenue, around the corner. It was from this vantage point that I witnessed, even from my mentally compromised point of view, what I understood to be the death of one subculture and the beginning of a more generic approach to the Village. Tish and Snooky's original 1970's punk rock hair dye store [Manic Panic] was closed down, and within weeks a GAP store was being constructed in its stead. Sure, there were some broken windows as the "Missing Foundation" generation realized what this meant for the future, and the neighborhood, but that only happened a few times, and then it was GAP, as part of the new general way the neighborhood would continue to be."

These were still the days of Mayor Koch; long before the arrival of Rudolph Giuliani. Mayor Koch liked a lively city and people would often see him on television asking his citizens,

"How'm I doing?" Most New Yorkers liked Ed Koch and elected him three consecutive times to office despite the economic hard times that existed in the city.

Although the gentrification process had begun and the first young urban professionals who were working for mainstream corporations in midtown were beginning to move into the neighborhood, for most people who lived in the East Village, money was still very tight and it was no surprise that business was initially very slow at Mission.

We were not yet on the neighborhood's radar screen and Mission, over by Avenue B, was located right on the edge of the safety zone, even for people who lived nearby.

I made up promotional cards and stood on a busy street corner giving them out to whoever seemed like a potential customer. It certainly helped get us started.

Mission: A Cast Of Characters
(First, Last, And Always)

William Tucker

William Tucker exposed me to industrial and industrial rock music. He was the first person that I knew who played albums from Nettwerk, Subway, and Wax Trax Records. William could also play guitar. One day, he told me that he was auditioning for Ministry. I had not yet heard William play guitar so I was pleasantly surprised when he told me that he had gotten the gig. Very soon thereafter, he was on a plane to Chicago where Ministry and many other Wax Trax bands were based. This would be the start of an exciting career for my friend. Whenever he was back in town, William would make his entrance with Chicago rocker friends in tow, jump up on the Mission bar and scream,

"Rob, what the fuck! How are you bro? We're here!" A night of partying would begin and take us into the following day. William's friends included Chris Connelly, and members of My Life With The Thrill Kill Cult, Meat Beat Manifesto, Front Line Assembly, Pigface, Smashing Pumpkins and other bands who were based in the rock music scene of Chicago.

Dave Kendall

Dave Kendall had created and hosted the most important alternative music show to ever run on MTV. It was called *120 Minutes* and it was not designed for the mainstream.

Although *120 Minutes* was relegated to late Sunday nights, its dedicated viewers helped build the careers of many of the artists whose music we played at the Mission. Dave was on MTV every week, and when William left to join Ministry, Dave stepped in and became one of our longest running deejays, staying to the last days of the club. Dave is now hosting *Party 360 with Dave Kendall* on Sirius Satellite Radio's First Wave Channel 22. Here's Dave and his thoughts about Mission,

"What made the Mission special was its size, or lack thereof. The place was tiny, so you could almost feel like you were in someone's living room. It was the place I learned to deejay. It was small and casual enough that the ten second pauses I left between tracks didn't matter all that much, or so I told myself. It was so different from the other alternative hangouts back then, like the Limelight on Sixth Avenue and The World, near Houston Street. It wasn't the place to be seen, 'cause it was basically a grotty little East Village bar. That made it quite anonymous and low-key, ideal for any musicians passing though town who didn't want all the razzmatazz. So, with no pretensions and expectations, it was a great place for interesting encounters and strange conversations. I remember sitting at the bar with Jaz Coleman of Killing Joke, discussing the relative merits of Friedrich Nietzsche and Aleister Crowley."

Michael Hilf

There's something about people from Detroit. I have always found them to be strong and savvy and they know how to get things done. Michael Hilf was from Detroit. We met while I was giving out Mission promotional cards; he would become a deejay at Mission and become my lifelong

William Tucker c. early 1990s

friend. We share a similar passion for music. Michael has some interesting ideas about how he would create a mood in the club. Michael relays his story,

"Being entrusted to spin the vinyl most Saturdays at the Mission probably should have included specific rules as to the adherence to manufacture's recommended revolutions per minute. For example, I would take this twelve inch record I had of that annoying Modern English song, "I Melt With You", and play it on 33RPM instead of 45RPM. The goths would all come out on the dance floor and sway happily back and forth like a black field of wheat. I would degrade the song further by turning the manual pitch further and further down throughout the song, eventually unplugging the entire contraption and let the record come to a grinding halt. It actually sounded really cool, and except for an occasional Jersey girl storming the deejay booth in a hysterical fit, it was a big hit. I got kind of known for playing records on the wrong speed and making people listen to Martin Luther King speeches.

I also soon had a "No Requests" sign I proudly hung in the booth; requests were always a hassle and almost never worked into the set. You would really have to have a great set of tits to avoid this otherwise stern rule (but this book is not about sex at the Mission, which never happened, and is not a part of this book).

On the subject of never happened, I also had a strip of black tape stuck across the mixer to keep the volume low so as not to upset the neighbors, I explained this in a hearing at the EPA, [the NYC environmental control bureaucracy which oversees enforcement for the city in regard to environmental issues] but for some reason, we still got a fine. Perhaps, it was because the woman who lived upstairs, rained down flower pots on our customers entering the club before the police took her away in a straightjacket one night. I did fail to mention that there were, and are, certain frequencies in Nine Inch Nails songs that, given the right volume and equalization, can certainly scrape out the inside of one's skull, and that tape, of course, can easily be repositioned."

Bryan Mechutan

Bryan Mechutan worked for TVT Records, as a telephone sales rep by day, and on weekend nights he was a deejay at the Mission.

Bryan once brought in a test pressing of a brand new band's first twelve-inch record and told me that his boss had asked him to play the song and see how it went over at the club. Our customers were dancing to it from the first night we put it on the turntable. The song was called "Down In It" and the band was called Nine Inch Nails.

These days, Bryan is the US label manager for Frontier Records, who distribute albums from melodic metal bands like White Lion, Asia, and Primal Fear. He also is the U.S. label manger for Demolition Records; releasing music from Twisted Sister, Nazareth, and Vixen.

Harold Kramer

Harold Kramer was a deejay at Mission. Harold also had an early interest in shooting video and has some amazing moments documented from Joey Ramone birthday parties held at the Mission and at Coney Island High; another East Village bar that was on Saint Mark's Place in the 1990s.

Harold's aunt and uncle ran and lived under the

Thunderbolt roller coaster in Coney Island for sixty years, as portrayed in the Woody Allen film, *Annie Hall*. Harold explains,

> "My aunt and uncle built the Thunderbolt over the Hotel Kennsington in 1925. Why they decided to live under the ride is still a mystery. It was always a lot of fun to visit them. The ride would make their house shake every time it passed over the house. They didn't mind because with every rattle, it was money in the bank. Former mayor, Giuliani, when he was still in power, had the Thunderbolt demolished, illegally, in 2000, at the request of the CEO of the New York Mets, who had just opened their minor league ballpark across the street. By that time, my family had long since sold the ride to Horrace Bullard."

Harold still spins 45s in his bar, Boulevard Tavern, in the Greenpoint section of Brooklyn.

Alex Coletti

We had a variety of fill-in deejays that would occasionally play music at Mission. Alex Coletti was the producer of *120 Minutes*. He usually filled in for Dave, if Dave had to be out of town on a MTV shoot. Alex was a very friendly, dependable guy and everyone liked him very much at the club. He went on to produce *Unplugged*, a milestone show on MTV. More recently, Alex is producing *Spectacle*, a very interesting talk and performance show with Elvis Costello.

Jonathan Daniel

Jonathan Daniel was one of the people who collected money at the door from customers upon entry. That job may have served him well as Jonathan has gone on to found Crush Management, a musician management company collecting profits in the millions with the mainstream success of pop rock artists, Train, and emo pop music artists Fall Out Boy, Panic at the Disco, and Cobra Starship. At the time that Jonathan was working at Mission, he was a member of Electric Angels, a glam metal band with punk pop influences; produced by Tony Visconti for Atlantic Records. I had known their vocalist, Shane, who used to come to the Sanctuary. Shane had grown up in Kingston, New York.

Jonathan had a dream to be a successful musician. When that dream did not materialize, he found a new important purpose to his life. When I mentioned that I was writing this book, Jonathan sent me this message,

"It was the best of times. It was the worst of times. I don't think it's a stretch to say that my band at the time, Electric Angels, qualified as a popular New York City rock n roll band in the late eighties/early nineties. It also doesn't mean that if you were a popular NYC rock n roll band at that time, you had a pot to piss in. Fortunately for us, there was a place we could go where the owner knew our name. The Mission was kinda like Cheers for the jet black hair set. The main man there, Rob, was the type of guy who'd come up with ideas like moving to Hawaii to rent camcorders to tourists or writing a letter to Animal Crackers to take the animals out of the cages on their boxes. I could never quite tell if Rob was joking or serious, but either way he was awesome. He had a soft spot in his heart for bands, which I will forever appreciate. He'd always let us deejay or look the other way on a drink or two while we'd discuss the latest three minute slice of heaven we were listening to at the moment. Every night from ten to eleven, he would have a five dollar, all you can drink special. I can't remember if the happy hour special was for everyone, or if it was just for bands, but we took full advantage of it.

I remember one Friday night I met a cute little blond number, from out of town there, and we proceeded to get so drunk that I could not drink any more. I don't know if that's happened to me. Ever. Before, nor since. So thank you Rob, I'll never forget that night. Oh and that cute little blonde number? I'm still with her today, eighteen years later!"

Psychedelic Furs
(Into You Like a Train)

We were only open for a month or two, when an attractive young lady came up to the window of the deejay booth and asked if I would play her boyfriend's record. To be nice, I said that I would, and a few days later she brought in a twelve-inch single of "All That Money Wants" by The Psychedelic Furs. I asked in a surprised tone,

"Your boyfriend is in The Furs?" She said,

"Yes", and that she and two other girlfriends wanted to have a home coming party for the band in the bar. The Psychedelic Furs was a post punk art rock band from England. I had no idea that they were now living in New York.

Their first two albums were always on my turntable back in my college days, long before they garnered mainstream success when their music was used in the movie, *Pretty In Pink*. I appreciated the way they blended late 1960s Velvet Underground influences with modern British punk rock attitude.

They would often start a concert with several minutes of ambient keyboards. Slowly, as the smoke billowed out above and in front of the stage and when the moment felt right under the dark blue lights, the members of the band would take their place on stage without playing a note. Creating a sense of excitement with guitars slung over their shoulders, they would look out at the crowd, eventually breaking into a fast tempo vamp that would drone on for several minutes. With the band chugging forward; the audience geared up for the ride, the singer, Richard Butler, would make his grand entrance onto the stage. The crowd would urge him forward as he made his way from one side of the stage to the other and then back to the center. All the while, he would acknowledge the people pressed up in front and make some sort of grand open arm gesture to the folks in the back of the room. As the band continued their fast paced guitar chugging drone, Richard Butler would yell out in his British accented voice,

"Hello! Hello New York!" and the crowd would roar back their approval.

"We are The Psychedelic Furs and we love you!" At that point, the band would burst right into their song entitled, "We Love You", off their first album. It was grand theatre and they certainly put the glam rock into punk. It brought the house down and that was just the start of the concert. By the end of the show, the Furs had seamlessly moved from their early punk rock gems and through their alternative hits, "Love My Way", "Heaven", "The Ghost In You", "Heartbreak Beat", "Here Come Cowboys", and "All That Money Wants"; finally ending with some of my favorite power chords of all time which open their colossal crossover hit, "Pretty In Pink". I've never seen a list of greatest power chord progressions in rock, but if I had a list, the opening guitar chords in this song would be near the top. Also, a sign of the success of a song is in the willingness of a band's audience to 'sing back' the chorus. Many great bands have 'sing backs' in their sets and the chorus in "Pretty In Pink" was always a moment of absolute joy as the crowd sang back those lines to the band,

"Isn't she pretty in pink?" I saw The Psychedelic Furs perform in concert more times than any other band with the exception of the Ramones.

    I eagerly anticipated the first party that we would have at Mission when the band wrapped up their tour come the following week. When it happened, it was a comfortable and somewhat laid-back event; nothing raucous or outrageous about the night and nothing crazy in any way. The band seemed road worn, but relaxed, happy to be home and in a very good mood. I had somewhat expected a bit of punk rock arrogance but there was absolutely no pretension in the room. That night, I spoke about microphone recording techniques with John Ashton, the lead guitarist, and raised a few beers with Tim Butler, who played bass. Both guys were friendly and easily accessible.

I received compliments about the bar from the band and was told that they would tell their friends and that they would often return. They did, and Dianne and I have both had a lasting friendship with John and Tim.

    Years later, after Dianne and I ended our relationship, it would be Tim who would introduce to Dianne, his friend and gold record recording engineer, Dan Grigsby. Dan and Dianne are still together after all these years.

I also met Joe McGinty that night, the keyboard player who played on the band's last few albums. It was Joe's girlfriend, Jessica, who first approached me with her request to play her boyfriend's music in the bar. I still count Joe as one of my close friends and that night when I got to meet The Psychedelic Furs is still one of my favorite nights that I had the pleasure of having had at the Mission.

Bjork, of The Sugarcubes, c. 1989

The Sugarcubes
(Party Out Of Bounds)

We hosted a party for The Sugarcubes who had completed a national tour in support of their second album. The tour ended in New York and they wanted to have a party to celebrate. They had a lot of Icelandic friends who lived in New York. Tens of thousands of people had seen them perform across the nation and their videos were in rotation on MTV. I was honored and a bit excited to have them hang with their friends at the bar.

Dianne and I were invited to their concert at the Beacon Theatre and we stayed until The Sugarcubes started their encore. Then, we caught a cab back downtown in order to get the bar ready for their party which was going to start in about an hour after their show. When our cab pulled up to Mission, as I was getting out, I noticed four well dressed guys leaning against a parked car in front of the building. I looked back over my shoulder as I was unlocking the door, and felt that about them there was something very special. They were dressed in that certain way of a British rock star. I didn't know who they were at that moment but intuition told me that they wanted to come into the bar. I told them that we were not yet open and that we had to prepare the club for a party but if they wanted to come in they were welcome to sit at the bar. I'm not sure why I did that, especially since this night was closed to the public. Something told me that these guys were cool and I went with my instincts.

Dianne and I poured ice into the bar sinks and put money into the cash registers while they sat respectfully at the bar waiting for us to finish our work. I asked them from where they had come as they looked really sharp. They said, in

English accents, they had just left their own party at some highbrow restaurant in Soho.

"It was boring," they said, and,

"Couldn't wait to get out of there." They had just left the record release party that their label was throwing for them for their new album, *Violator*. Dianne and I were hanging out with Depeche Mode. They had heard about The Sugarcubes' party and were the first to show up in the room.

The Sugarcubes' guests started to arrive about an hour later. I was surprised to hear so little English as almost everyone spoke in their native Icelandic language. The Sugarcubes picked up the tab for the entire party and I never saw so many people drink as much as their guests were drinking that night.

Mission had a dayglow mural behind the bar and had painted black walls with dayglow painted water pipes that ran the length of the club. Our next-door neighbor, Paul Ferguson, a former drummer in Killing Joke, had created the water pipes mural. The bar had a light cream pink-lavender Formica laminate top.

We had three florescent dayglow ultra violet black lights under the overhang on the front of the bar. They were evenly spaced about five feet apart. One of the lights had a short circuit, flickering on and off in a regular pattern throughout the course of the night. It's not something that anyone would easily notice, except that The Sugarcubes' drummer, Sigtryggur (Siggi) Baldursson, happened to be wearing a very colorful shirt that reacted to the ultraviolet light. When the light turned on, his shirt turned on, and when it turned off, his shirt turned off. It was weird and really very arty. Siggi sat in that seat for the entire night holding court with his friends as his shirt blinked on and off like a neon sign.

At one point when the party was in full gear, Bjork jumped up on the bar and started dancing to a James Brown song. I noticed that she had very, very large feet. Or, at least the sneakers that she was wearing that night were of a very large size. David, the singer from Depeche Mode, also jumped up on the bar and he was dancing too. I'm not sure if Bjork knew who he was as they were not dancing together but on opposite ends of the bar.

I guess a stage is a stage, and for certain performers the top of a bar can be a stage, too. I was holding onto the bar from the bartender's side, along with Dianne, hoping that the structure was built to withstand this moment. Bjork was really pounding up and down as her friends were cheering her on; beer bottles and cocktail glasses were flying in every direction.

Elliott, working that night, was holding the bar top too. When the song ended and the performers jumped down from the bar, Elliott turned to me and shook my hand. He reminded me of our conversation two years earlier up in New Paltz when I told him that I'd feel successful if Bjork was ever hanging out at the club. Not only was she hanging out, she was having a grand time dancing on the bar. I felt very good and it's something I will never forget; not so much because she is a famous star, rather, because Mission was a place in which she felt free and relaxed along with the rest of the band, and could comfortably be herself.

John Moore
(There's Something About You Girl)

Byron Guthrie was a drummer who had played in Ultra Vivid Scene, an East Village project by Kurt Ralske, and signed to 4AD Records. He became a regular a few weeks after we opened the Mission. He told me that a friend of his who had been in The Jesus and Mary Chain was coming to New York to form a band and that Byron was going to play drums in the group. One of my favorite bands, we played a whole lot of The Jesus And Mary Chain at the Mission.

A couple of weeks later, a few moments after we opened one night, a guy entered the club when I was busy getting the bar ready. I looked up and noticed him sitting alone. My first thought was,

"What a poser! What's he think he's in The Jesus and Mary Chain? I wonder where he got that pretentious haircut." As my thoughts were forming, his soft-spoken words formed in a gentle, inquiring kind of way and with an English accent he stated,

"I'm supposed to meet a friend here but I guess I'm a little bit early." I asked him for the name of his friend and he told me that it was Bryon.

"Holy shit!" I thought, "This is Bryon's friend and he really is, or just was, in the Mary Chain!"

Mission had only been open for two or three months and I was still surprised to find that musicians from some of my favorite bands would want to hang out at the bar. Without skipping a beat, and somewhat embarrassed by my own inner thoughts, I said,

"You must be John. Bryon told me that you were coming to New York. Welcome to the Mission." He replied that Byron had told him that we were one of Bryon's favorite bars and that Byron was here quite often. I told him that I agreed; that I did see Bryon here a lot and that he lived only a few blocks away on Avenue B. I think John had just arrived in New York that afternoon and this was the first place to which he had come after dropping his stuff off at his apartment. I was talking with John Moore, the drummer in The Jesus And Mary Chain from 1985 to 1987. John had replaced Bobby Gillespie when Bobby left to form Primal Scream. John became a very good friend and we spent quite a bit of time together at the Mission. He has a brilliant, self-deprecating sense of humor which I've always found endearing.

John's new band was called John Moore & The Expressway,

in which he sang and played rhythm guitar. He was signed to a record contract with a big major label. His manager, Jerry Jaffe, was also managing The Jesus and Mary Chain.

One night, John met a beautiful girl at the club. He was chatting her up at the bar which was very unusual for John. He was a shy guy so I could tell she was important to him. I had never seen him put any moves on any other ladies.

In order to impress her, he wanted to show her his album which we were starting to play at the bar. What John didn't know was that I had gotten his album in a record store in the East Village that was known for getting promo copies from people who worked at record labels. The copies were not meant for resale. There was a message on the cover that clearly said, "Promotional Copy. Not For Resale". But, the store would put a big sticker over the promo message with their store name and a ridiculously low price. I had bought John's album for $1.99.

John went into the booth and asked the deejay, Michael, if he could have our copy of his album for a moment. He wanted to show it to someone. When Michael pulled it out of the rack, John saw that his album had that gaudy sticker that said it cost only $1.99. He was bummed. He started to try and remove the sticker but it wouldn't come off easily. At that moment, I happened to enter the booth and John looked up at me and in an exasperated tone, he asked,

"How did you get my record so cheap?" He was struggling to remove the sticker but it was tearing the album cover apart. I said there's a store in the neighborhood but I didn't go into details. He finally removed the sticker and part of the cover came off; taking it back to the bar to show to his new lady friend. I'm not sure if she was impressed with the album cover, but I know that Veronica was certainly impressed with John. A short time later, John asked her to marry him and she said, yes. Several weeks later, we all went down to city hall and I greatly enjoyed being a witness at their beautiful marriage. I met John's

John Moore's album cover photo – 1989

mom and other members of his family who had flown in from England. After the formal papers were signed, we all went back to the Mission and had a wonderful wedding reception. Of all the events that I was honored to host at the Mission, this day was my favorite.

Unfortunately, the next several months did not fare as well for John as his band would fail to garner commercial success, and his marriage, strained by the stress of the moment would come to end in annulment. John exited from his recording contract and returned to his flat in London to begin a new phase in his life; eventually leading to a very short, but highly successful career in the UK with Black Box Recorder.

Jerry Jaffe
(People Are Strange)

Jerry Jaffe and I were at the bar discussing possible support acts for the upcoming tour. The Jesus And Mary Chain had a new record, *Automatic*, and it would be their biggest tour in America. Their single, "Head On", had a video on MTV and was receiving airplay on mainstream radio. Jerry said his choices were either Galaxy 500 or Nine Inch Nails. I told him that while I loved Galaxy 500, for this tour I felt that his band needed a high-energy support band. Nine Inch Nails was still unknown, and I think it was their first national tour, but I was betting that Trent and his band would make an impact on the fans that had come to see JAMC. I also told Jerry that their dance track, "Down In It", was going over exceptionally well at Mission. We speculated that the public would eventually hear Nine Inch Nails on the radio and see a cool video, but that would be a bit further up the road. Jerry agreed with me and I suppose that I only confirmed what he was already thinking.

Jerry Jaffe has an impressive record in the music business. In addition to working with JAMC, he managed Midge Ure, Dead Or Alive, and Saint Etienne. He was also head of the U.S. office of Creation Records and was involved with the promotion of the first album from Oasis. He also signed The Waitresses, Visage, Motorhead, Richard Thompson, and Bon Jovi. And, he also managed Electric Angels, the band in which Jonathan Daniel had been a member.

The Jesus and Mary Chain and Nine Inch Nails Party
(A Hard Day's Night)

By the time the tour reached New York City, both bands were breaking big across America. First, The Jesus And Mary Chain single, "Head On" had shot all the way up to the number two slot on *Billboard's* Modern Rock chart. In addition, The Pixies were about to release their version of the very same song; their single riding all the way up to number six on the very same chart. It's the only time I can recall two versions of the same song hitting the charts within a year of each other; both receiving critical reviews and both reaching into the top ten position. It was a tremendous salute from The Pixies to The Jesus and Mary Chain and both versions still hold a significant place in my music collection.

Meanwhile, the first Nine Inch Nails single, "Down In It", had made its way into the dance clubs of America; where deejays were spinning gothic and industrial rock records. Then, at the end of March 1990, and right after their successful JAMC supporting slot tour, the second Nine Inch Nails single, "Head Like A Hole" would be released and receive crossover airplay on many top forty stations. Also, the video, released that month, received a great deal of play on MTV.

TVT Records and Trent's manager had asked us to have a 'meet-n-greet' press party for Nine Inch Nails after their NYC performance. The band would arrive at Mission around 10:30PM and we needed to reserve space in the club for around forty or fifty music magazine writers and critics. This would be a very important opportunity for Trent to connect with the people who would be helping to launch his career. Alternative press and certain mainstream music critics were critical in garnering publicity and praise for new music artists.

Jerry told me that The Jesus and Mary Chain would come to Mission after their show and they wanted to have a party that would go afterhours; as they were not planning on arriving until around 2AM. Both bands could have their own time and space at Mission and I was looking forward to one night with two awesome parties.

There was a rap concert the night before at the Ritz. After the performance, there was a melee outside in front of the venue. The police were called and people were taken to jail. The following night, the date of the Nine Inch Nails and Jesus And Mary Chain show, the police showed up along with the NYC fire department to crack down on the so-called, unruly club.

The venue's booking agent, Chuck Beardsly, was a regular at Mission. He told me that the fire marshal told him that if the show was oversold, the fire marshal would have the police arrest him and take him off to jail. All shows at rock clubs are technically oversold. It does not actually mean that there is any danger as long as the fire suppression system is working properly and the exits are clearly marked;

Jim Reid, vocalist of The Jesus And Mary Chain – 1991

although lawyers could certainly argue the point. It is a law that city law enforcement agencies can use to close down clubs that they do not believe are in the best interest of the public good. Chuck called his boss and told him that he was going to cancel the show. He did not want to go to jail.

I got a call around 8:15PM from Gerry Gerrard, another regular at Mission, formerly the manager of Killing Joke and now the booking agent for Nine Inch Nails; asking if the band could come down early. I said sure but I wondered why they were coming so soon. I had no idea yet of what had happened up at the Ritz.

About twenty minutes later, I got a call from Jerry Jaffe asking if The Jesus And Mary Chain could come down to the club within the next hour. He told me that the show had been cancelled. I told him that it was no problem to start their party early. What I didn't know was that word somehow got out to the three thousand ticket holders that The Jesus And Mary Chain was playing downtown at a club called the Mission. They were not playing here. We had no stage and no live sound system. Mission was just a storefront bar on a side street with a deejay and tiny dance floor.

Trent Reznor and the band arrived just before 9PM along with around forty writers and magazine critics. All was going well for him and it seemed that everyone was having a good time. Although, his first big New York City show was unfortunately cancelled on this night, everyone seemed to be in good spirits. This tour was his first big success and there was a great deal of interest in his burgeoning career.

About forty-five minutes later, The Jesus and Mary Chain arrived with John Moore and a few of their other close friends. I escorted them to a back room where they could relax in private for awhile. It had been a stressful start to this evening up at The Ritz.

We never intended the back room to be used for guests. It was a space I used for storage and the only light back there was bright white florescent lighting. About a half hour went by when I noticed that our small club was really filling up. Our capacity was only around seventy-five people. I poked my head out of the front door and was shocked to see a line of people stretching down the block heading east to Avenue B, and then around the corner up Avenue B, and then turning west on East 6th Street. There were six hundred people on this line.

I asked several people on the line why they were waiting and they told me that they heard that The Jesus And Mary Chain was performing at Mission. I told them they were mistaken. They asked me if the band was hanging out inside and I said yes, but that we were already packed and there was no way we could fit any more people inside. Still, they would not leave and at least one hundred people were still standing on that line past 2AM when I next checked it out.

Police cars had stopped in the street at the front of the bar with their colored strobe lights turning. I went up to one car and told the officer that I was the club owner. I asked him why they were in front of my building and he asked me why there were hundreds of people lined up on the street trying to get into my club. I simply said that there was a famous British band having drinks at the bar. The police eventually left when they realized that the line was orderly and no problems occurred from the crowd.

Inside, the party was going strong. The friends that had managed to get in were having a blast. Jim and William Reid spent most of the night in the private back room under the glare of white florescent light; sitting around a bunch of cardboard boxes filled with my stuff from upstate.

At one point, I walked in to see how they were doing and if they needed something from me. William was holding my old acoustic guitar which had been lying around in the room. It was in need of new strings and he was trying to tune it but the strings were just too worn out to make any use of the guitar on that night.

Every so often, they would attempt to make a walk through the front room and mingle with their friends, but it was just too crowded to be comfortable and they retreated back to the private back room where each time I looked in on them they seemed to be in animated discussions. I had some difficulty understanding what they were saying through their Glasgow accents, but I could tell that they were doing OK and the stress of the earlier cancelled show had receded into the night.

Trent Reznor spent most of the night in the front room talking with new friends and fans. I never did see him in the back room.

I always wondered what the bands thought of that night; if it was special in any way, and if they even remembered their party. Many years later, sometime around 2004, I was in contact with Ben Lurie who had been in The Jesus And Mary and was at the party. In a very nice email to me, he told me that the band often spoke of that night and that the party had been a highlight of that tour. What could have been a miserable experience was turned into a really fun night for all.

Mission was getting very popular with many British bands that were coming over and performing in New York. Word spread among an inner circle of musicians. It would not be unusual to see members of the Sisters of Mercy, Cocteau Twins, Siouxsie And The Banshees, Psychedelic Furs, Lush, Killing Joke, and other UK artists drinking and hanging out with their friends and other musicians at the bar.

Al Jourgensen – c. 1990s

Ministry
The Industrial Music Scene
(You Know What You Are)

The innovative music we played at Mission included many different styles. On any given night you could hear our deejay segue modern rock, gothic rock, Manchester psychedelic dance, American noise rock, and industrial rock music. Although I loved all of the various formats, we had a very special relationship with the players in the industrial rock music scene by virtue of our friendship with William Tucker. William, who had been a deejay at Mission, had gone on to play guitar in several industrial rock bands including Pigface, My Life With The Thrill Kill Cult, Chemlab, with Chris Connelly, as well as his gig in Ministry. He also introduced me to many musicians who played in other bands with whom he was friendly.

William's tours would take him all over the world and, on occasion, I would receive a post card from him on which he would write a short note about some experience he just had in Japan, in Europe, or way down in Texas. He once told me that it seemed like he spent more time on tour in Texas than in any other place on the planet. William spent the better part of his life on the road in those days. But, sooner or later the tour he was on, and the band with whom he was playing, would arrive in New York for a show, or a series of shows in the city and tri state area. The band would check themselves into their hotel rooms, start a series of calls to their girlfriends, their male friends, the players they knew in New York, and to their connections that would lead them away, after their shows, about town. Sometimes,

William would call and let me know they were coming. Sometimes, they simply arrived at the bar.

We had parties with Killing Joke, Front 242, KMFDM, Psychic TV, My Life With The Thrill Kill Cult, Meat Beat Manifesto, Pigface, MC 900 Foot Jesus, Front Line Assembly, and Skinny Puppy. They were often raucous affairs fueled with all possible stimulants. Mission was a base for them, a place to meet their friends in New York. When they walked through the door, it was like the space shuttle had just set down in the bar. When I was momentarily within their orbit, I was fortunate to bear witness to the individuals whose creative explosion was unique in the history of rock. The leading industrial rock bands of the early 1990s were among the leading musical artists in the nation. Collectively, their album sales rivaled that of any other musical movement, including Seattle's great music scene at the time. However, they had become greater than the sound of their recordings; they became a political force of confrontation, a collective finger up the ass of the establishment. And, they did it in a way that young Americans could appreciate, with power and passion beyond limits previously acceptable to their parents. It wasn't contrived, but it was well conceived, although at the time many of the players may have been running on gut instinct rather than proper cerebral planning.

 Two of the primary bands were Ministry and Nine Inch Nails. Of the two, Ministry, along with their spin off projects, was the more prolific. However, Nine Inch Nails had a huge immediate impact with the release of their debut album, *Pretty Hate Machine*.
Ministry had serious underground credibility. They had been on the scene for years. Al Jourgensen was at the helm. He was the man in charge; the founding father and front man of the band. He assembled the musicians and produced the albums. In addition to his work with Ministry, Al had

side projects with Revolting Cocks, Skinny Puppy, Lard, and 1000 Homo DJs. Ministry had two gold albums and one platinum record for their three releases between 1988 and 1991. They were at the apex of their creativity and they had pushed hard against the mainstream.

We had lived through eight years of Ronald Reagan and we were in the middle of the first George Bush administration; a dozen years of Republican control of the government. Ministry captured underground anger at the political powers in charge. They railed against the hypocrisy found in the mainstream media. They successfully incorporated visual imagery into their performances and exploited their brilliant video releases through MTV, which at that time was targeting young adults who cared more about music than reality TV.

Trent Reznor, the main creator of the music on the Nine Inch Nails album, had to prove his worth among his peers. It wasn't easy. He had to work very hard, dig deeply inside, and find the artist that only he could be. There were people who thought Trent was a Johnny come lately who seemed to be rising too quickly into mainstream acceptance. His music was danceable but was he a bit of a lightweight? He was attractive but was he just a new teen idol? Some thought Ministry rocked harder, heavier, and faster but Nine Inch Nails had plenty of songs that made the kids want to jump up and down at their shows.

Trent seemed to incorporate his own personal demons into his writing; internalizing personal insecurities into songs about separation, loneliness, misery and anger. Al was more overtly political although his songs also explored issues about being marginalized, persecuted, alienated, and dehumanized. Together, and separately, Nine Inch Nails and Ministry became the cultural and commercial foundations of industrial rock music. Whatever it was that each was doing, it was certain that both had achieved success.

One night, after a party, Al had left something of great

importance to him in the bar. We found out where he was staying and had one of our employees return his possession. The following night, Al came back to the Mission and I was alone in the deejay booth. We had chicken wire against the window preventing people from reaching in and tapping you on the shoulder in order to make a request. I had my back to the window, the headphones on and was cueing up a record. Feeling a presence, not sure of what it was, I turned around to find Al pressing very hard against the chicken wire, making an imprint with his face. He was cutting himself and a small bit of blood was running down the outside of his nose. I looked up at him in surprise. He looked back at me with eyes very, very, dark; looking out from beyond the abyss of his soul. Quietly, he said,

"Thank you man, for last night." I replied,

"No problem, anytime." My voice trailed off as I smiled a half cocked, nervous smile. He scared me. He pulled his face out from the chicken wire and quietly left the club.

I have never known of a darker human soul in the world and I suspect that even the sun moved more quickly through the sky when Al was about in the day. Of course, that was a very long time ago…

The Ancients
(Touch The Fire)

I always had an interest in recording and producing music. Many years earlier, I had played in bands and wrote songs and had a short-lived publishing deal with a major music publisher. Nothing came of that, but I did learn how to record music and always enjoyed the studio process. I could talk equipment, techniques, and songs with anyone who cared. That led me into a relationship with a New York City goth band called The Ancients, whose album I produced in 1991.

I had met Fredric Schreck, a relatively unknown singer, when he was performing in a local band called Shoot The Doctor. He had one of the most powerful baritone voices that I have ever heard in rock. His voice was deep, reminiscent of Jim Morrison or Peter Murphy, but stronger and with greater power and range. Fred's voice was awesome. He could rival any other singer in the world. His songs were well constructed, bringing a melancholy, somewhat angry approach with which he engaged his audience. This was in the early 1990s and Fred's gothic manner also seemed to incorporate elements of Kurt Cobain attitude along with Fred's influences from The Dammed. I thought he truly had superstar potential and with a great band behind him, I could see him breaking through in the way that Trent Reznor was doing at that time.

Fred and I spoke at length about his music and his career. We also talked about the various styles of music that were on our turntables, including the Manchester sound of The Stone Roses, shoegaze from My Bloody Valentine and Blur, and 4AD bands like Lush and Cocteau Twins. He would occasionally deejay at the Mission too.

Eventually, we decided to go to a small studio in Queens, owned by an old friend, Barry Goldstein, who I had known up in New Paltz, and lay down a few tracks. Using Barry's drum loops, Fred recorded bass, rhythm guitar, and vocals on a few songs which we started playing at the bar. These were stripped down arrangements; just drums, bass, one guitar part, and a vocal but there was an immediate interest in his music from the regulars who came to dance to Bauhaus, Sisters Of Mercy, Joy Division, and Love And Rockets.

One night when we were playing one of Fred's songs, John Carruthers came up to me and asked me if I knew who was the singer and if I could tell him anything about the

Joey Ramone, Paul Ferguson, Fred Schreck, and Joe McGinty at The Ancients audition for Joey.

The Ancients performing members Geoff Green, Dana Locatell, Albert Zampino, Fred Schreck (kneeling), and Dianne Galliano.

band. John had just moved from England to New York. He had replaced Robert Smith in Siouxsie And The Banshees when Robert left to devote his time to perform in The Cure. I had seen Siouxsie And The Banshees ten years earlier when they came to New York and performed at The Peppermint Lounge. Their records were always interesting and I had been a fan going all the way back to their first album in 1978. Now, John had just left Siouxsie and was considering his opportunities in New York. John expressed an interest in playing guitar on some of Fred's songs.

At the same time, Paul Ferguson, a former drummer in Killing Joke, was playing with John in a new band called Pleasurehead. Paul lived right next door to the Mission and kept his drums in our back room. I gave him a set of keys to the club so he could come and go as he pleased and practice drumming without offending the neighbors. The back room of Mission was actually a concrete building extension into a former backyard and had no floors above it so he could make plenty of sound and racket. Paul also agreed to play on Fred's recordings.

Knox Chandler, who at the time was playing guitar with The Psychedelic Furs, came in to play cello on a song. Knox went on to play and co-write with Dave Gahan, of Depeche Mode, on Dave's solo album. Afterward, Knox played in Siouxsie And The Banshees, too. Most recently, Knox has been playing with Cyndi Lauper.

Joe McGinty, who had become a regular at the bar and was also in The Psychedelic Furs, played keyboards on Fred's recordings.

We decided to record an entire album through the autumn of 1990 and completed it in the spring of 1991. The players on Fred's album were of the highest pedigree. I came up with the name for the group, which Fred approved. The Ancients was now a new band in New York.

During this time, Dianne and I were regularly having dinner in a local pub, Capitol, on Avenue A, just around the corner from where we lived. There was a wonderful waitress there named Joyce Bowden, who also happened to be a back-up singer in the Tom Tom Club. We saw Joyce many nights of the week and we sometimes spoke about music. One night, I told Joyce about the new record that I was producing. She asked me to give her a tape of The Ancients. She told Dianne and me that she was a good friend with Joey Ramone and that she would play the tape for Joey. Honestly, I didn't think Joey would like it. The Ancients was not punk, but just the thought of Joey hearing it was pretty exciting for me. I had no idea that Joey would soon become a very important part of my life.

Joey Ramone
(I Remember You)

Dianne and I came home from work around 5AM. There was a message on our telephone answering machine and it was from Joey Ramone. He said that Joyce had played The Ancients tape for him and that he really liked it. He wanted to help get the band a record deal and that I should call him back soon. I called him back the very next day and he suggested that I come over and hang out, listen to records, and talk about the band. I had a play date with Joey Ramone!

I think Joey and I hit it off right away. Whenever he was home from touring, he would call and we would spend time together running errands, debating the qualities of good and bad pizza, listening to music, discussing politics, and just hanging out. He was a very passionate guy and had very strong convictions. Best of all, he had a great sense of humor.

Joey and I both shared a collective sense of the absurd and we had no problem in finding the humor in these affairs.

For example, the comedic actor Al Lewis, played Grandpa Munster in the 1960s TV show, *The Munsters*. By the early 1990s, Al's TV star days were long over but he would make paid personal appearances at parties and corporate events, dressed as his TV character, Grandpa Munster.

Al had something to do with a restaurant that had opened in the West Village. I'm not sure if he owned it, was a part owner, or was just a paid employee. In any event, Al Lewis would stand in front and insult people as they walked by the place. Some of those folks would stop and look back at Al and realize that he was the actor who had played Grandpa Munster. Then, Al would talk them into coming into the restaurant. It seemed to be a very strange business model. Absurd, for sure, and Joey and I laughed about the idea.

Joey had a passion for art. He and his mom were both collectors. He had a collection of original screen prints of San Francisco concert posters from the late 1960s, Grateful Dead and Jefferson Airplane at The Fillmore type posters. One day as we were about to leave his apartment, we heard a news story on the radio about the death of the artist who created his posters. We both stopped in our tracks. He looked down at me over the rim of his rose red glasses. We were silent for a moment and then he said,
"That's too bad about him dying." Then, a pregnant pause, a sly slight smile, and one last thought,
"Do you think they're worth more now?" I said,
"Oh yeah," and we quietly chuckled all the way out of his door and down the hall to the elevator.

Joey wanted to see the band perform before he invested his time and reputation in promoting The Ancients. I arranged to have the band play at a Chelsea rehearsal space. Joey didn't know who was in the band but he knew he loved the recording.

The band got to the rehearsal space about an hour before

Joey Ramone c. 1990

Joey, in order to warm up before his arrival. They went through a few of the songs and everyone felt pretty good. We went downstairs, back onto the street, and waited on a glorious late spring day when a yellow cab pulled up in the front of the building. The back, right side passenger door opened and we could see this sneaker attached to a long leg pushing the cab door open while the occupant paid the fare. At the same time, Joey was balancing a slice of pizza in one hand and receiving change in the other. Paul Ferguson said that it was an absolutely perfect way in which to meet the one and only, Joey Ramone!

I made the introductions and we all went upstairs to the rehearsal space. The band played with confidence and panache and after they ran through three or four songs, Joey had a wide smile that comes when a person has a sense of tremendous satisfaction. I was standing next to Joey when one of the musicians repeated the famous John Lennon quote from The Beatles' movie, *Let It Be*. It went something like,

"That's all folks and I hope we passed the audition." I'm sure Joey recognized the quote and the absurdity of the question at that moment. There could be no doubt. I then told Joey about the other bands in which the guys had played: Psychedelic Furs, Siouxsie And The Banshees, Killing Joke; it was one hell of a resume.

Joey arranged for record label people to come see The Ancients perform in concert. I made sure that everyone from the Mission would show up and show their support. Joey introduced the band when they played at CBGBs. The band had a palpable buzz and even secured a coveted opening slot for The Damned when that seminal British band performed before three thousand people at The Ritz.

Joey would mention The Ancients when writers would ask him to what new bands he was listening. On occasion, he would wear The Ancients tee shirt. Joey was The Ancients' number one fan and he did all that he could do to raise their profile and bring attention and credibility to the band.

The Ramones were having a resurgence at this time in the early 1990s. It's hard to believe, but Joey once told me that The Ramones never sold more than seventy thousand records of any one of their studio albums. Their brilliant early albums had each sold only half that number. It would not be until their greatest hits package was available that they would finally receive a gold record for sales in excess of half a million units. However, it seemed that everyone who had bought those albums in the 1970s would start a band of their own. The Ramones were being discovered by a new generation of kids who were already exposed to bands like Social Distortion, Pearl Jam, and Nirvana.

Also, the Ramones had just been recently discovered by a whole generation of South American teens. The band was now headlining festivals where tens of thousands of rabid Ramones fans would show up at their concerts. Joey told me that they even had problems coming and going from their hotels because the kids would want to touch them and be in their personal presence. They would swarm all over the mini van that the band used to move between the airport, hotel and concerts. Joey was often on tour and I felt really good for him. To accurately misquote Winston Churchill,

"Never a band was owed so much, by so many, for so long!" Their ship had finally come in and they were reaping the rewards of their decade and a half of effort.

Joey and I used to talk about opening a club together and we actually looked at a couple of spots. One day, we went to look at a small four-story building on the Bowery, just down the block from CBGBs. It was a ground level storefront and on the three floors above were supposed to be apartments. When we entered, we saw that the store had been turned into a locker room with benches installed in front of the lockers. We thought that was weird. Why should a store have lockers? Some were padlocked and some were completely wide open.

Discarded women's clothing was strewn all about the room. And, there were music cassettes with Asian writing scattered around on the floor. It looked as though some folks had certainly left in a hurry.

We went upstairs and noticed that the apartment on the second floor was not an apartment at all. It had no kitchen and no living room; just a series of several small bedrooms, each with an undersized bath. There were around twenty of these bedroom/bathroom combos in the building. Cheap sheets were still on the beds and cheap cassette players were plugged into the walls. Many more Asian cassettes were scattered around the floors. Joey said,
"There's something really weird about this place." And then it dawned on us both at the very same time. We were standing in the apparent remains of a brothel!
Joey and I thought that this building would make a great low budget hotel for bands that would come and play in New York. It is so rediculously expensive to stay in the city but this place could be a dive-y hotel with a super cool bar. In addition, it was in the East Village and could easily become part of the scene. There was one big problem, however. The entire building was on a serious slant with one side of it leaning a significant way to the west. Joey said,
"We can call it The Funhouse Hotel." And, I suggested that we could put those funhouse mirrors in the bar downstairs. While we thought that this would add a lot of character to our possible low budget rock hotel, we also worried that the building might someday fall down. It would really suck if we were responsible for taking out some of the nation's new up and coming bands with a possible building cave in. We both could imagine a photo on the cover of the New York Post, with the headline, "Rocker Ramone Indicted In Building Disaster!" We decided to come back to

this project at a later date, but that never came to be. However, I did keep some of the Asian cassettes and whenever I hear Asian pop music, I think of Joey Ramone.

Joey may have been seeing a girl who was a vegetarian at that time. We used to order lunch and have it delivered to his apartment. Almost every restaurant in New York City will have a delivery guy. That's one of my favorite things about living here. One day, we were trying to decide what to order from a nearby Chinese restaurant. I asked him what he liked from the menu. He thought about it for a moment and then he said,

"I really like pepper steak but I'm supposed to order something that's healthy. So, why don't I order the mixed Chinese vegetables and you get the pepper steak?" Then, after a brief pause, he added,

"Is it OK if we share?" I was pretty sure that later that evening when that special girl asked Joey what he had for lunch, he might simply have said,

"I ordered mixed vegetables from the Chinese restaurant." Joey was a very bright guy.

I never knew what was wrong with Joey but he had more bottles of medicine in his apartment than some pharmacies carry on shelves. I never asked him about his medication, but there was a lot of it. Joey's health was not great. Joey never mentioned what was wrong but I knew it was very serious. Later on, I read that Joey was diagnosed with Obsessive-Compulsive Disorder but I never witnessed him having an OCD moment. Perhaps, it may have been that he was at his most relaxed point in his life during those years, in the early 1990s.

The early formative years in Queens were long over. Being from Brooklyn myself, I could only imagine what kind of abuse Joey must have gone through as a kid growing up out there. He had to be a magnet for anyone who wanted to prove how tough he was by demeaning Joey in one way or another.

The difficult struggles for the band in their early days had passed. They had wanted radio hit songs and had hoped to become an American idea of The Beatles. When that did not happen, it had to be deflating and that could not have been any help for an already fragile ego. But, that was almost a decade earlier and by the early 1990s, Joey seemed to have made his peace with that issue.

He was no longer drinking and had been sober for two or three years when we met. The Ramones were receiving global recognition for their contribution to music and were paid very well, finally, for gigs. His voice sounded better than ever. He had really become a good singer.

The Ramones were headlining giant stadium shows in South America where tens of thousands of kids would chant, in Spanish accents, call back lines like 'Hey Ho, Let's Go' and 'Gabba Gabba Hey' at the band. It must have felt very good.

It was a year or two before Joey was diagnosed with lymphoma. Still, he must have been using that medication for something, but I have no idea. Sometimes he would break appointments because he wasn't feeling well. This seemed to be more often the case upon his return from touring. It must have been impossible for him to take care of himself on the road. The band was always cramped into a mini van and the relationship with John was never very good. When Joey referred to John, he never called him Johnny. It was always, John.

We rarely spoke about the other members of the Ramones but I do remember asking Joey if he ever saw any of the other guys in the band, apart from when they were on tour together. He asked,

"Do you mean socially?" I said,

"Yes." He thought about it for a moment. Joey would often refrain from answering questions until he had figured out what he wanted to say. Then, he said something to this effect,

"Well, John doesn't do anything but collect baseball cards. That's all he does." He said it with such disgust that I knew that it was not a topic for future consideration.

I then asked him about the other members of the group and his mood somewhat brightened. I asked about CJ who had replaced Dee Dee on bass a few years earlier. CJ was not an original member of the group, but from my perspective, CJ seemed to be a highly valuable part of the band's resurgence. Joey, looked down at me and said,

"CJ is a great kid." He didn't say anything else; Joey's response left me with an uncertain feeling about what he was really thinking.

Then, I brought up the member of the Ramones about whom I was most curious. Many years before, I remember Dee Dee approaching me on East 14th Street. I guess it was in the very early days of the band, maybe in 1977. We didn't know each other personally but I had seen his band perform at CBs. Punk rock was still relatively unknown. You knew that you had something in common if you saw someone who dressed like you. We were also about the same age.

I was walking west on East 14th Street when I noticed Dee Dee about ten or twelve feet in front of me. He was just standing there on that run down street. Our eyes met briefly and he walked straight up to me. He asked me, in that soft high-pitched Queens accented voice of his,

"Hey man, can I borrow two dollars?" He was panhandling. I looked straight at him and I realized for the first time that Dee Dee was a junkie. I felt sorry for him but at that same time, I thought of him as a brilliant bass player and songwriter. Dee Dee wrote most of the songs in the Ramones. I didn't want to bring up his band or say anything that a fan might say. I suppose that he already knew that I knew who he was. It was all so awkward. I reached into my pocket and pulled out a five-dollar bill and gave it to Dee Dee. He looked down at it. He looked back at me and said,

"Thanks, man. I'll get you back." I said,

"No problem, I'll see you around sometime."

I remember looking into his eyes at the moment we parted. It was just an instant, but in that fraction of a second I could feel Dee Dee's humanity, his pain, humility, and childlike awkwardness. I continued heading west and he went east on 14th Street. Even though this happened around fifteen years earlier, I never mentioned this to Joey. When I asked Joey about Dee Dee, Joey paused for a moment in his usual way, and he sort of sighed,

"I don't really see much of Dee Dee anymore. I hear he's in California." I think Joey spoke volumes in that moment for what he did not say to me. I realized that Joey felt as I did about Dee Dee but probably had to endure the pain of living with him in a band. I cannot imagine what it must have been like to be in a close relationship. My heart goes out to Dee Dee's two former wives, Vera and Barbara, as well as to the other members of the band and the other folks who were part of their organization.

I always wanted to know more about Joey's thoughts in regard to Dee Dee because I knew there was a great deal more that Joey thought and could say. Weird as this might sound, I have always thought that Joey could have written an interesting book about Dee Dee. However, it seemed too personal a matter for me to ever approach again.

Joey and I once had a conversation about the New York Rangers. If you go to a hockey game in New York, you will hear the 'Hey ho, let's go' line from "Blitzkrieg Bop". The New York Rangers use it to rev up the team and the crowd when they need to turn the momentum of the game in their favor. Being a big fan of the Rangers, I asked Joey what he thought about the team using a Ramones song. He thought about it for a moment and then said,

"I think it's cool, it's a New York thing, you know." Then, he paused for a short moment again and added,

"But the thing is, we don't get paid for that." I said,

"Really, I don't understand. Why not?" He replied,

"I don't know. It's something to do with the way royalties are collected or something." I said,

"That doesn't seem fair." Then, I asked Joey if he had ever seen a Ranger game at Madison Square Garden. He said that he had not and that he wasn't really that much into sports. I replied that it would be really fun to go to a game with him and that if he was sitting there in the Garden when they played The Ramones, he would feel proud to see how the chant would motivate the fans and the team. I also told him that if he went to a game, the place would go crazy if they saw him sitting in the arena. He said,

"I don't know, Rob, you think so?" I said,

"Yeah, I really do. I bet they would even have a shot of you on television, you know, sitting in a seat at the game." He said,

"Well, I've never been to a game but hockey seems kind of cool, but I don't know the rules." I replied,

"No problem, I'll explain what's happening to you." At that, he said,

"Oh right, if you get tickets, we'll go together."

Good seats to New York Ranger games are always sold out so I didn't follow up on the idea, but what I didn't think of at the time was that I could have contacted the Ranger's front office and ask them for a pair of guest tickets. It would have been a blast to share that moment with Joey and I do regret not giving it a try.

My older brother, Tommy, was a friend of Steve Rubell who was a co-owner of Studio 54. They had known each other back when they were kids in Brooklyn. Steve would greet my brother at the entrance to his club, ushering him straight past the line of others who might have been standing there for hours. I was not interested in going to Studio 54, but one night in the summer of 1977, my brother persuaded me to take the ride into the city in his red Buick Riviera.

Studio 54 was the first disco of the world, but not in the

sense that that was where disco music was first played. I'm sure that was not the case; it was the first disco of the world in that it was the premier dance club of its age. It was where the rich and famous went to party. Getting in was very special, even for me, a guy who had no interest in disco.

My brother was in a *Saturday Night Fever* white polyester suit, purchased at The Leading Male, on Kings Highway, in Brooklyn, the same place where the suit was obtained for John Travolta. I was in my usual attire; a black satin new wave light-weight baseball jacket with green dayglow trim, black tee shirt and straight black jeans. As brothers, we could not have been more different in our attire and tastes. But, as brothers in our twenties, we did share a taste for fun times and an interest in being where the action was, and Studio 54 was happening.

The music was loud, the girls were extraordinarily hot; it seemed as though we had entered a circus for adults. I think there was even a trapeze over the dance floor. Not being a dancer, I hung out at the bar, content to watch the beautiful people move in and out of my view.

My brother had been there many times and he had even partied with Jack Nicholson. I don't remember too much more about that night but I do remember persuading my brother, and his friend Howie Gertzman, to come downtown with me on another night. My brother had taken me to his favorite club and now I would take him to mine. I would also take him to see my favorite band.

We found a parking space on the Bowery right in front of the club. Getting out of the car, we approached CBGBs on a hot summer night. This neighborhood seemed dangerous and although my brother never had a problem in handling himself, his senses told him that he was out of his element and where we were heading could certainly be trouble.

The people outside had radical haircuts and holes in their jeans. They looked like 'freaks' to my brother who was in his *Saturday Night Fever* white polyester suit. He was probably right, but freaks come in all styles, all ages, and can hang out in all types of clubs. These freaks were my freaks.

We opened the front door to CBGBs and gained admission to the club. The Ramones were already on stage and they were playing very loud. My brother shouted something into my ear but it was really difficult to hear. Howie liked loud music but his tastes leaned towards metal. This was the first time either Howie or my brother had ever heard punk rock and it terribly upset my brother. The band was an assault upon his ears. The people were an assault upon his eyes and the scene was an assault upon his senses. My brother and Howie left after spending less less than ten minutes in the club; taking off and heading uptown to Studio 54, leaving me to enjoy the set.

I told Joey this story many years later when he and I were hanging out together in his living room. I was curious to know his reaction. He just looked at me and smiled. Then, Joey asked,

"Your brother really had one of those white suits?" I replied,

"Yeah. He might still have it although I'm sure it doesn't fit him anymore." He continued to smile. Then, after a short while, Joey said,

"You know, you just have to love 'em."

I think he was thinking about his brother, Mickey. And, I was thinking of Tommy.

Although Joey Ramone did quite a lot to bring attention to The Ancients, ultimately the band was not signed to a recording contract. John and Paul got busy playing in Pleasurehead. They would get signed to a major label and change their name to Crush.

Fred asked Dianne to play bass in The Ancients. She was a beginner so it was a real challenge for her. Morgan Visconti, the son of the famous producer, Tony Visconti, played keyboards for awhile until he left and was replaced by Geoff Green. Albert Zampino played guitar. Although the players were not well known, this live version of the band was still very, very good.

We decided to release the record on Mission Records, which was named after the nightclub. I pressed up a thousand copies of the album and sent them out to magazines and college radio stations. We received some airplay and there was a deejay at one particular station, in Iowa, that was playing the album a lot. I do not recall the station's call letters but I do remember that it was a public radio station that could blast their signal over the entire state.

We made arrangements with the deejay to do an 'on air' interview, over the telephone, from Joey's apartment. It was going to last thirty to forty minutes and the deejay would play some tracks from the album. Joey would go first and talk about The Ramones and then talk a little bit about The Ancients. Then, the deejay would interview Fred and Dianne.

What I didn't know before the interview began was that Joey had made arrangements for Handsome Dick Manitoba, from The Dictators, to be interviewed in the last part of the show. At the designated time, Joey's phone rang and it was the deejay from the radio station.

Joey had the speakerphone on and we could all hear the questions. It was live, 'over-the-air' in Iowa. The first part had pretty standard questions about The Ramones. The second part with Fred and Dianne was a basic interview too. Then, the deejay asked if he could speak with Handsome Dick Manitoba. Joey said that Dick was not here but that he would telephone Dick and add him to our conference call. Joey dialed Dick's phone number and you could hear the electronic telephone button sounds go out over the air, do-do-do, do-do-do-do-do, do do! Then, Dick's answering machine kicked in. This was in the days before voice mail. Dick's outgoing message said,

"You have reached," and then it proceeded to give out

his personal phone number over the air across the state of Iowa to anyone and everyone who was listening to the show.

Joey looked over at me with that 'oh shit' look on his face that comes when unintended circumstances fuck up good intentions. With an expression that seemed to ask,

"What should I do?" I said,

"See if he is home." So, Joey started to leave a message for Dick. It went something like,

"Dick, Dick. It's Joey. Are you home?" Short pause... Then again,

"Dick, it's Joey. Pick up the phone!" Silence. Then, one last time,

"Dick, It's Joey...."

This was going live, over-the-air across the state of Iowa. People could hear Joey Ramone leaving a phone message for Handsome Dick Manitoba. We all started to laugh. We didn't know what to do next. And, I'm sure it occurred to Joey that if he hung up now, Dick might still receive unwanted phone calls from all over the sate of Iowa. It was pretty funny in that awkward sought of way. At the very last moment, Dick picked up the phone. It sounded like he was in a thoroughly drunken haze; partying heavily for a day or two and had just fallen asleep. He was in a deep fog. The conversation went something like this:

Dick: "Hello."
Joey: "Dick, it's Joey."
Dick: "Who?"
Joey: "Joey!"
Dick: "Hey, what's up?"
Joey: "You're on the radio."
Dick: "On the radio?"
Joey: "Yeah."
Dick: "Where?"
Joey: "In Iowa."
Dick: "You're in Iowa?"
Joey: "No. I'm home."

A bit of silence....
And then the conversation continued:
Joey: "You're on the radio, in Iowa."
Dick: "How do you know I'm on the radio?"
Joey: "Because, it's live."
More silence...
Then, the conversation continued again:
Dick: "What's live?"
Joey: "You are. We're on the radio."
More silence.
We thought Dick might have fallen back asleep.
Then Dick continued:
Dick: "If you're home, then how do you know I'm on the radio in Iowa?"
We broke up laughing now. Dianne, Fred, and I were listening in on Joey's speakerphone.
Joey: "Cause it's live. Right now."
Then, more silence...
Then the DJ, who had one of those DJ voices, took this moment to interject something like:
DJ: "Hey, Dick, this is XXXX from radio station XXXX. You're live on the air and we want to ask you a few questions about your band!"
Dick: "Who the fuck is this?"
Dick seemed really drunk and could not comprehend that this radio interview was happening live, 'over-the-air' at that very moment, via a conference call over Joey's telephone. He was shocked when he heard another voice talk to him over Joey's phone!
Joey: "Dick. It's Joey. This is live on the radio."
Dick: "You're home?"
Joey: "Yeah."
By this point, Dianne, Joey, Fred, and I were laughing uncontrollably. Joey was trying not to laugh but the irony in this situation was getting the best of him.
Dick: "Who's that?"
Joey: "Some friends of mine. They were on the radio

too."
 Dick: "We're all on the radio?"
 More uncontrollable laughter...
 Joey: "Yeah. But now you're on the radio, live..."
 DJ: "This is XXXX from radio station XXXX. Can I ask you a few questions?"
 Dick: "Oh shit! That guy again!"

Dick, not comprehending that he should not curse on the air, was going to get this poor guy fired. The deejay just wanted to do an interview and ask Dick a few questions and play a Dictators song on the air, in Iowa.

We were laughing uncontrollably and could not stop for what seemed like the rest of the night, no matter how hard we tried. Handsome Dick was hilarious and I'm not even sure if he would remember the interview. It was the funniest moment that I have ever had in music. I never got the chance, but I would have liked to ask Joey if he felt the same way. Also, it is a pleasure to remember Joey laughing so hard and having such a good time with us on that day.

Joe McGinty
(Take It As It Comes)

The Ramones were working on *Mondo Bizarro*, a new album in 1992. Joey told me that they were going to cover, "Take It As It Comes", a Doors song. He said that they had asked Ray Manzarek, the original keyboardist in The Doors, to perform on their version and that Ray had politely declined. Ray said that he was no longer playing and that The Ramones version which was much faster than the original, was too fast for him to be able to play all the notes. There was a lot of organ soloing all over the track.

Joey asked me if I knew of the keyboard player in a Doors tribute band that was playing around the city at that time. He wanted to have their keyboard player perform on the new Ramones album. I suggested someone else. I knew Joe McGinty. Joey had briefly met Joe when The Ancients auditioned for Joey back at the rehearsal studio in Chelsea. Joe was also in The Psychedelic Furs. Joey had not thought of having Joe play on the recording and I told Joey that Joe could play the part, no problem. Joey then asked me if Joe was a good guy. I said,

"Oh yeah, definitely. You will love him. He's a great guy!" He seemed pleased and I gave him Joe McGinty's phone number. That was the start of a long relationship between Joey Ramone and Joe McGinty. Joe tells the story,

"Joey called me and asked me to play, and of course, I was thrilled. It's one of those telephone answer machine messages that I wish I had kept. I used to see Joey, and the Ramones, a lot around town. When I was in the Furs, we often sat near each other in the VIP section at the Ritz.

I didn't formally meet him until his birthday party at the Mission, on East 5th Street. I believe he became aware of me through my work with The Ancients, a band he was interested in managing or producing, and I think it was Rob that recommended me for the Ramones gig. I was excited and nervous at the same time.

Johnny [Ramone] had stipulated that he wanted it exactly like the record. By coincidence, one of the guys at Big Mike's rehearsal studio, where the Furs rehearsed, had just bought a vintage Vox Continental, so I rented it from him. I then learned the part note-for-note. When I got to the studio, I learned that they were playing the song a step lower and about twice as fast. Needless to say, it was a bit of a challenge to play those fast "all white key" A minor riffs, in the key of G minor. They asked me back for *Acid Eaters*, their follow-up record of 60s covers.

I really only met Johnny once, at that first session. CJ was super nice, I'd run into him randomly at clubs in the Lower East Side, and he was always great to hang out with. Marky, I would see at various Ramones related gigs. Of course, there will always be a special place in my heart for Joey. He was a kindred soul, very sensitive and passionate about music.

Joey had a side project called The Resistance. He enjoyed that band because it was a nice escape from the pressure of the Ramones. I think he mainly put the band together to show support for Jerry Brown's presidential campaign.

On a side note, one of the acts at one of the Jerry Brown rallies was Michael McClure and Ray Manzarek. Joey and I were waiting to go on, and he said to me,

"Should we go introduce ourselves, what do you think?" I, of course, said

"Yes!" So, we walked over to him, and I told him that I learned his part note for note on "Take It As It Comes". He replied, in a voice that was as much of a caricature as Kyle McLachlan's portrayal of him in the Doors movie,

"You have my deepest condolences. I really take pity on anyone that has to sit down and pick that stuff apart". Afterwards, Joey said to me,

"It was weird, right?"

Anyway, it was certainly a thrill to be introduced by a presidential candidate,

especially while in a band with Joey Ramone. I then did some tracks for his solo record. And, I even got him to sing at the *Loser's Lounge* [a popular ongoing New York City concert series] tribute to the Kinks.
He sang "So Tired" and "Set Me Free". It was awesome.

Playing with the Ramones was like being welcomed into an exclusive club. I can trace many of the people I've worked with, and still work with, back to the Ramones. Producer, Bryce Goggin, was the engineer on those sessions. He's since worked with Pavement, Phish, Apples In Stereo, and many others. I've worked with him on my Baby Steps and Circuit Parade projects, and also on records by Jesse Malin and Nada Surf. Ronnie Spector is another connection. Joey was a fan, and produced an EP for her. I'm pretty sure he recommended me for the gig. I started working with Debbie Harry when she called me to record a John Cage song with her. I'd recorded a song with Joey, and he sent Debbie to me. I subsequently played a bunch of shows with her in NYC around that time, before Blondie reunited."

Joe is an extraordinary keyboard player. He can sight read with the best, he can quickly learn existing parts, and he can create parts galore, so much so that a producer will have trouble selecting the one that works best. Joe is a master arranger and bandleader too. It's no accident that he is invited to play with some of the best musicians and bands in New York. And, like I told Joey, he's a great guy! I feel fortunate to have been able to make that worthy introduction for him so many years ago, and to know that his musical talent is still with us, and Joe's legacy is still years from being complete.

The Mentors
(My Erection Is Over)

Michael Hilf, Dianne and I were fans of a hard-core metal punk group called, The Mentors. Nobody else that we knew had any interest in this band and probably for good reason. The Mentors drummer and vocalist, known as El Duce, after the fascist Italian dictator, was fat, drunk, and stinky. He wrote and sang songs about degrading women, and in the process, he was perfectly comfortable in degrading himself. They would never be on the cover of Rolling Stone but we found them to be quite endearing in a subversive, politically incorrect kind of way.

One day, we all got very excited to discover that The Mentors were coming to our neighborhood and were playing in a nearby dive bar. We were the first people to arrive at the club on the day of their show. The room only held about twenty-five people. As we entered the club, we noticed a black and white printed sign on the wall that read, "Metal Blade Artist, The Mentors, Performing Live Tonight". The words "Metal Blade" were crossed out and above was scrawled the word, "Former", above the name of the record label. It was gloriously cheesy. That was a good sign for what would be coming for the rest of the night.

We took our seats at one of the only two tables in the room. We could reach out and touch the band when they arrived a few minutes later and started to set up their gear. They were directly in front of us on a small stage riser no more than a foot high. They had no roadies. They had no groupies. They had no fans except for us and some folks who came in behind us and took over the other table. At the start of the show there were a total of nine people there to see The Mentors.

The band was notorious for performing in black leather executioner hoods. However, they had planned to not wear them on this hot summer night. We were very disappointed. That was half the reason for seeing the band. Michael asked,

"Where are the hoods?" El Duce replied,

"No hoods tonight." Michael started leading a chant,

"Hoods! Hoods! Hoods!" and the other table joined in with us. The whole room was chanting,

"Hoods! Hoods! Hoods!" all nine of us.

Begrudgingly, El Duce got up from his drum kit and went back behind a small wall and came out wearing his black leather executioner hood. We all cheered! Now we could have a show.

Dr. Heathen Scum played bass guitar. Sicky Wife Beater, the guitarist, kept turning his amp up louder and louder. El Duce kept yelling at him,

"Sicky, turn down your amp! I can't hear my racket! Sicky, I can't hear my racket!" But, Sicky ignored El Duce's requests and continued to play louder and louder with each continuing song in the set. We had our own personal concert and before the show was over, we had heard "Golden Shower", "My Erection Is Over", "Sandwich Of Love", and "Four F Club" from their classic album, *You Axed For It!* Afterward, about twenty-five more people crammed into the tiny space to see Ween perform. We had no idea that Ween was even on the same bill on that night.

Ah, the joy of a subversive, silly rock-n-roll show; it's something missing in today's super serious indie rock world.

David Rockefeller c. 1992

David Rockefeller
(Down In It)

Dianne and I were bartending on a typical night at the Mission, when I noticed a gentleman around thirty years of age come in and sit at the bar by himself. This fellow was unusual; he had on a very nice grey suit. We never had anyone come into Mission wearing a suit. He spent the entire night at the bar, ordering several rounds and listening to the music. I thought that he certainly looked out of place but there was nothing unusual in regard to his behavior. He was quiet, relaxed, and confident in his demeanor.

He left shortly before closing and I went home with him in my mind; wondering about what he did for a living. He did not seem like a lawyer, architect, or similar type of professional. But, my impressions were from observations made across a busy night of serving other customers. I chalked the experience off as one of those oddities that we occasionally come across in the bar business, until he returned again on the following night. Now, Dianne and I were really curious as to who was this gentleman in the expensive grey suit and why was he hanging out at the bar.

After serving him a round or two, I began to engage him in small talk. He was quite receptive and spoke openly about who he was and what he did for a living. He told me that his name was James and that he had formerly been in the Secret Service; the federal law enforcement agency that protects the President and other very important members of government, foreign dignitaries, and their families. He had left working for Washington and was now employed as a personal assistant for a very important, highly regarded, and often maligned former secretary of state. I went through the short list in my head and came up with the name of Henry

Kissinger. He smiled; I got it on the first try. I had to ask,

"How does a man who works for Henry Kissinger, and I assume you are a Republican, find this bar and decide to spend his nights in New York listening to gothic and industrial rock music?" He replied,

"This is as far apart from my working life as possible. And, besides, I like what I'm hearing." He was an interesting man.

James continued by telling me that when he was on duty, the necessity for him to be at maximum attention was always part of his job. When he was off duty, he needed to relax and that would be easier for him if he were in a place where it would be very unlikely to meet someone by accident that might know him from his work. Also, he wasn't going to be satisfied with boring mainstream music when he was kicking back a few rounds. Ministry, The Cure and The Sisters Of Mercy spoke more to him than any radio hits.

He told me that he was leaving town the next day and would return when his boss would return to New York. Several weeks passed and he did return to the Mission. We spoke again and he would return, on and off, over the next couple of years. We became quite friendly over that time when on one particular evening he came in and told me that he no longer was working for Kissinger. The constant travel was wearing him down and through a mutual friend he had secured a position with David Rockefeller.

Mr. Rockefeller was much older and did not travel extensively and his job would be to accompany him from his home and to work most days. Also, Mr. Rockefeller had a home for James to use and he would no longer have to live out of hotels. Last, Mr. Rockefeller had a reputation for being a very nice guy, much nicer than Henry Kissinger. He was very happy with his new job.

Several months later, Dianne and I made arrangements with our new friend to go up and spend a weekend with him and his new wife at the home that David Rockefeller had provided. It was very near the vast Rockefeller family estate called Pocantico, located in Westchester County, about an hour's drive up from New York City.

We arrived on a Saturday afternoon and were there for about an hour when the phone rang. I could hear my friend's end of the conversation. He said,

"I have some friends who have come up to visit from the city." Then, while holding his palm over the receiver, he leaned over to Dianne and me and asked,

"It's the boss. Would you like to go over and see him for awhile?" That was a surprise for which we had not planned but we were quite interested in meeting David Rockefeller.

We jumped in our friend's car and made the short drive over to the entrance of the estate. After entering the grounds, we drove past the old mansion built by David Rockefeller's grandfather, the founding father of the family and the oil tycoon who founded Standard Oil, now known as Exxon and Mobil, John D. Rockefeller Sr..

The large stone structure, known as Kykuit, was closed as it was being prepared to become a museum as part of The National Trust. We drove by it, ogling one of the nation's most famous private residences, and fully expecting to arrive at a building of equal stature when we pulled up to the home of David Rockefeller.

Just a few moments later, we made a turn off of the private road into a driveway in front of a modest, almost typically suburban two-story home. The front door was open but there was a white screen door, so modest, that one could not imagine that the man who was coming through it, Mr. Rockefeller, himself, would be one of the wealthiest and most powerful men in the world. In fact, my family had the same type of screen door on my home in which I grew up back in Brooklyn.

Mr. Rockefeller, as we were instructed to call him, like a grandfather who was excited to see his family members arrive, came quickly through the door and greeted us as we exited from the car.

"Hello. Hello. It's so very nice to meet you," he said in a congenial sort of way.

My friend introduced us by our names and by saying that Dianne was a young artist from the East Village and that I was the owner of an establishment where many of the young artists and musicians spent their free time.

Upon entering Mr. Rockefeller's home, I noticed that he had original impressionist paintings on his wall, some of which may have been on loan from The Museum Of Modern Art in Manhattan; the museum he and his family have funded. Except for the value of the address, those paintings were worth considerably more than the cost of the house in which he lived.

We walked through a short hallway and made a left turn past a modest kitchen leading us into a lovely courtyard with a metal table suitable for outdoor weather. It was a mild sunny summer afternoon and we sat down at the table while Mr. Rockefeller excused himself for a moment. A butler emerged and asked us if we would like something to drink. James suggested that we try the iced tea.

"Mr. Rockefeller would like to know if you would kindly care for a slice of his birthday cake, leftover from his celebration of the day before yesterday?" the agreeable butler requested. In a moment, he had returned, along with Mr. Rockefeller, and we all enjoyed the cake and glasses of iced tea flavored with mint and orange citrus.

While we made small talk, I couldn't help but notice a wall several short paces away filled with many varieties of roses, many of which I had never before seen. I made a comment about their beauty and that my father had planted a few kinds in the garden of the home in which I had grown up. At that, Mr. Rockefeller jumped to his feet, more excited than at any point of the day, and said,

"Please, please let me show you my wall," and he and I walked over to his roses where he proceeded to give me a personal tour.

I had not known that horticulture was David Rockefeller's

passion and that he had spent many hours of his life in study and experimentation on the subject. He showed this rose and then that rose; carefully explaining to me how one and the other were associated. One, he created, was named after his wife, Peggy.

He explained their history and the reasons for this color and that and how on this wall was a unique history of the flower. I am always interested in the history of things and I will pay close attention in such matters. But, he was giving me so much information coming so quickly, all I could remember thinking is that here is a man who could make or do virtually anything in his life, and his heart truly beats faster for the beauty of a flower. How beautiful is that and how fortunate am I for having learned that about the man?

After our tea and cake, Mr. Rockefeller asked us if we would please join him in gathering strawberries from his patch. Being mid June, they were nearly ripe and would soon spoil without being pulled from the ground. He took us along the side of his home leading to a vast expanse of land with crops of varying kind, including several types of fruits and vegetables.

I allowed myself to linger back for a bit while the rest of the party moved ahead, bent down on their knees along each of the three or four rows, proceeding to pick strawberries until their was no longer any room in the baskets. Here again is a moment forever engraved in my mind, of one of the most powerful men in the world well over the age of seventy, joyously on his hands and knees in the dirt.

After we completed our picking, it was time to say goodbye. Mr. Rockefeller escorted us back to our friend's car and with a voice filled with friendship and gratitude, he said,

"You please be sure to come give me a call whenever you are back up in this neck of the woods." And then he added, and directing this comment towards James,

"You know, we can go down to the Mission and join

them for a drink after work sometime." At that, we all agreed, and bid our kind guest farewell. We had hardly left Mr. Rockefeller's driveway when I blurted out,

"Can you imagine him at the bar!" We all had a great laugh at the idea of the charming and venerable David Rockefeller sharing the goth and industrial scene at the Mission.

Sister Machine Gun/Warren Haynes
(Riders On The Storm)

Dianne and I were living in a tall building in the East Village. Our eleventh floor next door neighbor, Chris Randall, was making a living as a barback at Limelight, a large Chelsea nightclub carved out of the remains of a nineteenth century gothic cathedral. Chris was also an industrial rock musician and passed along his tapes for our deejays to play at the Mission. Eventually, his diligent efforts were rewarded with a Wax Trax record contract and he moved away to Chicago. His band, Sister Machine Gun, had a fair degree of success in the nineties.

Several months later, early one morning having returned after working all night at the bar, Dianne and I were walking down the hall on our floor of the building in which we lived. Just before we got to our door, I noticed that something new was coming from the directly adjacent apartment; the sound of an acoustic guitar. I stopped at the door, while Dianne proceeded into our place, only intending to spend a moment. But, the playing was so good that fifteen minutes had passed when Dianne came out from our apartment wanting to know what I was doing standing in the hall. I said,

"I don't know who this is, but whoever is playing guitar is good."

A couple of weeks passed when on another night upon returning home from work, we shared the elevator up to our floor with our new neighbors. We introduced ourselves to each other and that was my start of a friendly relationship with Warren Haynes and his lovely wife, Stefanie.

It's funny thinking back to those days in the early 1990s when we both shared opposite sides of the same wall, the dividing line between his living room and my bedroom; me on my side with my industrial rock records and Warren on his side, working out Allman Brothers lines and parts to his Government Mule. Sometimes, we would meet in the hall and he, or Stefanie, would invite me into their world.

"What are you doing?" they would ask. I would reply,

"Nothing special, what are you guys doing?"

"Come in and hang out for awhile, we were just about to have lunch," and I would join them for a time in their home. Warren would always be playing guitar while Stefanie would fix us a meal.

"How's the bar going?" she would ask from the kitchen and I would reply,

"Oh, about the same these days." I would continue,

"How are you guys doing?" and Stefanie would tell me about her new record label, Evil Teen Records. All the while, Warren would be working out parts on his couch. Sometimes, I would make a suggestion; the producer still lived in my ear, and Warren would play his guitar, writing, arranging the songs that the world would eventually hear.

Many years later, way after Dianne and I had moved out of that building and just before I reopened Luna Lounge in Brooklyn, Warren was performing at McCarren Pool, just a few blocks away from the bar. By this time, Government Mule was very successful and more than five thousand people had paid to come see his band perform. I was a friend of the concert promoter and was invited to the show. Just a few minutes before the concert began, I ran into Stefanie and Warren back stage.

"Rob, It's so great to see you. How have you been?" I was greeted like a long lost friend. It had been fourteen years since we had lived on opposite sides of the wall. I replied,

"I'm OK, opening up a new Luna Lounge here in a few months. Is everything good for you?"

"Yeah, everything is really good in our lives," and at that, the band was called to the stage. Just before going up, Warren took me by the shoulder and said,

"Come up with us. You can sit on the side of the stage."

What a friendly gesture I thought and I watched his performance sitting next to the monitor guy on that day. It was one of those moments in summer when a mild breeze comes off of the East River; the warm sun shines gently down, with beach balls and Brooklyn Lager, sunglasses and bikini tops; it was a fine place to be able to stay.

The crowd was very responsive and the outdoor show was a blast. About half way through the set, in the middle of one of his solos, Warren turned to me and smiled as he wailed away on guitar. I wondered why he was facing me when it occurred to me that the solo that he was playing might have been one of the songs that he had played for me when we were sitting together and hanging out so many years ago on his couch. Perhaps it was a tune to which I had lent a long lost hand. I really don't know, but what I do know for sure, is that Warren and Stefanie Haynes are two of the nicest people that I ever have known in New York.

Elliott And The End Of His Life
(The Long And Winding Road)

Almost a year to the day before Dianne and I sold the Mission, we got a phone call from our close friend, Elliott, who had moved back up to New Paltz. Elliott was very sick. His spleen had just been removed and he had leukemia. As is so often the case with cancer, Elliott seemed to make an improvement for a while. After a few months, he was out of the hospital and living with his girlfriend out in the country, several miles from downtown New Paltz.

Dianne and I rented a car and drove up to see him. He was in good spirit. He had an ancient dictionary from the nineteenth century; over one hundred years old. There were many archaic words that I had never before heard and we had great fun in trying to guess their meanings before Elliott would read them aloud from the book. It would have made a great game show, or at least, I would have enjoyed it. We spent the afternoon with Elliott and then returned to New York City, staying in touch by phone.

Several months later, I got a call from Elliott telling me that he was back in the hospital and things were not going well. Dianne and I went up to Albany to see him. It was very depressing. He was very weak. He was connected to an intravenous bottle and a host of hospital equipment set up to monitor his condition. His mother and sister had flown in to be with him. I could see him brighten up when Dianne and I walked into his hospital room. It made me feel good to know that after all he was going through, he still enjoyed our company. However, he was not awake for very long and he soon was sleeping deeply. It was about eleven o'clock in the morning. I looked out of his hospital room window. It was a gray overcast day. I stood at the end of the bed and watched my friend, now in an unconscious state. There was much in my heart and I wanted so very much to talk with him. But, after about an hour, Dianne and I decided to leave.

I should have waited and stayed with him until we could speak with each other one last time. Even in the company of his family, he seemed to be so alone. But, I was overwhelmed with sadness and I could not handle my emotions. Still, I should have reached deep down inside and took control of myself. I was unable to say goodbye and for that I am truly sorry.

On the drive back down the New York State Thruway, we decided to pull off the highway at New Paltz. We thought about staying there overnight and returning to the hospital in Albany on the very next day. But, after crying in the car for about twenty minutes, Dianne and I decided to get back on the highway and complete the four-hour drive back down to our apartment in Manhattan. There wasn't much to say and Dianne and I were both deep in our thoughts as we knew there was not much time left for our friend. A few weeks later, the week before we sold Mission, Elliott died.

There was to be a memorial service for him later that summer, but we missed it as we were in Europe at the time. Dianne did have a dream in which Elliott came to her and smiled. She felt that he was letting her know that everything was OK, not to miss him, and we should be happy. Even after his passing, we were still in benefit of his wisdom.

Selling Mission
(Rehab)

So much work goes into the creation and management of a nightclub. I was always in contact with band managers, publicity agents, and record label personnel in regard to hosting events with those artists whose music we played at the bar. In addition, Dianne and I both continued to bartend each night and that was certainly a job in itself.

After four or five years, the constant necessity to be 'on' and to be attentive to customers who would often come in with tales of the days of their lives, consumption of copious amounts of alcohol, and the continual late night hours began to wear down upon me with continuing dread and decay. I was in need of some daylight hours. I was truly tired of playing music for which people would come in to dance. I was bored with their requests. I had heard all those gothic hits for too long. Also, I was burnt out on the industrial music scene too. And, I was certainly in need of a change.

It had all been quite good fun but now I was thirty-seven years old and it was time to take stock of my life. I was sure that it was time to move on. But, what else in the world could I do? Were the best years of my life now complete? Perhaps, Elliott's illness and subsequent death had also affected my point of view.

I've heard it said that many a man may go through a mid life crisis. Well, if this is true, then I had arrived at mine. After five years of owning and running the Mission, Dianne and I would sell the bar to Michael and Harold; two of our continuing deejays. We also terminated our apartment lease and made arrangements to fly on a plane to London. We bought a three-month pass for riding the trains in Europe and prepared to have an awesome carefree summer.

It was the only time in my entire life that I did not have a key in my pocket. When we would return, we could live at my father's house in Queens until we found a new place of our own. But, for now, that was an issue we had no need to consider. Our last night at Mission was June 30th, 1993 and our last weekend at the club was filled with strong emotions; with cocktails equally strong as well. Many friends came by to say goodbye; having a sense that the nightclub was gone for good. It was.

Wisely, they would pull out the deejay booth; the first change that Michael and Harold would make, install a jukebox, and cut their historical cord to the Mission. Eventually, Michael bought out Harold and Harold opened up a bar called Raven, nearby on Avenue A, which catered to his friends who were still very much into the goth scene. When Raven burned down, he and his wife, Ria, moved to the Greenpoint section of Brooklyn and opened a bar called Boulevard Tavern.

Michael still owns the bar formerly known as Mission, which has been called ACE, since 1993. It is a very successful establishment filled with dart boards, pool tables, skee ball machines, and a collection of metal lunch boxes from the 60s and 70s; securely displayed behind a glass showcase. He makes a very good living while he develops other endeavors from Los Angeles, where he has lived for many years. In its own way, ACE has created its own legacy and is a current staple of the East Village.

London
(All Day And All Of The Night)

Dianne and I boarded our Virgin Air flight on Sunday evening, arriving in London on a busy Monday morning. While we were waiting to go through UK customs, Dianne went to the ladies room and I waited for her in line. A police official beckoned me to move to a new line that was forming in front of a different window. With a sign that I made with my fingers, I meant to let him know that I needed two minutes and I was waiting for Dianne to return. From about twenty feet away, he approached me and in an English accent, he said that I should know that I just gave him a very serious insult with my hand gesture, but since I had just arrived from America that I was not in any trouble. I had no idea to what he was referring but I apologized for my cultural ignorance. In America, when you give someone the finger, you use your middle finger. In England, they use two fingers. Who knew?

We got on the tube from the airport and arrived at John Moore's apartment in central London. John's flat would be our home for the next five days and he would be our gracious host and guide.

John took us out that afternoon and we walked around his neighborhood. I remember him telling us that Lulu lived in a certain house as we were walking by it. I was a big fan of her style and music when I was a kid growing up in the sixties. She still touches my heart whenever I hear her classic, "To Sir With Love". At the moment that John mentioned Lulu to us, as if she was waiting for her cue, Lulu pulled into her driveway in a mini van. We awkwardly stood there watching while Lulu removed her children and groceries. Lulu was a mom now and in her middle age.

John told us that we were invited to a party at a house later that evening. He said that we had already met some of his friends when they had come to the Mission when they were spending their time in New York. Dianne and I were looking forward to the party. John had a lot of very cool friends.

It was about 11PM when we arrived. I recall a very wide garage that could hold four or five cars side by side, and a stairway that led to a porch on the left side of the garage. The porch connected to the back entrance of a very nice home. Speakers were blaring really loud music directly out from the windows. I remember thinking that this would be impossible in New York. The police would show up in five minutes, bust up the party and cart someone off to jail. It was the first day of July and the weather was absolutely perfect. It was gloriously mild, a slight breeze in the air, and just about as perfect a summer night as one could ever imagine.

We ascended the stairs and went into the house. It was already very crowded. John introduced us as his friends from New York and told all there that we had owned the Mission. Everyone seemed interested in speaking with us and I felt like a New York celebrity. It wasn't until that moment that I realized just how popular Mission had been in England.

We were at Guy Chadwick's home. Guy is a songwriter, guitarist and vocalist in the band called The House Of Love, whose *Butterfly* album is filled with a unique blend of atmospheric melodic songs. Nearly twenty years later, I still enjoy his record and I still consider it to be a very near masterpiece.

The party spilled out onto the porch and steps. The music was really, really loud! I couldn't believe that anyone could get away with doing this in the middle of a crowded neighborhood; blasting the Stone Roses, Primal Scream, and My Bloody Valentine at rock concert levels.

I had met Liz Frasier once or twice at the Mission. I was a fan of the band, Cocteau Twins, in which she was the vocalist. They created their own unique melodic, atmospheric albums and their sound is the first branch we now call "dreampop"; rising out of the tree of music design.

Liz and I talked for hours that night on the steps and I really enjoyed her company. She was so friendly, unpretentious, and filled with positive energy. She was reaching out to make a connection with me among this party filled with people; helping to make my first night in England, and my first night no longer an owner of Mission, a relaxed and comfortable experience. Hours had passed on those steps before either one of us had realized that we had spent so much time together that evening. This was a few years before Liz would go on to sing with Massive Attack; another band whose sound would define a new genre, trip hop, and is still popular today.

Dianne and I had a wonderful time with John and his gracious friends. To this day, it still ranks as one of the best parties to which I have had the honor to be invited. We spent the rest of that week with John, meeting more of the people he knew in London, sharing meals, touring the pubs, walking the town, and having a very good time.

Phillip Boa And The Voodoo Club
(Satellite Man)

Our next stop was in Amsterdam. Dianne and I had made advance arrangements with our friend, Dave 'Taif' Ball, who had been the bass player in Killing Joke when we met at the

Mission, in 1989. By this time, Taif had spent some time playing bass with Lloyd Cole and now had a gig playing with a German indie punk and new wave group called Phillip Boa And The Voodoo Club.

They were on tour in Germany and Taif told us that we could all connect a few weeks ahead in Dresden, where the band was scheduled to perform. Dianne and I took in the sights of Amsterdam and then traveled down through Germany eventually reaching Dresden on the proper day. We arrived at the train station late morning and walked around with our backpacks for a while in that beautiful city.

Taif had told us that the band was performing at an outside facility in a park near the river. We found the park and were surprised to see that several thousand people were expected. I had not heard of Phillip Boa and was happy to see that Taif was playing in a very successful band.

We had been given instructions to meet Taif at a hotel that was just on the other side of the river. We crossed over the bridge, a stone structure some hundreds of years old, and came to the front door of a magnificent building that looked like it was the former home of some kind of king or queen. This was not only a five star hotel in which the band was staying. It was a palace!

We entered the hotel and headed over to the front desk where the concierge was as nice as the building was beautiful. He told us that the band was waiting for our arrival and pointed to a salon just off of the main lobby. We left our backpacks behind his desk and went over to the room. It had plush couches and a rich, classic European elegant decor.

There were only a few people in the plush and luxurious chamber. We introduced ourselves to Phillip Boa and his lovely lady, Pia. They were as gracious and inviting as two people could ever be and they told us that Taif was up in his room. Someone telephoned him and Taif came down right away. He had already told the band all about us, and that we were his good friends that had come all the way from New

York City.

Dianne and I had not made plans to stay anywhere yet in Dresden when Philip took the initiative and upgraded Taif's room to a double so that we could spend the night in this amazing hotel. That was incredibly nice and we greatly appreciated his generosity.

We chatted for awhile and then someone told us that it was time to go to the band's soundcheck. By now it was around 4PM. The band gathered on their tour bus and we hitched a ride with them back over the bridge to the other side of the river. By this point, at least a thousand people had arrived and were all enjoying a beautiful afternoon on the grass. We pulled into the backstage area and got a bit of a feel for the rock star life when we exited from the bus. Dianne and I were greeted as if we too were in the band. We were given all-access passes so that we could come and go as we pleased.

The band did their soundcheck. It was at that moment that I realized that I had been hearing one of their songs all over European radio stations that summer. It was called "And Then She Kissed Her", and was sung by Pia. It is still one of my all time favorite songs and I was thrilled, along with several thousand other people who saw their performance later that night.

The band had an interesting sound. Their songs often had a very melodic, somewhat anthemic chorus punctuated on either side by verses that featured atmospheric, almost ambient breakdowns. Sometimes, Philip would sing in a majestic throaty style and Pia would counter with her warm angelic voice. It was an odd, but quite original approach to making music. I've never heard another band employing this style in the making of records. It creatively worked very well and the band seemed to have a great deal of commercial success. Philip Boa was the number one selling artist in Germany at that time; the fourth largest market in the world. I recall him proudly telling me that his band sold more records than Metallica, the second largest seller in

Germany.

Dianne and I parted company with Taif and Phillip Boa and The Voodoo Club the next day, and we continued upon our European vacation. We spent some time in Italy, making our way down from Venice to Florence to Rome and to Naples. We camped for a couple of nights in Pompeii, the ancient Roman city completely covered in ash, decimated by the volcano, Versuvius. What an eerie sight, but how fascinating was that experience to see a city preserved exactly as it was on the day that it died nearly two thousand years ago. We continued south and then east to Greece before making our way back north, and our final weeks lost in the cafes of Amsterdam. It was not until late September when we finally returned to America. We had had a glorious vacation. It was a good cure for the mid life crisis in which I had been immersed.

In Between Days
(Halfway To Crazy)

I called my father when we arrived back at JFK airport in New York. Before we left, we had made arrangements to stay at his home in Queens. We expected to stay there for a week or two while Dianne and I looked for a new apartment to rent in Manhattan. What we did not know was that my father had sold his home that summer and was now living in a small apartment with his wife. This was before email and cell phones. We had been completely out of touch for three months.

They had found a new home in Florida and were taking an airplane south on the very next day. We had arrived just in time. Also, new tenants were moving into this apartment in about a week so we had to move fast to find a place for ourselves to live.

We found a studio apartment listed in the classified which

would be shown in a couple of days. There were thirty people that showed up to look at the Chelsea space. We were desperate to get it so I offered the owner six months advance rent. It was a lot of money but we could afford it since it came from the sale of the bar. The owner accepted the offer and Dianne and I moved into that tiny Chelsea apartment. It would be the last apartment that we would ever share together.

Now that we were back in New York, I still had to figure out what I wanted to do with the next stage of my life. I did not yet think that I wanted to be back in the bar business. I dabbled with the idea of opening a video store or a coffee house. I love coffee and the coffee craze was just starting in New York. Starbucks had only just arrived and I thought about opening an independent cafe in the East Village. I also went through the massive New York Yellow Pages and looked at every category listing of existing businesses in the city. Of all the categories, starting with A and ending with Z, I could not find anything about which I could get excited. Time was passing and the money on which we were living would not last forever. We saw the end come of 1993 and lived through the following year. With the exception of the New York Rangers winning their Stanley Cup championship, 1994 was a bust.

I managed stock investments made with the money received from the sale of the bar and Dianne got a job working as a bartender at catered events around town. Doing this, she met Leonard Nimoy, the actor who played Spock, on *Star Trek*, when he impatiently leaned over and grabbed a warm bottle of seltzer which exploded all over the bar.

"Not too bright are we Mr. Spock?" she thought to herself as she helped him to clean up the spill. She also met Peter Jennings, the anchor of ABC's nightly newscast, on the day ABC received an Emmy award for the broadcast. Immediately swamped at the makeshift bar set up on the side of the set that evening, Jennings jumped behind the temporary bar and started serving drinks to his thirsty staff. Dianne told me that he must have been a professional bartender at some point in his life because he really knew how to handle himself. It must have been strange to be bartending with the man from whom millions of people had just received their news.

Johnny Lydon
(God Save The Queen)

Another interesting event took place during this time. Johnny Lydon, aka Johnny Rotten, wrote his autobiography. It was published in 1995 and we were invited to attend a book signing where he was scheduled to appear. It was in a small club in the East Village with two or three levels. Dianne and I arrived and made our way through the main floor of the club. There were people hanging out at the bar but nobody that we knew and nobody that looked very interesting. A bit bored, we went upstairs to the second floor where we found a small empty room. There was a small couch against a wall. Dianne and I sat down on the couch and figured that we would go back downstairs in a little while. About five minutes later, Johnny Lydon came into the room and sat down next to us on the couch.

Almost immediately, the room filled with his fans who were mostly girls around twenty-one years of age. They had disposable cameras and were taking dozens of snap shots of him sitting on the couch. Nobody asked us to get up so we sat there on the couch while Johnny Lydon made characteristic facial contortions and primed for the cameras. I wish that I had a camera too. I would have asked Johnny Lydon to take my photograph so that I could tell my friends that this is the photograph that Johnny Lydon took of me. I think he would have appreciated my request.

The Lower East Side (1995)
(Fairytale Of New York)

Although the steady influx of urban professionals continued to transform the East Village, it was still several years before the tipping point would be reached. Yes, new restaurants were opening all over the place but most of these were not yet the obnoxious trendy type bistros that would come to dominate the Lower East Side. The neighborhood still had a great many drug dealers and tenement rents were still fairly reasonable. Thousands of musicians still lived on the Lower East Side and in the nearby East Village.

The new mayor, Rudolf Giuliani, was cracking down with a new series of lifestyle laws designed to change the permissive atmosphere in New York City. People who played their car radios too loud were receiving expensive tickets. The open container laws that prohibited drinking alcoholic beverages on the street were strictly enforced. People who jumped the subway turnstiles were apprehended and sent through the judiciary system. People who neglected to show up in court to answer minor warrants, such as smoking on a subway platform, were seized and made to spend time in the city jail.

Crime rates were reduced as a result of a score of quality of life initiatives. Although many New Yorkers thought the mayor was absolutely foolish when it came to his ultra conservative stand on matters of art, culture, and civil rights, he was generally appreciated for his efforts in bringing peace and security to the city.

Eventually, we decided it was time to get back into the bar business. I still had to figure out exactly what I would do, but first I needed to find the right building in which I knew I would do it. I was sure that I didn't want to do a gothic industrial dance club again. Then, on a night just a couple of days before the end of 1994, a friend told me about a one-story building on Ludlow Street that had a "For Rent" sign up on it.

I knew about that building but it had been previously been up for sale and not for rent. I felt pretty sure that he had probably got it wrong. However, the next day just to be sure and not miss an opportunity, I went down to look at it and saw that he was correct. The sign now said that the building was for rent. I called the broker and made arrangements to look at it on the last day of the year, just hours before New Year's Eve.

As soon as the agent opened the door, I immediately knew it was right although it was filled with bails of Chinese herbs. The landlord, Mr. Kong, had used the building as a warehouse for his Chinese imports until his business outgrew the capacity. I could see that its location and size were perfect for where I wanted to be and for what I wanted to do. Dianne agreed and we told the broker that we wanted to look at the lease. It had taken a year and a half but on the very last day of the year we found the new space that awaited us had finally come to appear.

It took a few months to negotiate and five months of construction too, but eventually on a hot summer Sunday night in mid August of 1995, Dianne and I opened the doors to our new bar. We called it Luna Lounge, in part for my love of the band, Luna, and for the park that once existed in Coney Island.

The Luna Lounge jukebox below the show calendar board.

Luna Lounge
(We're A Happy Family)

In the beginning, Luna Lounge was not a live music venue. We built two rooms into the building. The back room was initially filled with old upholstered reclining chairs with footrests that could rise and fold out in front; the kind that your grandparents may have had in their basement or den. Dianne and I bought a dozen of them at a Salvation Army store in Allentown, Pennsylvania for fifteen dollars a piece. We put several small handmade wood coffee tables near the chairs and put candles on each one. We kept the light very low in the back room. It was kind of weird but it was a cheap way to fill the room and create an unusual atmosphere.

Maybe ten or twenty people would hang out in the back room at any given time. Sometimes, customers would move the chairs around and change their configurations in order to meet the needs of various groups of friends. The seating arrangement was fluid and it seemed to be redefined every few days. There was no stage, no PA, no sound booth, and no live music.

The bar was in the front room where there were also a foosball table, jukebox, bathrooms, and a couple of 1950s diner-style booths with blue Naugerhide vinyl benches. A

Bar back, Zee, bringing up new glasses from the basement.

Luna's front room (looking towards front doors) – 2002.

few years after we opened, we moved the benches and booths to the back room and bought a used blue vinyl couch and a couple of 1970s easy chairs. No dark colored paint was used anywhere in the building; I was completely over the Mission black walls and goth motif. I covered one wall with an extremely thick coat of joint compound, using a large sponge to form it into a cave-like coating with nooks and crannies and painted it with a gallon of very expensive gold leaf. There was a warm glow reflected from that wall when we placed amber floodlights above it.

The dry wall behind the diner booths was originally painted a dark hunter green. We removed it a few years after we opened to find an old brick wall we exposed when we relocated the booths. The concrete floor was painted fire engine red. With those colors Luna always had the subliminal feel of Christmas and was a particularly festive room around the holidays.

We could comfortably fit about sixty or seventy people in the front room but on extremely busy nights we could shoehorn about twice as many into the space. That was never any fun but there were some nights when we all had to live with it. But, those crowded nights would be a thing of the future for when we first opened and for the first three or four months we were simply a neighborhood bar hoping to draw some friendly locals into our worthy establishment.

Luna Lounge had no entrance fee, never had a velvet rope outside, and rarely had a guest list unless it was a very special event. But, again, those special events would come a bit up the road. In our first few months of business on the Lower East Side, many of the locals were cautious and very slowly came in for a look, a drink, and a conversation with our bartender. They worried about gentrification, assuming the worst about the new bar until they would eventually get to know us, our staff, and slowly get over their fear.

Dianne, Rob, and Joe McGinty – Halloween 1995

Jim Ferguson, of Lotion, with Valentino.

Lotion
(First We Take Manhattan)

Back at the beginning of our time on Ludlow Street there was a show running on MTV called *Unplugged*. Produced by Alex Coletti, the same person who had been a fill in deejay at the Mission, the show featured famous rock bands performing acoustic versions of their popular songs. The performances of note featured Paul McCartney, Eric Clapton, Bob Dylan, Neil Young, and Nirvana.

The guys in the band, Lotion, started hanging out at Luna Lounge very soon after we opened. They were friendly with Joe McGinty and it was through Joe that they had discovered the bar. They would come in with a gaggle of friends; it always felt like the party arrived whenever they walked through our doors. Always upbeat, smart, and very much on top of the scene, Lotion was the band that put Luna Lounge on the map of the Lower East Side.

The Village Voice had named Lotion's debut album, *Full Isaac*, the album of the year in 1994 and they were touring with Pavement and Mercury Rev. The idea of doing an acoustic set in a small room really appealed to the band but Lotion was not commercially successful enough to perform on MTV's *Unplugged*. So, they approached me with their idea of doing an acoustic show at Luna Lounge. It would be a night of unusual arrangements and intelligent offbeat songs. In addition, they agreed to teach me the game of foosball, a table I had set up in the bar but with which I had little skill. This set events into motion that would lead to a change in our direction and a new way of presenting live music on the Lower East Side.

We built a small one foot high riser in the back room on which we placed a couple of reclining chairs and a table between them with a small candle. We also had a life size ceramic pink pig we moved around on the riser every couple of nights. There was something quite Norman Rockwell in a Lower East Side kind of way about the scene in the back of the bar. The riser was set back against the rear wall and was about fifteen feet wide by about eight feet deep. Some people would be quite psyched if the riser was empty and they would rush to the old reclining chairs so that they could appear in the motif.

Without a PA, no monitors, and without a soundboard, it was on that riser that Lotion created their unplugged set. They were the first band to ever perform at Luna Lounge. The band played through their first record and then introduced some new songs that would soon be released on their second album. Lotion certainly knew how to make the quirky room work to their advantage. That night was a blast. The room was filled to capacity with some of the notable music elite of the Lower East Side and it made me want to do it again.

Sun Studio
(That's All Right)

Sun Studio, in Memphis, Tennessee, may be the birthplace of recorded rock'n'roll music. In the early 1950s, the list of recorded artists there includes, among others, Ike Turner, Howlin' Wolf, B.B. King, James Cotton, Johnny Cash, Elvis Presley, Carl Perkins, Roy Orbison, and Jerry Lee Lewis.

I have always been impressed with the exciting live sound

of those early recordings in Memphis so I decided to take a trip down from New York and see if I could pick up a few pointers in the development of our live room at the bar. The one story building at 706 Union Avenue in which Sun Studio is located is nearly the same width and length as the building in which Luna Lounge was located. The ceiling height was about the same too.

Sun Studio had closed their doors to recording in 1959 when the owner, Sam Philips, decided to move to a larger facility. The original building then housed several other businesses over the years, until in 1987, Gary Hardy reopened the studio and added a museum and restaurant, making the new Sun Studio one of the hottest tourist attractions for fans and musicians from all over the world.

They had an available tour given by an assistant recording engineer of which I took full advantage. With the exception of the old school sound absorbing ceiling tiles, I noticed that there was not a lot of sound absorbing material in the room. The floor was covered with hard vinyl tiles, not wood as what is often used in expensive modern studios. The walls were simple drywall or plaster with no bass absorbing sound baffles in the corners. I wasn't sure if this was the layout of the room when those recordings were originally made, but after others on the tour had left the room, I lingered behind and measured by ear the resident noise in the room by clapping my hands and timing the length of the decay of the sound. It was only a bit splashy, not too bad, and I had a feeling that that splash was what gave those early recordings some of their distinctive live sound.

I returned from Memphis with a confident approach to the design of our performance space. With just a small amount of sound absorbing foam rubber over the stage mainly used to absorb the sound of the cymbals, and accounting for when people would fill up the space by standing in front of the band, the back room at Luna became one of the best rooms in which to perform in New York.

We decided to buy a set of speakers from Sean Schertell; a friend who was soon leaving for the West Coast. They were not really meant for a club, rather, they were designed for a large apartment. But, they were a bargain. It was all that we could afford at that time and we made them work well in the room. We also bought a Mackie four channel soundboard and I sat off to one side of the stage mixing vocals when we started presenting live bands. It wasn't much but it was how we learned our craft. And, by working with less, it taught me that things could not be fixed in the booth. So, if the band needed help we would have to work it out in the soundcheck and make their sound coming off the stage the sound we intended to hear. That made the bands better too.

Valentino
(The Lion Sleeps Tonight)

Valentino was the door person at Luna Lounge for most of the ten years that we were on Ludlow Street. Val, as he was affectionately known, is a very tall large black man with long dreadlocks. He had previously been the door person at The Scrap Bar, a metal and hard rock bar with a history well known by those in that social circle. The Scrap Bar was not the first club in which you could find Val at the door. By the time Val and I found each other at Luna in 1995, I think he was happy to be at a relatively violence free club. Of course, I'm sure that he kept out most of the people who were looking for trouble.

Val was also an accomplished guitarist and singer, having once pursued that dream, and now he was our sound engineer on Sunday nights for awhile. I remember one night when I came into Luna Lounge to check out a band on a night when Val was in the booth. There were only a handful of people in the room. I could hear an additional harmony part coming through the PA while listening to the band but there was only one vocalist on stage. I looked over at Val and saw him adding his harmony part using a microphone in the soundbooth while the singer was looking all over the room. He could not figure out from where this excellent harmony was coming. Val just looked at me and smiled. It really was a very good harmony.

Adam Green
(My Shadow Tags On Behind)

One other Sunday night, Adam Green, from Moldy Peaches, was performing at Luna Lounge. I had seen him in the bar and was pleased when he asked for a gig. But on the night he performed at Luna there was no one in the room except for my girlfriend, Val who was behind the soundboard, and myself. Absolutely no one was there but that didn't bother me. I knew of Adam Green through my friend, Lach, who booked him along with other anti-folk artists in the nearby back room of Sidewalk Cafe, which Lach called The Fort.

Lach and I went back to the days just before Mission. Actually, it was he who suggested that I come up with a better name than the one I originally had and after giving it some thought I knew that he was probably right. So, Mission it became, instead of something inane. I always respected Lach's intelligence and he has a great history himself in the picking and choosing of bands.

On this particular night, Adam was alone on the stage and Val was alone in the booth. I had been listening to Moldy Peaches all week and found his songs entertaining

Val, in the Luna Lounge basement with road case and beer.

and certainly funny as well. Adam has some unusual ways of rhyming words and I can remember hearing Val groan out loud when Adam sung out,

"Who mistook the steak for chicken; who'm I gonna stick my dick in?"

Jim Thirlwell And William Tucker
(Steal Your Life Away)

It was on a quiet midweek night at Luna Lounge when a flamboyant character with flaming red hair entered the club from the street. He stood at the front of the building, inside of the front glass door and made a proclamation as if he were announcing his intentions from a lofty theatrical stage. With his right arm raised up in the air and his hand thus pointing towards heaven,

"Uli has sent me to spy on your new bar!" I was the only person apart from our bartender who was in the club. Uli owned Max Fish, a bar that had opened a few years earlier directly across the street

"Well then," I returned, "I think you should join me for a drink or two at the bar. It's the best place from where we may make our observations."

I had just met Jim Thirlwell, one of the founding fathers of industrial music in the 1980s and a brilliant composer whose music is at the apex of twenty-first century modernism. I already knew who he was; Jim was an icon in the music scene on the Lower East Side. Jim's music really defies description. If the Rock-N-Roll Hall Of Fame could be more sophisticated, Jim would be there on the walls. His influence, his diversity, his complexity and his musical pedigree are without match by anyone else in the world.

Alcohol by itself is of little interest to me. But, I have learned that enlightenment may come through inebriation in the presence of an appropriate drinking partner. Over the years I have had several partners. Jim and I spent more than a few nights together employing our time at the bar. One night, he told me that he was putting a new version of his band, Foetus, together and was getting ready to go out on tour. He knew that some bands had started to play at Luna. He wanted to do an unplugged set as a going away party that month. I didn't see how that was possible with the style of music he was playing but Jim was an artist and I believed that he knew what he was doing.

About a week before the show, Jim walked in with William Tucker who was now playing guitar in Foetus. What a surprise! I had no idea that William was playing with Jim and Jim had no idea that William and I went back to the Mission. I had not seen William since Dianne and I had sold the bar as he was either on tour somewhere in the world or was living at home in Chicago.

William and I never had a telephone relationship. Our friendship was solely based on being in each other's presence. William looked great and he was in good spirit and seemed to be in charge of his life. I had always thought of William Tucker as a human version of Daffy Duck. He did have a tendency to bounce off a wall or two in the world but at this time he seemed more settled and at ease with a new calm and a new kind of maturity. We got to spend quite a bit of time together that week as the band would come by each night and hang out after their practice. He told me that he had grown tired of 'down strokes', a style of guitar employed to grind out a beat. That had been his job in Chicago and now he wanted to leave that method behind. He was working on quieter music and playing some acoustic guitar.

At the end of the week, the unannounced Foetus show

played to a completely packed room. It seemed like more of a ball than a concert; Jim's star was shining so bright. It was a night to remember; the folks who had come to the party were part of a wonderful night. It was a grand gala affair and even though there was no charge to enter the club, it was the hottest ticket in town.

Elysian Fields, featuring Oren Bloedow and the beautiful Jennifer Charles, were the opening act on stage. Elysian Fields, a very sexy and vampy lounge style group is one of Jim's favorite bands and we had their album in the jukebox. My good friend, Phil Schuster, was their A & R guy at the label.

Foetus was very loud. So much for playing an unplugged show! They played through their set they would take on the road. So tight, professional, and well rehearsed; it was the only time I saw that band play out. They closed with a brilliant version of "I Am The Walrus", which to this day is the only time I have ever heard a live performance of that song. What a moment in rock! I will never forget it.

Unfortunately, that week was the last time that I ever saw William. I read that he had become ill with severe testicular pain the following year, in 1997. After seeing doctors for most of the next three years who were unable to improve his condition, I guess that the unrelenting pain became too much for him to bear. On May 14th, 1999, William Tucker took his own life in his apartment in Chicago. I still think of him quite a lot and I wish that he was still here somewhere on the face of this earth, playing guitar, making music, and being the man that only William Tucker could be.

I got in touch with Chris Connelly, former vocalist and keyboardist in Ministry, who sent me these words about William,

"I first met Tucker when he appeared out of
nowhere one day at the dress rehearsal. I use
that term loosely and humorously for Ministry's

late 1989 early 1990, *Mind Is A Terrible Thing To Taste*, tour. When I arrived, he appeared to be setting up my keyboards, and I had no idea from where he had come, but, in the world of Ministry, I had learned quickly to just not ask where things came from, things appeared out of nowhere, usually they were drugs or insane people. It was one of these wonderful moments where a friendship begins, it feels so familiar, like a conversation you maybe started years ago that you are easily picking up again. We talked about music, bands we liked, records we were into, and I found out he lived, very proudly, in New York City. I grew very close to him over the two month course of the tour, eventually building a pharmacological arsenal, recording ideas on his Teac 4 track, the famous 'band in a box', and seeking out stoned and rabid goth girls.

    Tucker was one of these guys who absolutely thrived in chaotic situations, it gave him an unholy energy and an ugly stamina; I'd like to think I helped ground him a bit, but the chaos he thrived on, animated him as if possessed, and it infected those around him. Fans scaling dangerous hotel walls, there was Tucker, forty people skinny dipping in a hotel pool at 3AM, with the alarm going off, Tucker! Hotel room packed with teenagers with the cops outside, yup, Tucker! Fast asleep under a record rack at 11AM in the morning in a New Orleans record shop, Tucker!

    He moved to Chicago to become more involved in my musical circle, and helped me navigate through the dim twilight ebb that my life had become at that point . He was a gothic Ratso Rizzo with the charisma of a Johnny Thunders. He had an unflappable spirit and his incendiary passion could take him to incredible highs and down to furious lows.

We had an excellent working relationship, when I would grow restless or bored with whatever music we were tackling (as I am wont to do) he'd either take over himself and go at it meticulously and doggedly until it's completion, or he would gently and skillfully persuade me to keep at it.

We toured and toured, made records, stole drugs from people, and shoplifted food. I tried to tame him on long international flights, to no avail. We conducted interviews with tearful journalists; he made an Italian TV presenter cry and tell him she couldn't fuck him because she had her period. He threw a college radio DJ's cassette recorder into a Boulder, Colorado motel pool for asking a stupid question.

I would yell at him when his drug intake became stupid and dangerous. I remember him sobbing when my girlfriend died and I remember laughing really hard when I saw him slapped by girls, numerous times.

I remember being so late for a gig in Atlanta that he shaved in the back of our van using Diet Pepsi, instead of water.

I remember him brazenly stealing cash from our tour money to buy aerosol whipped cream in order to inhale the nitrous oxide. And, there was the time when we climbed trees on Halstead Street after huffing anyl nitrate.

William and I eventually, regrettably, drifted apart, but we never fell out, we were always friends, but we started to move in different circles, however, I knew he was always there for me, even when he became so sick and no doctor could work out what was wrong with him. He was in agony, and not once did he complain. Eventually the pain overtook him, and he took his life.

I often talk to my friend, Chris Bruce, about Tucker. Something current will come up in conversation. We'll say "Tucker would have LOVED that"; things like Youtube, recording on an i-pad, sophisticated internet porn, Larry David, Jackass, young noisy bands from Brooklyn, Adult Swim, Tru Blood, flavoured vodkas, Suicide Girls, Amy Winehouse, Lady Gaga (perhaps)...then again there are things he would have loathed, like the universal ban on smoking.

I think about him every day, there is always a Tucker moment, and I truly regret not being with him more at the end. I am sad he didn't get to meet my children. My son's middle name is Tucker. He would have adored them."

Lydia Lunch
(Are You Glad To Be In America)

A couple of weeks after we met, Jim Thirlwell mentioned that he would recommend that Lydia Lunch come by and talk with me about curating art for the walls of Luna Lounge. I knew of her as a member of the 'no wave' scene in the eighties but I didn't know of her as an artist. When Lydia came by, she also made a grand theatrical entrance. Like Jim, she stood just inside the front door and made her announcement,

"I am Lydia Lunch. I have come to see your walls." I approached her from the other side of the room and introduced myself. She told me that Jim had told her that we had very good walls. I hadn't really thought about it but I guess they were quite nice. I took her into the back room

and said,
"This is the back room. These are our walls." Then we walked back into the front room where I said,
"And this is our front room." What else could I say about the walls? Impressed, and in a sort of gothic manner, she agreed,
"Yes, these are very good walls." Then, she added,
"I will come back. I will put art on your walls." I said,
"That sounds great. I look forward to it." But, unfortunately, I never saw her again.

Club Concept
(Add Some Music To Your Day)

We never charged an admission fee to see a music performance at Luna Lounge and Luna was never intended to be a regular live music venue. Rather, live music would be presented as special performances in addition to our series of art openings, and a great jukebox and bar.

We encouraged musicians to introduce new material and take chances that they may not have been comfortable doing in other venues where people were paying to come see them perform. Many small live music clubs in New York will book five, six, or even seven bands on any given night. Often, the bands are not given an opportunity to come in and do a proper soundcheck. Instead, the club owner's philosophy is to keep turning over the room and rotating people through the bar. It makes the venue money but those clubs are rarely very interesting.

We only had two or three bands perform on most weekday evenings and on weekends there would usually be three or four, forty-minute shows. I never endeavored to fill up the club with sub par bands just to make sound and hope that they brought people out to the club. I felt that on those nights we could let the front room work its magic and hope for a decent bar ring on its own. A club is only as good as the people who come through the doors. We were lucky to have a great deal of talent living so close and we were fortunate to have them perform in the bar.

Eating It
(What's So Funny 'Bout Peace Love And Understanding)

I was in the bar early one evening just a few weeks after we opened when three people walked in and asked if they could have a look around the club. They were Michael O'Brien, Greg Fitzsimmons and his brother, Bob Fitzsimmons. Bob and Greg's father, Bob Fitzsimmons Sr., was a very well known radio and television personality in the New York area for more than twenty-five years. He had one of the first talk radio shows back in the early 1970s when I was still a student in high school. His son, Greg, at the time that we first met, was about to host *Idiot Savants*, a game show on MTV. Although that show would only last for a year, later on, Greg would regularly appear as a commentator on two shows on VH1, *I Love The....* and VH1's *Best Week Ever*. Greg has gone on to write and produce *The Ellen DeGeneres Show* and host his own show on Sirius XM Satellite radio. In addition, he regularly performs on late night television, Comedy Central, and on *The Howard Stern Show*.

Michael O'Brien is a publicist in the comedic area of the entertainment industry. He, along with Amanda Schatz and Dave Becky were producing a comedy show at another bar in Chelsea and they wanted to move the show to another venue, preferably a room on the Lower East Side. Amanda continues the story,

> "Dave and I worked together at 3 Arts Entertainment, an LA based management company. We opened their NY office shortly before starting the show. We mostly represented comedians and Michael was a publicist that represented many of our clients so the three of us spent a lot of time together.
>
> The show grew out of our desire, and the desire of the comedy talent community, to have a place where comedic performers could try out material other than what they were doing at traditional comedy clubs."

Michael said that Luna Lounge would be perfect because our club had a separate back room. I told him that I didn't think so as Luna was an indie rock bar and that comedy hardly seemed appropriate for the space.

I had a bias against comedy as it seemed like something designed for the tourist trade of New York. The comedy rooms of which I knew where in mid town or on the Upper East Side; areas of the city not noted for their cultural significance. To me, comedy seemed at home with the mainstream theatre of midtown and something akin to Times Square. This was the Lower East Side, a bastion for creative art, music, and cultural design. However, there was something in their approach to me that made me think that I might be mistaken about their intentions and the importance of their show. They talked me into presenting the show by telling me that we could try it once and if it didn't work out they would move on to some other bar. That was one of the smartest decisions that I have ever made in my life.

The *Eating It* comedy show ran on Monday nights for the entire ten years that we were on Ludlow Street, and in addition to presenting original live music, this show became one of the most important cultural experiences Luna Lounge offered up on the Lower East Side in that decade. Amanda adds her thoughts,

> "*Eating It* was exciting because it not only harnessed up and coming talent (UCB, Zach Galifianakis, Sarah Silverman, Jeffrey Ross), it also attracted "of the moment" talent (Janeane Garofalo, David Cross, SNL cast), as well as the well established talent (Roseanne Barr, Robert Klein). It went against the tradition of doing polished/crafted "bits" and instead offered performance, music, films, and sketches that pushed the envelope. It made comedy feel cutting edge and cool, which comedy clubs at that moment, were really not, at least in NY and LA.
>
> We regularly had actors and cool bands coming by to check out what was going on."

Dave Becky is a producer, manager, and consultant in the movie and television industry. As a producer, he has helped develop ideas for the comedians with whom he has worked; bringing their talent to many television projects. He has arranged for the financing, marketing, and distribution of their shows. Some of the projects that Dave has produced include *The Hughleys*, featuring DL Hughley, *Everybody Hates Chris*, featuring Chris Rock, and nearly a score of stand up comedy shows on Comedy Central and H.B.O. featuring Louis C.K., Jeff Garlin, Dana Gould, Kevin Hart, Bill Burr, Jim Norton, Mike Birbiglia, Dave Attell, Tommy Tiernan, and Tracy Morgan.

Every Monday evening, the comedians would work out new jokes, new stories, and new routines in front of a dedicated loyal following. There was only one rule the comedians were obliged to follow; they could only perform new material. They were forced to live on the edge. They could not fall back on any previous success. If their routine was a bomb, there was no way out but through the routine.

A lot of the comedy worked but some of it fell on its

face. But, the audience was generous and they were rooting for the comic's success. If the material bombed, quite often the comedian would ask from the stage what was wrong with the joke. The sophisticated audience would often reply with an intelligent and supportive critique. These were not a bunch of drunks sitting in a roadside bar. Greg Fitzsimmons adds his thoughts,

"I was used to doing anywhere form two to seven sets a night at the regular comedy clubs in the city. Luna was a chance to do newer, more daring material without the fear of losing the crowd. It was cult comedy, so it was looked down on by most of the regular comics I worked with at the Comedy Cellar or The Comic Strip. I almost felt embarrassed in the sense that it was comedy by educated white kids for educated white kids. I just knew that it helped me experiment with loosening up my edge and trying to tell more stories.

I did the show every Monday night, if I was in town, because it forced me to come up with five to ten new minutes every week. I never did jokes I'd done before, on stage there. It was a pure workshop. The room, physically, lent itself to this because it was small enough to be packed all the time and it had a soundbooth in the room for audio and video. The bar was outside [in the front room] so it was a good intimate space.

The UCB folks were unknown and hungry and prolific. Wanda Sykes would come in with other writers form Chris Rock's show. Zach Galifianakis and Nick Swardson and Marc Maron were all unknown and there was no agenda in terms of being "discovered" or getting a following. The East Village was not a place people went to for

Sarah Silverman – 2007

entertainment when *Eating It* started there. Luna was really just the only place where they would have us.

Since then, that part of town has become a parody of what is hip or cool, much like the rest of the city. It's a shame that what started there as an "alternative" to mainstream clubs did not lead to a more sustained movement that was more similar to the roots.

People like Michael Portnoy, Ross Brockley, Todd Barry and Jon Groff were really doing something different. Now when I go to "alternative" comedy nights there is no diversity of style or opinion. Like most avant garde entertainment, it got a singular voice of irony and self satisfaction. There are stars in the alternative world, and many of them have gone on to do some of the most uninteresting things on TV, including beer commercials and horrible sitcoms and animated kids movies. For one brief shining moment, it was Comedy Camelot."

Marc Maron adds his thoughts,

"Luna Lounge was as a place and phase in my life that changed the way I performed. The *Eating It* show at Luna Lounge had an impact on my creativity and style that changed the way I saw comedy and what I could do with it. Luna Lounge was magic. I miss it."

I learned a lot by watching the show. For example, the 'call back' is when a comic sets up a joke by giving us a piece of pertinent information in the early part of a story. But, the listener does not yet realize that that piece of information is important. The comic continues and eventually comes to the end of the story; using what he or she had told us earlier as the punch line of the joke. I hear the 'call back' used all of the time and it's fun to try and discover it as a comic's routine moves along. The really good comics are very crafty and like a good magician who may conceal the movement of their hands, a good comedian can often conceal the directed movement of the humor.

We had almost no physical comedy performed on the stage, no slapstick, no clowning, and almost no insult comedy, either. We had a fair amount of sketch, some cringe routines, a bit of word play, a whole lot of satire, some deadpan, a small amount of prop comedy, occasional musical routines, some surreal routines, a bit of improvisational moments, some off color comedy, and some black comedy too.

Many of the comedians were observationists. Masters at seeing reality from a point of view where no one has gone before, they would observe and then relate to us what they had learned. And, in the process, they would provide us a new context in which we could now see the situation; never forgetting to bring the humor along for the ride.

Some of the comedians were shockers. They would attack with their anger and confrontation hoping to compel the audience into a reaction. Some of the comics were performance artists, bringing to the stage an entire sketch routine based on an unusual character. Some were political satirists who would poke a pointed finger at the powerful, the government, or the bureaucracy. Some of the comics used their bodies to make us laugh at ourselves.

The comedians who were often at Luna Lounge included Janeane Garofalo, Todd Barry, Louis C.K., Marc Maron, Jim Norton, Greg Fitzsimmons, Dave Attell, Colin Quinn, Eugene Mirman, Demetri Martin, Lewis Black, Michael Showalter, Christian Finnegan, Andy Blitz, Sarah Silverman, Jeff Garlin, Patrick Borelli, David Cross, Rick Shapiro, Margaret Cho, Kristen Schaal, Reverend Jen, Judy Gold, Rob Corrdry, Tammy Faye Starlight, Eddie Pepitone, and Steven Schirripa.

Some comedians who performed there occasionally included Jon Stewart, Roseanne Barr, Ed Helms, Wanda Sykes, and Dave Chappelle.

The list speaks for itself and for the people that were there as performers, Luna was a good room in the sense that the conduit that flowed out of the performer's brain would pass through the brains of an audience of interested followers. Not followers in the sense of a cult, but followers in the way someone might follow a team or follow a really good band. It was all of that energy all wrapped up in itself and they really did create a scene of their own. But even more than that, they created, or at the very least, profoundly developed a new school of alternative comedy.

Amanda adds her thoughts,

"The fans of the show were beyond loyal. It was almost like being a fan of a television show - you needed to tune in and see what happened on this week's episode. Initially, the show attracted a somewhat "industry" following but then they told two friends, and they told two friends. . . . There was also the post-show "party" which became very popular. You'd see the show, then hang out with everyone who performed, after, at the bar. It WAS pretty cool. It was also set at Luna, which was very low-key but cool, and people would be sitting on all of these couches and mismatched chairs that we would move into place, week after week. Also, it was on the Lower East Side, which was somewhat undiscovered by a lot of people at that time - it was exotic."

Almost all of the talent on Monday nights could be seen before and after the show at the bar in Luna in frantic discussions about things that to them always seemed really important.

The comedians would come in by themselves, one at a time through the front door. We never had a backstage dressing room or a backstage entrance. Everyone had to come through the same door. Whether you were David Cross or anyone else, the front door was the place to come and go through the club.

On those nights, my particular job was to manage the front door with Dianne, and she would collect the money. Yes, we did charge money at the front door for comedy. But, it really was a one-drink purchase because we gave the patron a Luna Lounge token that was good for any drink at the bar. So, I liked to think of it as a free comedy show with the beer you just bought.

As the comedians arrived, a palpable energy would start to kick in that led up to the start of the show. I would see Colin Quinn being himself in one corner by the bar with Todd Barry standing at his side. But, Todd would only be half listening to Colin because he just saw a girl come in who had been coming to the club a lot recently. Todd always had a ready eye for the ladies. Or, maybe not, maybe Todd was really listening. I could never be quite sure what Todd was really thinking. But, I like to think it was all good.

Louie C.K. might be talking with Jim Norton. In my mind, I saw them as kindred spirits. Sarah Silverman was the sexy one at the bar; a good-looking woman and a marvelous dispenser of irony. I can picture her in a Woody Allen film that somehow is yet to be made.

Lewis Black would arrive alone. He was very soft spoken at the bar and I never saw him with a drink. He seemed very professional and controlled until he got up on stage. Then he would let the audience know how insane the modern world had become. He would rant, he would rave and it all was absolutely hilarious. I think I can still hear him saying from the stage,

"I don't understand it!"

Judy Gold had a very strong will. I could feel it from across the room. She is very powerful. Steven Schirripa would often come by and people would take a double look at him, as if it was out of place to see him in Luna Lounge. Steven played the character of Bobby "Bacala" Baccalier, on the H.B.O. hit, *The Sopranos*. Bobby was the lovable gangster. He was not a complicated character. Bobby was earnest. He had a very good heart. You rooted for him because he was a good guy. What most people didn't know was that Steven is a very funny man.

Marc Maron would be very intense and very funny. Being the host as the morning man on the Air America radio network was not the right spot for him. It was too confining. It was too political. Marc needs a bigger canvas. His current podcast, *WTF*, is brilliant and I try to listen to it regularly. I recently read that Marc has made forty-two appearances on Conan O'Brien's shows, more than any other guest.

Janeane Garofalo once partook in a vodka shot taste test with a couple of other people who happened to be sitting at the bar. A new brand of vodka was getting a great deal of advertising and we started to carry it at Luna. I tasted it. I didn't think much of it. It was almost twice the price of Absolut or Stoly so I wondered if it was twice as good. I didn't think so. In fact, I thought it was not half as good. So, to test my own tastes with those of three other random people, I offered Janeane and two other people four free shots of chilled vodka. Each one was a different brand but they didn't know which brand was in each shot glass. The verdict was unanimous. The voting was that Absolut was the best, followed by Stoly. The new brand was third and the cheap well brand came in last. Ah, good times...

Demetri Martin was so likable. He would sometimes come in with an easel, or a guitar, or his mom; like a kid bringing a really cool homework assignment to school. I once saw Demetri on the local news because there was a fire in his building. He just happened to be the tenant who lost his apartment and had to find a new place to live. It was heartbreaking. The news reporter had no idea of who he was but I guess most of the world had not yet discovered him at that time. There were so many talented comedians. I wish that I could remember them all.

About five years into the show, the production of *Eating It* was taken over by Naiomi Steinberg and Jeff Singer. They both gave a great deal of their time and effort in maintaining the high quality booking and they helped to promote the show within the comedy industry, often having casting directors, television producers, agents, managers, and festival scouts in the seats.

Jon Stewart
(Mr. Big Stuff)

Jon Stewart came by after taping *The Daily Show* for a performance at Luna on a very hot day at the beginning of September.

We used to take the summer off from presenting comedy as many of the comedians would be in Los Angeles trying to get a television role going on the West Coast. Then, in the first week of September most would return to New York and perform at Luna Lounge. For this particular year's grand opening show of the season, Jon Stewart had agreed to make an appearance.

The room was absolutely packed and everyone was excited with Jon being at Luna. It was a very hot and extremely humid day and, of course, the air conditioning system broke down. It was a hundred degrees in the back room. There were no windows, no doors and no air circulation of any kind. It's hard to laugh when you are uncomfortable and people were feeling miserable, but no one even thought about leaving the club for a moment.

Jon took the stage and looked out at the audience packed together in the sweltering room, and said,

"What am I doing here? I'm a big star! I don't have to do this. This place is a dump!" He took the energy in the room with which we all had to work and he turned it into an expression of irony. He wasn't really belittling the club. He was making it work for the room.

Well, maybe he was, but it was still funny...

Eviction Proceedings
(Breakin' The Law)

At one point in the middle of our lease, the landlord wanted to get us out of the building in a most underhanded way. Our lease was written in order to cover two periods of time. The first period was the first five years of the lease. The second period was called an option.

The amount of the rent in both periods was established when we originally signed the lease but the landlord required that we notify him in writing of our intention to exercise our option, no less than thirty days and no more than one hundred and twenty days before our first period ended. It's a crafty way to screw a tenant because most tenants will not remember to notify the landlord in writing and in the required time frame. Most people put their lease away in a draw and go on with building their business and living their everyday lives. Then, bam! You're out of a building and you've lost everything for which you have worked. And, in our case, it's the end of something really valuable to the community. However, we did send him a letter notifying him of our intent to exercise our option. We sent it by registered mail. It arrived in his office and someone there signed for it. But, the landlord claimed that there was a different document in the envelope. Trying to intimidate us, he served us with an eviction order stating that we were to immediately vacate the building, leave it in a broom swept condition, and return the keys to his office.

We ran to our lawyers and had a consultation with the firm's senior attorney, Dudley Gaffin. Dudley had been our lawyer going back to the time we opened the Mission. Chris Morik is also an attorney in the office and he handles a great deal of legal issues too. Dudley and Chris agreed that we should fight the eviction in court. They gave Dianne and me confidence and we had high hopes on the stressful day of our trial.

When it came, Dudley had the building owner on the stand for six hours. He asked him the same question in ten different ways. It was a revealing cross-examination and the landlord unraveled on the stand under oath, contradicting his testimony.

Jeff Singer, who by this point was producing *Eating It* along with Naomi Steinberg, and the comedian, Eugene Mirman, sat with us throughout the trial. It started at 8AM and ended at 5PM. We had a recess for lunch and we all went together to a nearby restaurant. Eugene was very concerned for the club's welfare. His support meant a great deal to me.

Upon retuning to court, the attorneys made their summations. The judge had the court break while she went to her chambers in recess. After about thirty minutes she returned and read her verdict, telling those gathered before her that she believed that the compelling evidence pointed in favor of the defendants. She found that the contract was legal and binding and that we had the right to stay in the building until the end of our option. Everyone rose to their feet and shouted for joy, except for the landlord. But he had nothing about which to worry. Real estate prices continued to soar and he probably sold the building to a real estate developer for a great deal more money at the end of the following five years that came.

Reverend Jen (and friend) with Dianne at Luna Lounge.

Zee, Dianne, and Dana Distortion in Luna Lounge office.

The foosball table with band stickers – 2001.

Steve Brockway, of the Ton Ups, after a show.

Dianne (part two)
(When A Man Loves A Woman)

Dianne and I broke up as a couple less than three months after we opened the Luna Lounge. We had been together through the years at the Sanctuary and at Mission, working together in the clubs. Much time had passed and I believed that we would grow old together, continuing to create new bars until we finally retired together on some little piece of land in some little town some place up in the country. We had merged our personal and professional lives for so long that it almost seemed inconceivable to me that the two could exist separately from each other. However, what may seem impossible on one day may quickly be possible on another, and that is what happened in October of 1995.

When a new bar or nightclub opens, local members of the community are usually the first to become your regulars. That girl who lives down the block or that guy who works across the street may suddenly become your favorite new friend. There were many interesting people on Ludlow Street. One of those interesting people took an interest in Dianne. Dianne took an interest in him. Not much more has to be said. Even though their interest was very short lived, it was enough to break the loving chain that bound us to together for thirteen years. In the short space of about thirty days, the long space of our lives would be ultimately changed forever.

I'm sure that there were other issues, both conscious and subconscious. There is always something that needs to be addressed in every personal relationship. Perhaps, this was Dianne's mid life crisis. I really don't know. She never gave

Jon Spencer (center), with friends.

Dianne, John, and Harri behind the bar on Halloween 2004.

me a reason. I am sure that I'll live out the rest of my life never knowing what I did wrong or what I could have changed to keep her in love with me 'till the end. In any event, I was grateful for her honesty and that did eventually help us to reestablish a friendship after the anger finally subsided. While we struggled with our personal issues, we did our best to maintain a positive approach in the bar. There was no wisdom in bringing our drama to the staff. They and the bar would have suffered. Smartly, we decided to work on separate nights giving us a chance to be apart and have more time to think through our situation. We each only worked three or four nights, instead of us both being there on every night of the week.

Incredibly, I immediately found an affordable East Village apartment and moved out of our Chelsea studio on the third day of November of 1995. It was really weird being alone in my new empty space on that first night; all that I had was a pillow and a blanket. I could hear my thoughts feedback in that little empty room. I thought of Dianne. I wondered if she missed me. I wondered if she was alone.

It was a ground floor apartment on East Second Street, between Avenue A and Avenue B. The neighborhood was still very rough and I could hear drug deals going down just on the other side of my window. The walls were so thin, it sounded as if they were hanging with me in the room. I could hear people arguing in Spanish. Somebody said something about Julio. And, the money was coming up short. My four years of high school Spanish wasn't helping to make me feel safe. I slept furthest away from the windows, afraid that a stray gunshot would kill me in my sleep. Silly, what I really needed was a bulletproof blanket, but I awoke alive in that room and I spent the first day of the rest of my life with nothing but my thoughts in a lonely time on my own.

Time passed and Dianne and I fell into our new routines. She never called me. I never called her. We never spoke about 'us'. We just went on with our lives. We took care of our business and we tried not to argue. Eventually, we started to occasionally meet at an East Village diner to discuss our business affairs. But, we never really talked about each other. On the few occasions when we did, it never ended up well. There was a lot of anger. I was hurt and I suppose that she felt unhappy with me before she did what she did. It was a very sad time in my life. I was lost and adrift and unable to set a new course.

    I stayed home a lot and read books about Taoism and self-discovery when I wasn't working at Luna. I looked for the way to regain what I lost: my confidence, my belief in myself, my pride. Above all, I wanted to love and be loved once again. I tried to be strong, be smart, and be open to the wisdom in the words I read on those pages. I had a great deal of my life to be lived and I wanted to live it well. Still, I retreated back into my inner world; the world I had known as a boy, and attempted to seek out the reason for why my life was missing the joy.

    At first, I didn't really think that our separation would last forever. In the back of my mind, I wondered if somehow we would end up together. But, that road was closed and no way to get on that line. No future existed for the sake of the past; our sandglass had run out of time. It never happened.

Elliott Smith
(Somebody That I Used To Know — Bled White)

I first met Elliott Smith when he started coming into Luna Lounge in winter, around the beginning of 1997. Luna's bar was shaped like the letter 'L', with the small part of the 'L' coming out from the wall closest to the front door. Elliott would often sit at the small part of the 'L' at the bar. He was a solitary figure and I had no idea of who he was or what he had already done. Every night he would sit alone, filling page after page in his book. He was not yet a star in New York.

He had a couple of albums recorded and a bit of a following too, but leaving his world back in Portland for a place where he wanted to write, Elliott traded in a town that he knew for a place where he had not yet arrived. Just another musician making his way through the Lower East Side; it was still most of a year before his music appeared in the film, *Good Will Hunting*, and the newfound fame that would come from his Academy Award nomination.

After a few months, on one particular night, having just completed something giving him pause for a smile, Elliott glanced up from his book to find me looking for something behind the bar. By now he had seen me in Luna dozens of times but to each other we had not yet spoken. I used to think to myself,

"That man is very far into his jar and the lid's on tight."

But, on this night there was a brief opening and I took a chance and sought to make an entrance into his world. I said,

"Nice day, today. I think it's getting warmer." He thought about it for a moment and then with a slight smile replied,

"Yeah, it was nice today." I smiled back at him and walked out from behind the bar. On my way home I thought to myself that he seemed like an interesting guy. But, I still had no idea who was this solitary man.

Elliott Smith and I had broken the ice but he continued to bring his notebook into the club and I would not disturb him when he would write. But, it was almost spring in New York and like the new thaw coming, he slowly began to warm up in the world in which he now lived.

Elliott had made great use of his freedom while writing his new album at Luna. By April, it seemed like his work was complete. I got the feeling that Elliott had escaped from his people in Portland. His feelings expressed, he seemed a little bit lighter now having set down what he had set out to say.

We two knew of sadness; both winners and losers the same, but he was driven by something inside which was bringing him anger and pain. Sometimes we would talk about life and how love could abandon us all; pursuing a notion of happiness, we chase a beckoning call. We never spoke of his music.

I was working at bringing some Taoist ideas into my life and in a conversation that we had at the bar, I once spoke with Elliott about a Taoist poem that was helping me to find some balance. The poem suggests that it is not the pot in which we boil water, but the space inside. The poem may mean many things. I told Elliott that I believed that the Taoist poem expressed the idea that the essence of energy is created in a place not seen and not easily understood, hidden by the hard and tangible outer shell. However, it is within the inner space where matter and energy will bond and where the process of change will occur.

In addition, in specific regard to the human condition, I also believed that the poem suggested that it may be that our intellect was represented by the pot, seeking hard and tangible evidence for a position and point of view, and that the space inside is represented by the heart; not seen and not easily understood and hidden by the cold will of the mind. The heart is, never the less, the inner space where the essence of our energy is created and where the power and beauty of our lives will be manifest.

I continued along this line and expressed to Elliott the idea that perhaps seeking to understand ourselves by using our minds to pay heed to our internal dialogue was keeping us set on the outside of our lives. Rather, we may better serve ourselves clearly by seeking to feel the heart of the person for whom we ask the question; as the heart is where matter and energy will bond and the process of change will occur.

When one is able to feel the heart of the question then there is no longer a need to seek an answer. Its meaning is clear. The expressions, "Trust your heart", "Follow your heart", and "Feel the answer", are expressions meant to place us on this path of enlightenment.

Elliott thought about what I had said and was taking it in for a moment. Then, I continued,

"The hard part for me is applying this to myself; feeling the heart of myself. I judge myself a lot and that blocks the way of the heart." He continued to listen closely. And, I continued,

"Judgement is the will of the intellect; the cold will of the mind, and like the pot in which we boil water it is the barrier which keeps us from knowing the inner space where the true beauty of our heart resides." By referring to myself, Elliott knew that I had opened a window through which we both could peer in, and by not giving him advice I was hoping to help him find a way to appreciate the good heart I knew he himself had inside.

Elliott Smith - 1997

For me, the study of Taoism was a way through my loneliness. I knew that something had to change in my life, and that I needed a new approach. Dianne had left me a year and a half earlier. Even though I was the one who had walked out the door; I knew in my heart that she was the first to let go. Elliott knew Dianne. She was always in Luna too.

Spring passed into the summer of 1997 when on one evening Elliott approached me in the bar. He told me that he was going to play at Fez, a nearby basement cabaret with a capacity of around two hundred people. He asked me if I would like to come see him perform. I was surprised that he would be thinking of me but I immediately said yes. I had become a small shelf on a wall in his life. I still had no idea of what kind of music he would be making but there was something about him that I found absolutely compelling. He told me that his show was sold out but he would have me placed on his guest list.

When I arrived at Fez, I noticed that there were around four hundred people on a line stretching down the block. In the space of less than a year, Elliott was becoming a star in New York. I said to myself,

"All these people don't have a prayer of getting in. They must be really dedicated fans if they are willing to stand on this line; hoping that others will not show up. There must be something to what Elliott is doing." I stood outside for a moment and took in the scene on the street. Then, I entered and gained admission on Elliott's list and went down into the club. It was packed, really packed.

There were about seven or eight long rows of narrow tables that ran perpendicular out from the stage. People had to sit cramped in their seat turning their head to the left or the right; depending on what side of the table they faced.

Along the back wall were the best seats in the room but to which only reserved guests could attend. They were large plush padded booths for groups of eight or nine and were raised above the floor. While I coveted the luxury seating, I found a spot on the far side of the room by the bar, and stood there for the entire show; less than a couple of dozen feet from the stage.

Elliott came out by himself and proceeded to play through his set. I did not know any of the songs that night but they were all brilliant little gems filled with emotion and perfectly executed on his acoustic guitar. His voice was soft and he sang in a slightly high range. He introduced his last song at the end of his set. He started and stopped twice, and then quit in mid song during his third attempt. He got up and walked off the stage. I turned to a person standing next to me and asked him to tell me what happened. He said,

"Oh that's just Elliott. He always does that. It's the end of the show." It seemed unprofessional, but at the same time, it was an example of Elliott's depressive emotional state.

His audience seemed to accept it and actually seemed to expect it. It was part of the Elliott Smith show. I wondered if his breakdown was real or contrived for the scene. But, regardless of how the show had ended, I was absolutely sure that I had been in the presence of a great singer songwriter. I was honored to have been invited by Elliott Smith to come see him perform at the club.

Meanwhile, Gus Van Sant had made a good movie. He had made movies before with some success and some failure, but this movie would be different. *Good Will Hunting* was a box office sensation; nominated for several Academy Awards, including Best Director. It won Academy Awards for best screenplay and for Robin Williams, an Academy Award for best supporting actor.

Elliott was also nominated for an Academy Award for his music that Van Sant, a fellow Portland resident, had placed in his movie. Out of the blue, Elliott Smith would become a national sensation. He bought a white suit and he wore it to the Hollywood show.

Elliott came by the bar a few nights before he flew out to Los Angeles to sing his song at the *Academy Awards*. He had just taped his first performance on national television on *Late Night With Conan O'Brien*. Elliott asked Harri, the bartender, and me, if we would go across the street later that night and watch his performance on the TV set in Max Fish. He wanted to share in the moment with two of his friends.

Just after 1AM, I locked the door at Luna Lounge and put a sign up that said, "Went To Max Fish." There was no one in Luna but we left the lights on until we returned.

The bartender at Max Fish, also named Harry, turned up the sound on the TV and turned off the jukebox. Marc Maron, who regularly performed at the Luna Lounge Monday night comedy show, was sitting in the chair opposite Conan. They finished up their conversation and broke for a commercial. I felt very special. I knew Marc and I was standing next to Elliott. The commercial ended and Conan made the introduction. The camera cut to Elliott Smith. He was singing "Miss Misery" alone; with an acoustic guitar.

Elliott was watching his performance on television, carefully noting himself; while I stood behind Elliott watching Elliott watching himself on TV. Silent and intense in the bar, Elliott knew he was on the cusp of a world in which he was rapidly becoming a star. When his song was complete, Elliott Smith was happy, really happy, and it was the only time I ever saw him really, really smile.

Nothing lasts forever, not the good and not the bad. But, depression can seem like an endless night in the rain and Elliott and I shared the same space under that blue umbrella.

For some people, depression is the conduit through which we find our self-expression. It might not be pretty and it might not be safe, but in the end this is a tool from the chest of tools we've been given. No prescription drug in the world can change that, nor ought it do so, and this may especially be true for an artist. In time, with self-discipline and a bit of mastery if the depression is manageable, we can evolve by understanding our experience with depression.

Depression is the absence of love for ourself, by our self. But, we must never lose our capacity to believe in something other than our own demise. When we have passed through that night in the rain, we have survived. We are reconnected and have to now grow from the experience. Maybe, after depression's purpose has been fulfilled, it might go away. Elliott seemed to find a sort of drive powered by his depression, but unfortunately, that same energy could overwhelm him and incapacitate him for long periods of time.

For Elliott, being in close proximity to other musicians was uplifting. He became an exalted member in the community of the brethren of players. His peers knew him and Elliott had gained their respect. It was all around him in the bars; all around him in New York. For example, I was friendly with an alt country band from Chapel Hill, North Carolina. They were called The Mayflies USA. They had a few albums out and this time up in New York they were scheduled to perform at Brownies, a small club nearby in the East Village. I thought that Elliott might also enjoy them and told him about the band.

On the night that The Mayflies performed at Brownies, Elliott was in a seat off on one side in front of the stage. The band looked over and couldn't believe that he was there, in the room, and that he had come to see them perform. It was a testament to the respect that Elliott Smith had garnered among his peers. Matt Long, former guitarist in The Mayflies USA and now a founding member of The Library, has often spoken of that night.

Tabitha Tindale, of the band Joy Zipper, tells her version of a similar story,
"The week before we were leaving for a
UK tour, we had the pleasure of playing at
Luna Lounge. We played there a few times
before and thought it would be the perfect

place to do a warm up show for the tour and also have a going away party with our friends.

When we arrived for soundcheck, the place was empty except for one guy sitting at the bar. He was wearing all black and never picked his head up from the notebook in which he was writing.

I whispered to my friend, Nicole, that I thought that that was Elliott Smith. We only recently had started listening to his music so she got really excited and ran up to him and started asking him questions. She also told him that my band, Joy Zipper, was playing in the other room in about an hour and that he should come and watch. He was so quiet, she was so excited, and I was so embarrassed that she was badgering this guy that clearly just wanted to be alone.

Sure enough, just as we were going on stage, Nicole ran back into the bar area, grabbed Elliott right from his bar stool and forced him to come and watch our show. She sat with him the whole time. I'll never forget looking out into the audience that night and seeing Elliott Smith's sweet face looking back at me, Elliott Smith, the hostage."

When Elliott first came to New York, he was living where he needed to be, without fanfare; an anonymous presence among the writers and artists of the city. Later on, I was disturbed when Elliott told me that he was moving to Los Angeles; even though I knew that he needed a change.

After the attention garnered through the movie, the Academy Award nomination, and the brilliant album, *XO*, which was released in 1998, people were starting to crowd in on him at Luna Lounge. One night, I counted seven guys wearing the same signature wool hat, a night in which Elliott was sitting at the bar. The people who believe that they discover their own style, their own identity, by emulating the identity of an artist whose work they admire had finally found their master. He had come to escape from his friends in Portland and now a timely escape from New York was at hand. But, there were issues to consider that would affect his health and wellbeing.

In Los Angeles, he would drive himself in a car but he was better off served by a subway. He wrote about the subway. He used the subway map as metaphorical imagery in his music. Elliott was still anonymous on the subway; in the company of other hard working, real living individuals who had no interest in the man with the cap in a seat. He was a writer and needed stimulation from the close proximity of other human beings. It was important that he not be a recluse. He needed to have people close-by and he had to be out and about each day.

He needed to observe, but observation is passive when you are driving on a highway. It's redundant; the same thing for miles behind and miles ahead and what you do see is somewhere out there in the distance. Standing on a street corner in New York, a dozen interesting faces may move through the crosswalk in any given moment. You can reach out and touch one and she, or he, can reach back and touch you too.

The weather was too predictable in Los Angeles. It was too nice, too much sunshine. He needed a good storm from time to time in his face and not far away. He was not a surfer nor could I see him going to the beach. In Los Angeles, his darker elements would work their way up through his soul.

I kept all of this to myself and never mentioned to him how I felt. I knew that Elliott had to be leaving and moving further along on his road. He would only have deflected advice. I knew why he was going to Los Angeles; I saw that on the night we stood at the bar at Max Fish. Elliott was driven to success and now he would drive himself to excess; testing the limits of the people who loved him as an artist and as a friend.

I flew out to Los Angeles and hung out with him at Spaceland, a club in the Silverlake section where he was living. He was already starting to change. We spoke for awhile but it wasn't what he said, it was now how he looked. I had a strong feeling that Elliott had begun to use heroin; not yet full tilt but Elliott was more than recreationally using the drug. There was no weekend warrior in this man. If he was going there, he was going all the way there.

Yes, he was a drinker and he drank more than a few glasses of Jameson in New York. But he never lost his powerful will or his ability to compose and to perform. He played at an extraordinary level of expertise. Under the influence of heroin there would be a downward slope to his playing and the nuance in his vocals would suffer. Some guys can play while heroin is in a place in their lives and some guys cannot. It depends on their style. It depends on their personalities. Elliott would not play well. And when Elliott knew that he was not playing well, a downward spiral of self-loathing and demise would occur.

He could still write and compose but Elliott needed to play. When he performed, he was always best when he was there by himself in a room. The closer the people were to him, the more he got out of the experience.

Time passed. His next album, *Figure 8*, was released and I put it into the jukebox at Luna Lounge. At first, I played it a lot. Then, I stopped playing it. Every time someone else in the bar played a song from that album, I started to feel worse. In his songs and in his voice on that album, I could hear Elliott moving closer to his end. The man I had known and admired; the man who had sat at the bar while creating the album *XO*, may have been out of control and heading for the wall.

I took *Figure 8* out of the jukebox at Luna Lounge, but I left *in XO*. I put in *Either/Or*, his last album recorded while he still lived in Portland. I also put in Quasi albums. I put in The Spinanes, who were his friends, and I put in the Heatmiser record; anything that could bring a positive mojo into the room and perhaps send a message of love and good will to Elliott wherever he was in Los Angeles.

I was hoping that he could find his way out of addiction and out of the associated depression concurred. We all need a resurrection and it's best to have one while one is still living a life on this Earth. I was hoping for his personal resurrection. Elliott was a determined individual. He was not likely to fail under pressure. He was a powerful man. But, sometimes it is better to cry than to raise one's fist in the air; better to be soft than to be firm, and better to bend than to break. Elliott had a powerful ego. His birth sign was Leo, the lion. You cannot change their mind. Only they will change their mind.

Elliott came back to New York on a visit. I heard that he was hanging out at another bar in the neighborhood and I knew drugs could be bought in that bar. Then, I got a phone call from Harri. It was around midnight and I was home on this night. He told me that Elliott was at Luna Lounge. I asked Harri if Elliott had asked for me. He said,

"No." I asked Harri how Elliott looked. He said,

"Not good." I told Harri that unless Elliott asked for me that I was going to stay home on that night. I couldn't go in and see him; although now in retrospect I wish that I had, but it hurt too much at the time.

The last time I saw Elliott Smith was at Spaceland, and he more or less was still the person I had come to know at Luna Lounge. By the time he came back to New York, the man I knew may have been gone. I was reluctant to find out.

I heard that at the time of his death, Elliott had cleaned himself up and that the autopsy had found no drugs in his system; except for those powerful psychoactive drugs that pharmaceutical companies have designed and sold to the public. In the end, perhaps Elliott had made it through his addiction. He had the will and the power from within to do it, and of that I am absolutely sure.

I have taken one of those prescription drugs. It was no fun. It was the most difficult experience of my life. I felt like I was going through shock treatment. My brain had electrical pulses, some people call zaps, that kept happening over the course of the first few months on my prescription. My mood swings were through the roof and I was nauseous for hours every day. I had to take the pill before I went to sleep. If I took it in the morning, it would incapacitate me for several hours, making it impossible for me to work.

I checked the pharmaceutical company website and found only the mildest of statements in regard to possible side effects. They left out a whole lot of stuff going on in my head. I got through it but it took a dozen weeks. Perhaps, the combination of these powerful pharmaceutical psychoactive drugs, and the illegal drugs that Elliott may have combined with them, had seriously compromised important mood altering chemicals in his brain. Maybe, it would have helped if he could have had a longer period of recovery with experienced, intelligent supervision. Rehab is never long enough, anyway.

Perhaps, he just got tired of coming to the same place again and again; tired of hearing his inner voice express the same words that he had before so often heard. Elliott was passionate and creative. Maybe, he was angry at his own redundancy.

Maybe, he felt that his time in Los Angeles had come to an end and again it was time to move on. But, now where was he to go? Perhaps, the thought of his starting over again was finally too much to bear.

Maybe, Elliott had been worn down by the hard friction received in living those last few years, and like a space shuttle, he disintegrated upon reentry into a drug free life.

Or maybe, in his last moment, Elliott Smith used his

powerful will to cross over in exploration of some place to which he had not yet arrived; some place on the other side of his life. I have, like most fans, spent time thinking about the end of Elliott's days.

Ultimately, for whatever the reason, or reasons, why Elliott Smith has died, I am reminded of the night in which I spoke with him at Luna Lounge in regard of that Taoist poem. Perhaps, it is wise for us to avoid seeking the will of our intellect in trying to know his action, for like the pot in which we boil our water; our intellect is the barrier which keeps us from seeing the inner space where the beauty of Elliott's heart resides.

As the heart is where matter and energy will bond and the process of change will occur; we may better serve ourselves clearly by seeking to feel the heart of the person for whom we ask the question.

And, in seeking the heart of this artist, we need only seek him out singing his song.

Elliott Smith at Luna Lounge.

Sound Engineers
(I Can Hear Music)

I had the privilege of working with a few thousand bands over the course of a decade at Luna Lounge. I became a very good, dedicated sound engineer. Much was often worked out at soundchecks and they were immensely important to the development of the band's expertise in front of an audience.

When I worked with young musicians, after I initially got the sound levels for each instrument, the band would run through one or two songs in their set. This is where I could tell what had to be improved, taking into consideration the volume and the equalization of each instrument in comparison to each other and to the vocalist in the group. Most players had only focused on their own sound and paid little or no attention to how the part coordinated with the sound being created by the other members of the band.

A typical issue would involve having to consider that one or more guitarists would have their instrument equalized, or eq'd, in the same exact frequency range. I learned from listening night after night that when this was the case, the listener could not adequately distinguish the difference between the two musical parts being played. In effect, the guitarists were canceling each other out. Inevitably, they would both resort to raising the volume of their amplifiers in order to more adequately hear the parts they were playing. This caused a cycle of 'loud and then louder' to be constantly happening in the band.

Eventually, the vocalist would ask me to turn up the

volume on his or her microphone because they could no longer comfortably hear their voice in the song. This was the most common problem in working with bands that performed at Luna Lounge. Fortunately, the solution was simple and I found most players willing to work through the issue. I would explain to the band what was happening from what I could hear in my booth. Then, I would suggest that one of the guitarists cut back on the high end while the other guitar would cut back on their low. Thus, the two guitars became properly eq'd and their parts became easy to hear. Now, the vocalist could sing without having to scream at the top of their range.

Another typical issue, but a bit more difficult to execute, would be that of a quiet singer in a band with a very loud drummer. Cymbals can cover the frequency range of most vocals. It can be hard to become a good singer when the drummer is smashing these loud metal plates. Again, the first line of defense would be to ask for more volume but that wasn't making the singer sound better. The cymbals were still canceling out vocals competing for range in one's ear. I would politely ask if the drummer could pay closer attention to the power being used to strike the cymbals. Many young drummers cannot control their dynamics, playing more or less, at one single volume. This was often the weakest link in a band and there wasn't much that I could fix in the booth.

On a few dozen occasions over the years, a great drummer would come and play in the room. Often already in successful bands, they would play in side projects and on these various nights I would clearly notice the difference. Some drummers that come to mind were Stanley Demeski, who played in The Feelies and Luna, Dennis Diken, of the Smithereens, Jaleel Bunton, the drummer in TV On The Radio, Ira Eliott, the drummer in Nada Surf, and Clem Burke, the amazing drummer in Blondie.

One more issue that was sometimes at hand in a soundcheck was the case of the very shy female singer;

lacking in confidence, their voice so slight that almost no sound could be heard through the system, I would take a special tact with these groups.

In a soundcheck, I would dramatically stop the band in mid song and walk directly up to the stage. Then, I would ask that only the vocalist sing and have one guitar play underneath; reducing his or her volume to properly support the vocal. Then, I would say to the band,

"If you want her beautiful voice to be heard, we need to have you play at this level." Of course, they would ask,

"Can't you turn up the vocal?" I would reply,

"I would if my system went up to eleven," referencing the *Spinal Tap* movie, "But unfortunately, we only go up to ten." It was the only polite way that I could explain that you cannot increase what is not there without hurting anyone's feelings. Sometimes it really helped.

We had a carpet on the stage at Luna Lounge and it took me years to figure out that we were harnessing the power of static electricity. Occasionally, during a soundcheck, a vocalist would reach out and grab the mic only to receive a slight shock in return. I could not remove the carpet as it was permanently nailed to the floor. The singer would yell out,

"Hey, I'm getting a shock when I touch the mic," and I would return,

"Well then, I suggest you not touch the mic." Of course, the singer would then grab the mic several times over the course of their set.

Sometimes, a band might bring in another sound engineer. Often, in those cases, it was someone who was recording the band who knew all the delicate intricacies of what they were putting down on record. A few of those engineers were brilliant and from them I had the good fortune of learning a few tricks of the trade. Some of them were really better off in the studio when lacking experience working a 'room'. On those nights I had to be patient and hope for the best. Unless, there was some form of audio pain being inflicted upon the band and audience, I would sit quietly by and be available if the engineer would shout out for a life preserver, but that very rarely happened.

Luna was also a club where record producers and studio owners would often be seen, especially those who lived, worked, or had studios in the neighborhood. I used to say that the East Village and Lower East Side had thirty thousand musicians because in the 1990s it seemed like almost everyone carried a guitar. There were five recording and rehearsal studios on Ludlow Street at that time. There were another dozen within walking distance. Just a few blocks away on Avenue A, there was Context, a massive rehearsal space that could accommodate a dozen bands at any given time. One of these recording studios was co-owned by Gordon Raphael. Gordon relates,

"After rehab in Seattle, coming down off my New York trip, late 80's chapter- I did a year in Hollywood, faring pretty well, and then a return to Seattle where in the height of the grunge revolution I was in a signed tribal space rock band called, Sky Cries Mary. We toured the US and made bi-annual trips to play in Manhattan, appearing on the *Jon Stewart* and *Conan O'Brien* shows, at our peak.

Then, I formed Absinthee, with Anna Mercedes, and had an opportunity to take her to New York on her twentieth birthday. Part of the allure, as the Seattle rock and roll star was waning, post Cobain and post Soundgarden demise, was that we were offered a show performing at Luna Lounge! We were an unknown band, even in Seattle, but my pal Alan Bezozi from the cool band, Dog's Eye View, arranged this gig for us.

Absinthee's two person excursion to New York City was so much fun and so inspiring, made more so by the fact that at our performance at Luna Lounge, we met and chatted with a real live record company executive who was there randomly, and took it upon himself to say hello after our show.

Anna fairly insisted we move directly to Manhattan and try to live there and promote our music, which I hesitated about because of my deep failure there a decade earlier, and the fact that we'd just gotten ourselves a very fancy and huge house to live in that was really cool, in Seattle. But, off we went, to become NYC rockers and try our fortune in the Big Apple once again.

I had two good friends, Chad and Dorit, who were in an amazing band called Halcion, that performed regularly in the East Village. Chad introduced me to a circle of almost entirely Austrian, Swiss and German ladies and gentleman, most of whom were artists and musicians and journalists, in many cases, all three simultaneously! From the beginning of my new residency in New York (1998 May), every night centered around the Ludlow Street configuration of hotspots, as it was for all intents and purposes, the only place with a pulse in town if you valued new music, intelligence, creativity, friendliness and fun."

The neighborhood was a home for musicians from all over the country and more than a few from the United Kingdom, Ireland and continental Europe. I knew a musician who told me that he had grown up behind the iron curtain and that he swam across the Danube River in order to escape from the communists. He was caught twice.

Finally, he was able to legally get out of that country by claiming that he was a religious zealot and that he had found God. Then, the communist bureaucrats let him emigrate to Italy where he had to live with Jehovah's Witnesses for more than a year. Finally, he made it to America and now he was living on my block and he was playing in a hardcore band called, Molotov Cocktail.

When a group started to go out on the road, they would always promote themselves as being from New York. The band was from New York but the individual members were almost always from some other place. It made me smile. It is still the case today although these days it is more fashionable to hail from Brooklyn.

Jody Porter
(Life Is Good)

I had been dating a girl who would eventually become my wife for awhile. We had been hanging around each other for a few weeks and the time came to go out on our first date. That was on May 25th, 1999.

I had some friends that played at Luna Lounge quite often. They had called themselves Cardinal Woolsey but had recently changed their name. They were now Phono, the opening act that night at The Bowery Ballroom. I got us on their guest list and we went to see my friends and the headliner band from New Jersey, the indomitable Fountains Of Wayne.

May 25th is also the birthday of Fountain's lead guitarist, Jody Porter, and the other members of the band had a very pretty girl present him with a birthday cake on stage. The concert was a great deal of fun; smart pop songs for the indie rock set, Beatles influenced harmonies, and very good guitar work in support of the tunes. I had never seen

Fountains Of Wayne before but I was a fan of the two studio albums I knew. I had both records in the jukebox at Luna Lounge and I played songs from them every night. After the show, my date and I went back to the bar. It wasn't long before the members of Fountains Of Wayne walked in behind us. I had no idea they were coming to Luna that night. Jody was celebrating his birthday in fine style, holding court with a bevy of friends.

Jody is an American, born in South Carolina, but you would not know that from the way he plays guitar. As a young member of The Belltower, an American band who played within the British shoegazing scene, Jody garnered critical notice from his British peers. NME Magazine named The Belltower EP as a single of the week in 1990.

After releasing a couple of additional UK singles and a full-length album too, The Belltower moved back to the United States. Now living in New York, Jody met Adam Schlesinger who joined The Belltower and played bass guitar in the band. Eventually, The Belltower disbanded and a couple of years later, Adam asked Jody to join Adam's newly formed band, Fountains Of Wayne, before their self-titled debut was released.

Fountains would go on to have some success with their singles, "Radiation Vibe" and "Sink To The Bottom With You" off their first album and they incessantly toured for a year. The second album, while critically reviewed, failed to garner much radio play. The band, disappointed with the label, was able to leave their grasp and ultimately signed with another company. Their third album, *Welcome Interstate Managers*, spawned a colossal hit called, "Stacy's Mom", an anthem for the thirteen something set. It would earn a gold record and sold more than a half million copies.

Jody and I would spend plenty of time together in the following years to come. And, he would become a person

Jody Porter at soundcheck in Madison Square Garden.

whose company to which I would look forward whenever he came to the bar. He enriched my life; bringing his rock star world and his bon vivant way through my doors.

The Basement
(Yellow Submarine)

There was a basement in Luna Lounge, not open to the public, it was where we kept the liquor and beer, a walk-in refrigerator, a bathroom for the staff, washing machine and dryer for bar towels, and an assortment of discarded cymbal stands, broken instruments, and guitar amplifiers that somehow were left behind and never claimed by their owners.

There was only a bright white florescent light that hung from the low basement ceiling. There was an old, round, 1970s style, white Formica kitchen table down there, too. I had originally bought that table for my empty apartment but it never quite fit in and it was consigned to the basement where it remained for the entire decade. The table came with four vinyl kitchen chairs in very groovy 1970s colors. They could rotate completely around and that could be fun on the right night at Luna. The table was fairly accommodating and we usually had a couple of boxes and an old amp on which folks could comfortably sit. We could fit as many as eight or nine people around that table, and we did, whenever the moment was right.

But, for the most part the basement was my escape from the people one floor above. It was a quiet private place to gather my thoughts. I spent many hours downstairs in the basement.

I often had twenty or thirty minutes to myself after the last band's soundcheck and before the beginning of the first band's set. I might have my dinner at that time or I just might want to be alone for awhile before the club filled up on that night. I found it to be peaceful, meditative, and a hidden treasure just below the chaos of a crowded bar.

Occasionally, when a friend would come by, we would go downstairs together where it was relatively quiet and we could talk without interruption. It was also comfortable in those old kitchen chairs.

Some bands knew about the basement although I did try and keep it a secret. I did not want it to become a dressing room or a backstage area. I wanted to keep the basement for Dianne, a few friends, our staff, and myself.

However, as time went on and we became friendly with a number of bands, it would not be unusual to go downstairs and find those musicians tuning up and rehearsing before their set. There were Olivia Tremor Control, playing New York for the CMJ Festival, and Orange Park who would practice their vocal harmonies. There was Peter Kember, aka Sonic Boom, whose indie drone psychedelic sound driven work in Spacemen 3 and in Spectrum would continue to be one of my favorite experimental sounds. You could find members of stellastarr*, Falcon, Longwave, The Inevitable Break Ups, Nada Surf, The Astrojet, Billionaire Boys Club, Kitty In The Tree, Travis Pickle, Skywriter, Railroad Jerk, Fooled By April, Interpol, Helicopter Helicopter, Dave Pirner of Soul Asylum, and other bands in acoustic rehearsal before their sets.

Sean Lennon
(All You Need Is Love)

One night, Jody came into the club as I was about to go down into the basement. He and I met at the cellar door inside the club. By this time, we had become good friends. He asked me if he and his friends from Cibo Mato could go downstairs for awhile. Without even looking at them, I said sure and I told him that I was just about to go downstairs, too.

I didn't really know anything about Cibo Mato but when we all gathered around that white kitchen table I noticed that there were two beautiful Asian women sitting to my left. I really had trouble in keeping myself from staring at them; they had a very powerful presence. It wasn't just that they looked good, which they did, but they had something elegant and earthy in great detail. They had star power; not the kind of star power manufactured in Hollywood but real star power with which certain creative people are born.

Jody introduced the girls to me but their exotic Japanese names went through my ears before my brain could properly catch their phonetic sounds. I just smiled and said that it was very nice to meet them. Jody then introduced the guys but I didn't quite catch their names. However, I had already met one of them and his name was Timo Ellis. Timo sat to my right and Jody was sitting to Timo's right.

The band was comfortable and engaged in conversation to which I mostly observed. They had performed somewhere earlier that night and they seemed to be in that after show spirit that comes from a good performance. After several minutes, I found myself looking across the table at the fellow who was to Jody's right as he was sitting directly across the table from me. In a quick moment, I thought to myself,

"Gee, that guy looks like John Lennon." Then, in a flash, my little brain went though the following sequence,

"He doesn't look like John Lennon. He looks like Sean Lennon. Oh, my god! That is Sean Lennon. I'm sitting across from Sean Lennon. " Then my thought progressed to,

"Oh, I feel so bad for him. He lost his father when he was just five and he grew up without a dad." I personally felt for the first time the effect of what happened on that cold night in December. It made me angry and it made me well up with compassion for Sean. I didn't think about The Beatles. I didn't think about John. I thought about Sean and how much was taken from him when he was still just a little boy. I sat there while their conversation freely flowed round and around the table. No one gets over something like that; they just have to move on. They have to find their own way in the world.

No matter what happens in Sean's career, I will always respect him. The ignorant in this world may choose to see him as a person living in the afterglow of his father's fame but I see him as a man who has struggled, and with determination, has become a man in his own right. He is his own musician and a very good player too. Sean has played in a variety of interesting projects, many of which I play in the bars I have owned.

Later, on that night when we met, I saw Sean playing foosball and having a ball upstairs with his friends. He was happy and I was happy to know that he had in that moment a joyous time in the bar.

Disaster In The Basement
(Sink To The Bottom With You)

The basement was becoming an iconic part of Luna Lounge. It was the scene of many nights of conversation and camaraderie for Dianne, myself, and our friends. However, there was one time when the basement became a scene of disaster a few months after we first opened.

Lotion was making a video and the band stored their equipment down in the basement after the filming was completed that day. Next day, I was the first to arrive for work. I turned on the lights and proceeded to go down into the basement where I beheld a horrible sight. Something had gone terribly wrong; sewage had flowed in from the street. The band's amps were submerged, the bass drum floated by in the murk. Later that night, the city plumbers repaired the main pipe on Ludlow Street and the sewage receded back into the city sewage system but not before leaving its mark on everything below the water line in the basement. It took a week to properly clean up the cellar.

The band had upcoming out of town dates and they came by and picked up their gear. I never imagined that their amps would ever be working again. But, they told me that when their amps had dried out, they seemed to sound better than ever! Even the smell had disappeared. I have never figured out how that possibly could have happened.

Camper Van Beethoven
(That Gum You Like Is Back In Style)

After Lotion made their video at Luna, we were honored to occasionally work with some of our other favorite artists in the making of their videos, too.

I seem to have an affinity for bands that come from the small cities and towns in California. Among my favorites is the group known as Camper Van Beethoven. They have an eclectic mix of influences, an honest do it yourself attitude, and above all, a collection of brilliantly written songs I still enjoy more than a dozen years after their creation.

Somehow, the band discovered Luna Lounge and kept company there whenever they played in New York. It was a great thrill for me to see their singer and songwriter, David Lowery, hanging with his friends at the bar.

The stage in Luna Lounge was immortalized in the Camper Van Beethoven video, "Discotheque CVB", a song off their brilliant 2004 release, *New Roman Times*. The video image of our stage is all that is left of the room where so many bands once performed. It was exactly, in reality, as it is portrayed in the video. The camera angle in the Camper video duplicated the camera angle that we used to send the

Jeff Moore and Harve, of Orange Park, with a drink token.

French Kicks at Luna Lounge after a performance.

Mayflies USA in concert on the Luna Lounge stage.

Dianne and Paul Dillon (Mercury Rev, Longwave, Silver Rockets) downstairs in the Luna Lounge basement.

Gordon Wright of Fooled By April and Julie Chadwick of Helicopter Helicopter.

Travis Pickle's Pete and Carla in one of their performances.

closed circuit video image to our television above the bar in the front room. Apparently, David Lowery was sitting at the bar when he got the idea for this video.

Jon Spencer
(Blowing My Mind)

    I had the privilege of spending an afternoon with Jon Spencer when he shot part of a documentary film about the theremin, an electronic musical instrument invented in the 1920s. It is a strange instrument; controlled without contact by a player. The idea is to place your hands in specific spots between two metal antennas. By moving your hands either up and down, or from side to side, you can get the instrument to make sounds and control the pitch and volume. The theremin is often associated with the eerie music found in 1950s science fiction movies.

Jon played the instrument but not in the way that classical and jazz virtuosos perform on it. On the day that the film crew was in Luna recording Jon's method of playing the instrument, I observed Jon doing stage dives between the antennas creating his own sound through the instrument's electronic field. It was one of the weirdest things that I had ever observed at Luna, but at the same time, it was really interesting and great fun to see.

I have followed John's career and have enjoyed the music he made with Pussy Galore, Boss Hog, and Heavy Trash. Years later, after Luna had closed on Ludlow Street and had moved to the Williamsburg section of Brooklyn, Jon would come to the new Luna Lounge with his friend, Matt Verta-Ray (formerly of Madder Rose and Speedball Baby) and give an electric performance on our new stage. I will always appreciate Jon's rock'n'roll attitude and the way he reinvents himself as an artist over and over again. His career has had commercial peaks and valleys but he has never failed to rock; he makes his own way through the indie rock world and I respect him very much.

LunaSea Records
(I Know It's Only Rock-n-Roll But I Like It)

I noticed that we were starting to have a number of good bands performing regularly at Luna Lounge sometime around the middle of our ten-year run on Ludlow Street. I also noticed that although our room was filled to capacity when they performed, no one from a major record label was in the audience. It was still a year or two before The Strokes broke down the walls through which a flood of talented bands came crashing. Just before that time, some of my favorite groups were Scout, Orange Park, Joy Zipper, Probe, Kitty In The Tree, Travis Pickle, Northern State, Wheatus, Pop Star Kids, Individual Fruit Pie, The Compulsions, Dirty On Purpose, Semi-Gloss, Moths, The Twenty Twos, The Cogs, The Hong Kong, Toss, Skywriter, The Inevitable Break Ups, Helicopter Helicopter, Asobi Seksu, stellastarr*, The Astrojet, Pony Express, Highspire, Aerial Love Feed, Motel Creeps, Motel Girl, The Soft Explosions, The Irreversible Slacks, Mike Daly (of Whiskeytown), The Hold Steady, Hula, Sea Ray, Fooled By April, The Ton Ups, The Comas, The Mayflies USA, We Are Scientists, Moonrats, Clara Venus, Human Drama, Certain Distant Suns, Mini King, Stupid, French Kicks, Skywave, and Pleasure Unit.

I decided that I would do what I could to get the process started if no one else was going to help get these bands get heard beyond the walls of the Luna Lounge. I never imagined earning any profits from owning a tiny record label. Back when I sent The Ancients album out to radio and pressed up five hundred copies for sale in retail stores, not much really came of it in a financial sense. Still, by this time, Luna Lounge was doing well and I wanted to give it another try. Dianne was willing to partner with me and that helped ease the financial expense. We called the label, LunaSea Records.

I approached Travis Pickle, one of my favorite bands who regularly performed at the bar. They had a well-crafted, slightly warped sense of humor expressed in their sophisticated blend of pop, rock, and lounge pop music. They also had recorded a full album's worth of worthy material.

Pete Min played guitar in the band and recorded and produced their album. Pete has gone on to record and produce many bands, including The Airborne Toxic Event, whose single, "Sometime Around Midnight", garnered a great deal of radio play in 2009.

Ten years earlier, Pete Min was in Travis Pickle, along with Carla Capretto, a very attractive lead singer, accomplished keyboard player and guitarist. Yianni Naslas played bass and Steve Wickins was the drummer. Their songs were quirky, as was the name of the band, and I always enjoyed their performances. Carla Capretto provides her impressions,

> "All four of us were in a backing band with another singer and Pete decided that he wanted to start a new group. So, we auditioned tons of singers but we couldn't find anybody that we liked. So, we said, let's just sing, do it ourselves, and that's how the four of us started Travis Pickle.
>
> I loved playing at Luna. Rob made it so easy and fun. It felt like we were playing in our living room, that's how he made us feel. It always seemed to be the same people there. Including the other bands and friends, it felt like family. I always knew that on the nights that we had a show there, it was going to be a great time. Even on other nights when we were not performing,

going to see other bands and just going to hang out, it was going to be fun. I liked the way the stage wasn't too high. I felt like the audience was right there with us when we played. And, of course, hanging out downstairs in the basement..."

Yanni Naslas adds,

"I had known Rob and Dianne since 1991 Luna was laid back, the bartenders appreciated the drinking crowd that we could bring in, and the bartenders could be generous to us in return."

In an interesting side note, a few months before the opening of Luna Lounge, while walking down Saint Mark's Place in the East Village, I noticed a throng of people spilling out of a small Irish run coffee house called, Sin-e. Travis Pickle was performing their very first gig in this tiny space. People were pressed up against the plate glass window trying to hear what was going on inside. I couldn't see all of the members of the group as they were sitting on chairs normally used for the tables and many were standing in front of them.

As I stood outside observing the phenomena, Joey Ramone just happened to come down the block. He stopped behind me and tried to figure out what was the reason for the crowd spilling out of the cafe when he noticed me standing on the street pressed up against the window. He called out,

"Rob, what's going on in there?" Recognizing Joey's voice, I turned my head back to him and answered,

"I don't know. It's a band and I think they sound pretty good."

I took a more active role in the recording of Kitty In The Tree, a band of pleasure seeking hedonists who I used to say were the only band that could fall onto the stage before a performance. I could not book Kitty In The Tree to play after 11PM because they were always partying so hard. However, if they went on stage no later than 11PM, they were one of the greatest party bands in New York.

The guys in Lotion introduced me to Kitty In The Tree and for awhile, Carla Capretto and Pete Min were doing double duty, playing and singing in Travis Pickle and Kitty In The Tree.

I co-produced, along with a great deal of work from Bob O'Gureck and Randy Staley, their eponymous album which we also released on LunaSea Records.

Apart from some good reviews and a few college stations that played those recordings, not much came of the Travis Pickle and Kitty In The Tree albums. There were too many bands competing for a listener's attention and without a five or six figure promotional budget spent willingly at radio and other media outlets, worthy bands were simply washed away in the rain of releases from larger indie and major labels.

There was only so much that I could do unless those bands decided to perform outside of New York City. That would mean they would have to buy a van and commit to the process of becoming a regional touring act. They would have to develop followings in the nearby large cities of Boston, Philadelphia, Baltimore, and Washington DC. In addition, they would have to play in some of the smaller college towns. Last, they would have to perform at some far off music conventions including South By Southwest, in Austin, Texas.

The idea behind becoming a regional act is to substantially increase the band's following beyond their own city in order to gain the respect and interest of people in the music industry. People will take a band for granted when a group continues to perform every month somewhere in New York City. They simply become another bar band and people feel that they can see them play anytime. However, once a band has become a regional act, they can cut down the number of performances in New York by playing the out of town dates.

By diminishing the number of local appearances, a band will draw more people to each show whenever they do perform in the city. Then, instead of performing in front of forty, they can expect to play in front of one hundred and forty people. This makes the band look like they have a buzz and they can start to sell out larger rooms. Record labels and the music press will take notice when a band starts to sell out larger venues. In addition, they have the benefit of having developed followings in several additional markets.

It's not rocket science but it takes a certain determination and a serious will to succeed. It is very difficult as it requires the musicians to have a total commitment to the band. Jobs might have to be sacrificed, players will find themselves sleeping in strange locales, vans will break down, and musicians will find themselves driving great distances to play in front of handfuls of people who may initially have no interest in seeing them perform. It's all part of the process of building a career for yourself when no one else will do it for you. Unfortunately, though both bands were among the best to perform at Luna, for various reasons, Travis Pickle and Kitty In The Tree were unwilling, or unable to successfully follow this course.

We put together a compilation album that was called *A Tribute To Big Star (With Additional Songs By Chris Bell)*. It had twenty-three different Luna Lounge bands performing their versions of Big Star compositions. The album received good reviews. Among the highlights on the album, were Nada Surf's rendition of "Blue Moon", Marty Willson-Piper's version of "Thirteen", Longwave's version of "Holocaust", and Fooled By April's recording of "Oh Dana". I was particularly pleased with this album. I am a fan of the band and recall them performing at Ultrasonic Sound Studios way back when I was an intern in 1974. Although

Big Star was never a commercial success, they created music that influenced some of the brilliant indie rock bands in the following decades to come.

We released an album from the New York alt country post punk band, Moths, and an album from a punk power pop band called, The Cogs. While both groups delivered very good records, each band broke up within a short time after their albums were pressed and sent to college radio for play. Actually, The Cogs broke up even before the record was pressed.

    I am grateful for having had the experience of running LunaSea Records. I would have liked to continue to do it and to have helped launch the careers of other good bands from New York. But, as it would turn out, there would be other issues that would come to affect the bar, and consequently, I would have to rein in my available funds. But, there would be one other band with whom I would share some success and they would go on to sign with RCA Records.

Longwave
(Make Me A Believer)

I had wanted to release an album by the band Scout, which I wanted Pete Min, from Travis Pickle, to record and produce. I put together a meeting at Luna to talk about my idea with the band and introduce them to Pete. The meeting went well but the band knew of another person who would ultimately record and release their album.

    Steve Schiltz, at that time, was the lead guitarist in Scout. He was twenty years old and had only recently joined the band; having just arrived in New York City from upstate in Rochester. Steve approached me soon after that meeting. He mentioned that he had written some of his own songs and asked if I would be interested in hearing them, with the possibility of booking a performance at Luna. To be nice, I simply said yes. In Steve's own words,

"I first came to Luna as a member of the band Scout. I had been playing shows with a rag tag group in the West Village, but Luna was a more serious venue to my mind, and I hadn't dared to try and get a gig there. I was fresh off the bus from Rochester. I had just started playing guitar in Scout and this was the big time. I had just turned twenty years old and I was too young to be in the club, let alone playing.

After I performed one or two Scout gigs at Luna, Rob approached us and said he'd like to meet with Scout about doing a record for his new label. He invited us to come to Luna on a Saturday afternoon to talk, and he brought with him a guy named Pete Min. Pete was going to record the band, and Rob was going to put out the record.

My memory of that meeting is that Scout was a little unfocused, and lacked a real direction. Maybe the other guys just didn't want to do the record. I don't know. Pete was very interesting to me, and I knew I wanted to spend more time with him. Rob was a wild card. I didn't know what he was thinking, only that he really seemed to like my new band.

About three days later, on a Tuesday night, I was at Luna again. I was just hanging out. I saw Rob and I decided, this is my chance. I was going to ask him for a Longwave show. I figured he liked Scout so much, he had to give me a gig. I went up to him and we talked for about two or three minutes. He asked me about Longwave, and told me he could book us on a Wednesday night, at nine, I believe. I had to bring twenty people. He couldn't promise me much in the way of money, but I didn't care. I

was so psyched. Longwave was going to play at Luna. My connection to Scout must really mean something to him. I said thanks a lot, and I'd talk to him soon. As I was walking away, he stopped me and asked,
"Wait, what band are you in again?"

Steve had not yet really made an impact upon me. I had seen Scout many times before he had joined the band. I might have only been half listening when he was pitching his own band for a gig at the club. He was just a new kid in town and I received about thirty similar requests each week. Although, he impressed me as a guitarist in Scout, I could not have imagined that what I would soon hear on his demo recording would affect me so very deeply. Steve continues the story,

"After the Wednesday gig, Longwave played again at Luna on a Tuesday. I remember feeling demoted. Then I gave Rob a three song CDR with rough mixes of the Longwave songs "Escape", "Best Kept Secret", and "Make Me Whole". I had brought these songs with me from Rochester. All of a sudden we were playing on a Saturday!"

I did not work at Luna on Wednesdays; that was a night of the week when Dianne would mix sound for the bands. That Wednesday was probably the first available date on our schedule. I had not seen Longwave and had not yet heard Steve's songs when Longwave first performed at the club. I simply provided a gig for him on the strength of his presence in Scout. It was one of the very few times when I would book a band without hearing them first on a tape.

When I finally did hear his recording, the effect upon me would not have been greater if John Lennon had sat down and played "Imagine" for me on his piano. How could someone so young write with so much intensity? These were heartfelt and deeply moving songs with an original evocative nature. I looked at this young twenty year old and knew I was in the presence of a great talent who was at the very start of his career. Steve continues,

> "Rob offered to put out a Longwave record. I initially said no. Longwave wasn't a serious band then really, although I took the writing and the playing seriously. I subsequently gave Rob another CDR with three more songs, although I don't remember which they were. I know one was called "Pretty Face". It wasn't until I convinced Shannon to join the band that we decided to put out our record with Rob. In my mind, the band could now be a force, which was ironic since Shannon, of course, had never before played guitar. I just had a feeling about it."

The other songs were "Something" and "Ending", two songs along with the other four which would be the foundation of Longwave's first album.

I almost couldn't believe that I had the good fortune to release that recording. Some people in the record business have asked me why I did not sign Steve, or any of the other artists to a multi-album contract. I could have had some leverage in future considerations if and when it came time for a major label to sign them to a million dollar deal. I was told that I had made a mistake. I only signed a short-term deal to license a first album for five years. Afterward, the artists would retain all rights to the record. They had no obligations to me in anyway.

I have always told those record company people that I had started LunaSea Records in order to bring attention to the talent that was performing at Luna Lounge. I was not in the record business to become rich and powerful. If an artist was able to move on to a major label after doing their first album with me, then I had accomplished what I had set out to do.

Steve continues the story,
> "I remember signing the deal with Rob on a case of Red Stripe in the basement of Luna. That seemed appropriate. I also remember Rob giving us a thousand dollars to mix with Pete. The entire record. Pete did a great job, but even he seemed to think the number too low and I remember we paid five hundred dollars from our own pockets to remix the songs "Ending" and "Make Me A Believer"."

Obviously, Steve was an unknown talent and the deal to which we agreed would help launch his career. He would be making a small investment in mixing his album and this would be only the start of a process of commitment and leadership which he would develop continuously over the years.

Steve finishes this part of the story,
> "The thing was, the deal with Rob was fair, and I always felt like we never really needed to have a piece of paper anyhow. I didn't feel like Rob was going to screw us in any way. Ever since that time, with the exception of other record deals, I have never had a piece of paper between people I deal with. I just go with my gut. We were fortunate to meet Rob when we did, because he believed in the band. He was our first champion and we were lucky that it was a guy like him."

Shannon Ferguson was living in a storefront on Grand Street in Williamsburg. He was a bass player but he and Steve had decided that Shannon would play guitar in the band. Steve continues,
> "When I moved to New York, I got a job pretty quickly working in the back office of a Citibank branch on Wall Street. The office

was all young guys. We listened to music all day. It was a great job. We would always get temps in to help with extra work, and Shannon was one of the temps. Shannon smiled a lot, even though he wouldn't speak. Eventually I started talking to him and found out he was a musician. He played the bass. One day I brought in my Scout pedal board, probably because I had a gig at Luna that night. Shannon asked me a lot of questions about the pedals, and I showed him my guitar, and we became friends. It took me about a year, I think, but I eventually convinced him to play guitar and join my new band. We were just starting to play at Luna. I would walk by his desk at work and ask him, and he would say no. He would say,
"I play bass." But I kept on him. It was like Peppermint Patty in Peanuts", how she would always press on Linus' head so he wouldn't grow up to be bigger than her. I would ask Shannon every time I walked by. Finally, he gave in, probably to shut me up."

Shannon also had a very good feel for recording. Using only a few microphones, it was in a basement rehearsal space near that storefront on Grand Street in Williamsburg that the band laid down the tracks that would become their debut release. Although they had used a collection of inexpensive equipment, they had created a warm endearing album perfectly recorded to compliment Steve's dreamy impressionist songs. Shannon adds to the story,
"We recorded on an Otari MX5050. It was an analog half inch tape machine with eight tracks but only seven were working at the time. I bought it with Neil [Neil Rosen, of the

band, Falcon] from Main Drag Music in Williamsburg, in 1998. We were told that it was previously owned by They Might Be Giants. The front cover of the manual had TMBG written across the front in black marker. Neil and I are still co-owners of the machine which now resides at Neil's house in Saugerties, New York."

We decided to bring the master tape to a top-mastering studio because of the lofi nature of the recording. Mastering is the process in which a recording is sonically improved before copies are mass-produced. It is the final step in the recording process. The method used in improving the sound on the recording primarily has to do with selecting the sound frequencies of each instrument used in the recording and boosting or reducing their presence at particular places in each song. Your bass and treble controls on your home stereo sort of do the same thing, but without the same level of precision that is used in a mastering studio.

We were fortunate to work at a great mastering house, and our engineer, Roger Lian, was one of the best. When we walked out of Masterdisk Studios, Longwave had a great sounding album. Roger has gone on to master recordings for The White Stripes, Ian Brown, Grizzly Bear, The Strokes, The Killers, and Madonna.

The band included Dave Marchese, on bass, and Jeremy Greene, on drums. They would call the album, *Endsongs*. For awhile, Steve was doing double duty in Scout and in Longwave, but he soon realized that he had to fully commit to his own band and he amicably parted company with the members of the band with whom he first played in New York. Eventually, Steve and Ashen, the lead vocalist and songwriter in Scout, would work together again, but that would be several years up the road. For now, Longwave was a brand new band and they began to build their following in

Steve Schiltz, of Longwave, on stage at Terminal Five, NYC.

a slow but steady way by performing regularly at Luna Lounge; taking their time to mature as musicians and in finding their own original sound.

Steve Schiltz was a highly competent bandleader in addition to being an accomplished songwriter and guitarist. Because of his hard work, Longwave was able to purchase and maintain a van, book their own out of town shows, and perform regularly in other regional cities from Boston down to Atlanta.

I had made an arrangement with Steve. If he got in contact with a club, I would mail out a Longwave press kit but Steve would have to follow up with the next round of phone calls and get the bookings. Every week, he would call me and give me the names of five or six clubs and my assistant, Brandee Boyle, would send out the press kits. After a couple of months, we had sent out over fifty packages and each one was a potential new show.

After a few months, Longwave began going up to Boston and down to Philadelphia and Washington D.C. and were well on their way to becoming a regional act. The group began playing in support of the best new bands that were living in those cities, playing before strong local followings. They were well embraced at clubs like The Velvet Lounge in Washington D.C. and The Middle East Room in Boston. Longwave was off to a very good start but there was plenty ahead to accomplish.

Eventually, I decided to go see just how well they were doing on the road. They were playing in a brand new club in South Carolina in support of Candella, a local band that had a very good following in Myrtle Beach. Candella had made sure that all of their friends and fans knew to come out early and see Longwave perform, and on that evening I believe Longwave achieved a milestone. I was taken aback by the quality and professionalism that they had achieved as I watched them perform on that night. They had become a

Rob, Steve Schiltz and Ashen Keilyn (Scout)

Longwave at Luna Lounge – 2005. Photo: Mayumi Nashida

very good band with a well-balanced sound and an energetic approach which complimented their original songs. The band was starting to rock, and while they still retained their original evocative style, they now were delivering a bigger stage sound that could reach to the back of the room. For the very first time, I knew that the band was going to be special.

Longwave had been slowly building their following over the course of a year and a half. In the beginning, they played at Luna Lounge once every month. After several months, they were regularly performing in other cities and we cut back on their number of shows at the club. By the summer of 2000, when they did play at Luna, the club would be packed and the buzz was certainly palpable. They were succeeding in becoming a regional act, a huge step towards earning the interest and respect of their peers. Still, this was a year before they would find a manager who had major label connections, and in the meantime, they continued to grind it out on the road.

Marty Willson-Piper
(Let Me Tell You A Secret)

I was not on line until late 1999, but once I got my first Mac there was no turning back. It was the start of the age of the internet for me. I would stay up all night and listen to radio stations using the Real Audio program. I remember finding a radio station in Algeria. It was five or six hours later there and it was probably around 3AM in the middle of their night. The deejay was speaking in his native language, very close to the microphone and very sexy. He spoke slowly and played Arabic trip hop music. I had never heard trip hop in that language before and it really impressed upon me the idea that people may share similar tastes in music

Shannon Ferguson in his current studio – 2011.

Artist, Jason Oliva and Matt Long, of The Mayflies USA.

even though cultures may appear to be vastly different. The internet brought the rest of the world so much closer to me.

One night, while surfing through some of the world's other radio stations, I was surprised to receive an email from Marty Willson-Piper. Marty is a guitarist and a founding member of The Church, best known for the 1988 hit song, "Under The Milky Way."

I was a life long fan going all the way back to their first album in 1982. I had almost met him that year when I was standing outside of a New York City club one afternoon in conversation with a friend who was that club's day manager. The Church was scheduled to perform that night and when they arrived for their soundcheck, they stopped in front of my friend and me when a few fans asked them to sign some autographs.

Longwave's debut album was getting rave reviews and some writers thought that their album reminded them of The Church, if not in sound, certainly in its emotive spirit. Marty is an avid record collector. His letter would ask if I could send him a copy of *Endsongs*.

Marty must have checked out Luna Lounge on line from where he was living in England. A few weeks later, his manager and I made arrangements to have him play at the club during the CMJ Music Festival. Luna was a small room in which to perform, especially for a member of The Church. Also, it was a free music venue. He would not be paid very much to appear at the club. Still, he was coming to New York and Luna Lounge was where he wanted to play.

Marty had come straight from the airport on the day of his CMJ show. It was in the mid afternoon and I was the only person in the club waiting for him as it was a few hours before we were scheduled to open. A cab pulled up in front of the building and the front door of the club was unlocked. He opened it, carrying a guitar case in with him. I was standing about thirty feet back towards the middle of the room. He approached me and in a cheerful British accent, said,

"Hello, I'm Marty." I said,

"Hello, I'm Rob. Welcome to Luna Lounge." He replied,

"Well then. Let's have a look at your place." I took him into the back room where the stage was located. He said,

"This looks great. It's quite lived in, this room, isn't it?" I answered,

"Yes, we've had many shows here."

I told him that I had been a fan of The Church for many years and that I was very pleased to have him perform at the club. He said that he had many friends in New York and that everyone spoke highly of Luna Lounge. It seemed to me that Marty had a history in New York City and that his friends were well connected to what was artistically current and musically happening. He asked to leave his guitar in the club while he made his way around town. I put it in our office and assured him that it was safe to leave it there, and at that, he left the building and was gone into the mid afternoon sun. I looked at his guitar case and remembered the first time when we crossed paths in 1982. I thought about my life and was pleased to know that somehow, so many years later, our lives had woven their way back to a meeting.

I introduced Marty Willson-Piper and Steve Schiltz to each other several hours later. Steve was twenty years old and Marty was around forty. Marty had played on more than a dozen records and Steve had just released his first album. There was a third person, from another band, interrupting the conversation and distracted Steve from hearing what Marty was saying to Steve. The bar was quite noisy and very crowded; full of bands and their friends who were excited to be part of the CMJ/Luna Lounge scene. In that conversation, Marty told Steve that no matter what happened with Longwave in the future, that Steve would always make a living playing guitar. I thought that was a high compliment coming from Marty.

I mentioned that comment to Steve recently and he has no recollection of the conversation. I find that amusing because not only has Steve earned a living from Longwave, he has also played guitar with Albert Hammond Jr., a member of The Strokes, when Albert tours in support of his solo albums. Steve has also played with Teddy Thompson, Blue October, and other artists who respect Steve's guitar playing skills. Marty's opinion was spot on although I bet Marty cannot either recall the advice.

Sometimes, no matter what the best of intentions may be, plans may go awry due to circumstances beyond one's control. That is what happened later that night at Luna.

I had thought that it would be a good idea to have Longwave perform after Marty's set. It would be late, but that would be a good thing. My logic was that there were hundreds of bands performing during the CMJ Music Festival. The big bands all performed between 9PM and midnight. My thought was that by putting Longwave on the stage at 1AM we would give people time to see the big acts and then come down to the club and see their set. This way, Longwave would not be in competition with the other more established artists. People would still be out and about looking for something to do when they came out of those big shows. They were not going to go home. It was a weekend night in New York.

Also, by putting Longwave on after Marty's set, the band could receive some of Marty's crowd. After all, Longwave was being compared more often to The Church than to any other band. It all seemed like a good idea at the time.

The first problem that occurred that night was with our own sound engineer. The person working was inexperienced, especially with CMJ issues. We had seven bands perform on that day starting at 7PM in the evening.

Each band is supposed to start their set on the hour and finish by forty minutes past the hour. The sound engineer must be like a marine core sergeant and make sure that we stay on schedule. If a band arrived late, we would have to cut their set to have it end at forty minutes past the hour. It is harsh, especially if they have come hundreds of miles to perform. However, it is necessary in order to be fair to the bands that are performing later in the night. Unfortunately, our sound engineer on duty that night dropped the ball. He couldn't be the marine core sergeant we needed.

We were running about an hour behind when Marty took the stage. To make things worse, we were getting awful, random, electronic noise coming from the stage monitors when Marty tried to start his set. It was loud and abrasive, not something any one would want to hear.

Marty had brought his own sound engineer and he just happened to be a friend of mine. Robin Danar had been the live sound engineer for The Church for many years. He knew his business and I knew the sound problem was not coming from him. It took awhile to trouble shoot the issue and we were falling further behind schedule for Longwave. Finally, Robin figured out that a previous band had partially severed the cable that connected the stage monitors to the soundboard. It was intermittent; meaning that the splice in the wire was not complete but only partially through the wire. That's why the awful crackling sound was coming through the system randomly and not in a continuous loop. I had been a sound engineer for three or four years at Luna and that was the first time that had ever happened. When Robin figured out the problem, we got a new cable and connected it through the monitors. All was finally working well and the sound in the room was good.

This all happened in front of a packed house and Marty's fans had shown great patience, but when his set was over we were running an hour and a half behind schedule. It was nearly 3AM and Longwave's crowd had lost their will to hang on, and when the band finally got to the stage, the room was only half filled. I felt terrible. It was quite a letdown for the young band and they were truly unhappy that night. But, it was only a bump in the road and they would recover quite well for sure.

Marty stayed in New York after his CMJ show. He was sharing an apartment in Brooklyn with Jonny Cragg, the drummer in Spacehog, whose first album, *Resident Alien*, was constantly played in our bar.

We were in the middle of compiling the tracks that would appear on *A Tribute To Big Star*. Marty had covered Big Star's, "Thirteen", in his live solo set. We told him about our tribute album and he graciously agreed to record his version for our release. Although Marty never knew this, Elliott Smith was thinking about doing that song too. But, Marty got to it first and Elliott was busy on tour. Could I have had two versions from two of my favorite musicians? Definitely.

Dianne's boyfriend, Dan Grigsby, is a sound recording engineer with a considerable amount of experience and time behind the console and he engineered on the session. It was great fun for Dianne and me to witness Marty recording for LunaSea Records. A couple of Marty's friends that Marty knew in New York performed on bass and drums. They ran through the song two or three times while Dan got his levels in the room. Then, when Dan was ready to record, the band laid down the song in two quick takes, seamlessly, as if they were playing together for years. That track on *A Tribute To Big Star* was recorded practically live with only a couple of additional passes for vocals and a second guitar.

Dan has maintained a friendship and professional association with Marty and has subsequently engineered and mastered music, both, for The Church and for Marty's solo recordings.

Dianne, Dan, Marty, and Rob at LunaSea recording session.

Marty Willson-Piper performing at Luna Lounge – 2000

Rob and Robin Danar, sound engineer for The Church.

Ellen Ferguson, Neil Rosen (Falcon) and Shawn Christensen, (stellastarr*) in the Luna Lounge basement after a show.

The Strokes at Luna Lounge back for their second show.

Kerri Black with Fab, drummer in The Strokes.

The Strokes (part one)
(Last Night)

I am not really sure as to how I first came to book The Strokes at Luna Lounge. Albert Hammond Jr. told me in an email during the research for this book that he had contacted me and that we made the arrangements together for their first show. And, that later, their singer, Julian Casablancas, was in touch to book their subsequent shows.

I suppose that they dropped off a tape in the typical manner that any band would employ in order to get a gig. Honestly, I don't recall ever hearing that tape but I have a strong feeling that their first demo, while good enough to get a show at Luna on a non weekend night, might not have been strong enough to have made a lasting impression on me. I feel pretty sure that I must have heard something that I liked, but if I did, that demo tape along with the hundreds of other demo tapes that I received that year was long ago discarded and is probably buried deep somewhere in a New York City landfill. This tape is not to be confused with the recordings that they would soon make with Gordon Raphael.

In any event, we did book a show and I was the sound engineer on that night. Oddly, I clearly remember their soundcheck. The band showed up on time and ran through a few of their songs. They were loud and the balance between the instruments was a bit off, but for a first show their soundcheck went well and there were no glaring issues. They seemed just a bit nervous but that was to be expected. They were serious but not stressed. Above all, they seemed very respectful to each other. They were getting focused and that's what a soundcheck is supposed to accomplish.

After meeting the guys and working with them for no

more than twenty or thirty minutes, there was something in them that I immediately recognized as interesting. They were powerful; more powerful as individuals and as a collective than any other group with whom I had previously worked. And, even though they were still a moderate distance from being the polished, professional group that the world would soon come to know, The Strokes had a defined presence on the Luna stage. They reminded me of The Ramones, as they were in the late 1970s, not in their sound or songs, but in their commitment to the power they called forth from themselves in the process of seizing and defining their moment on stage. And, that's saying a lot, because in 1978, The Ramones were the greatest live band in the world.

Later that night, there were about forty people in the room. It wasn't filled but it was a respectable turnout for a band's first show. At this time, I didn't know any of their songs. The band opened their set, playing the intro of a good first tune, when without hesitation, Julian jumped off our small two foot high stage and started to move among the folks who had come out to see the band perform at the club. Effortlessly, seizing the moment he began to sing to people, face to face in the crowd. I thought to myself, in the following sequence,

"What the hell is he doing?" Then,
"Hey, he sounds pretty good." Then,
"This guy has a pair of balls!" Then,
"Wow, what a great moment."

After singing most of a verse, he hopped back up on the stage and rejoined the band at the chorus. I was very impressed. In the first thirty seconds of their first show at Luna, Julian Casablancas was fearless. He grabbed the attention of absolutely everyone in the room.

Later that night, my girlfriend who was asleep when I got home, awoke and asked me how was my night. Sitting on the edge of the bed, I told her,

"I might have just worked with the best band that I will

ever see at Luna. If they don't implode, they are going to be huge." Returning to her dreamy state, she said,
"That's nice," and she rolled over and fell back asleep.

Albert Hammond Jr. recalls his feelings about that night, "I don't remember if we had been in Luna before but it was definitely one of the clubs that was on the ladder up. There was an excitement in us when we arrived for our first show. We were gonna play two new songs, "Modern Age" and "Last Nite".
The room was so beautifully lit. The bar was dark and the live room was darker, with a black light vibe radiating. Looking back, it was probably a very small room but at the time, Luna looked like a masterpiece, a square in the middle of the room, orange walls, and a thing that was starting to happen, fans!
I remember feeling great, another notch on the belt. We hung out all night at the bar. I think we met Kerri Black after that show. I remember we had asked you to be on a weekend and I think you hesitated and put us on a Thursday. But, when you saw we brought people after that, it got easier.
That night was the beginning of asking for things we wanted that maybe we hadn't earned yet, but getting it, I think because of our music. I don't think we looked at the final goal at that time. We just always had baby steps and mini goals that kept arriving faster and faster 'till you no longer have control over them. Actually, looking back, you realize you don't have control over any of it. All you can control is the playing, the vibe and the music, and in those days, we, all five, in our own way brought everything we had to The Strokes."

Kerri Sweeny was a regular at Luna Lounge. She, along with Terri O'Rourke, were two of the biggest fans of the music scene going on in downtown Manhattan.

Kerri formed a company and taking on a new professional last name, she became known as Kerri Black. KerriBlack Promotions worked with some of the young bands, helping them to get gigs. Sometimes, she would tell me that I should book a particular band. And, even though I received countless numbers of tapes, I would pay attention to what Kerri believed was good. Kerri tells her story,

"Luna Lounge had a great walk-in crowd since it was one of the few no cover venues for bands to perform in. Because of this, bands had a chance to gain exposure, new fans and grow. Also, bands liked to play at Luna Lounge because it had a great sound system for a small venue.

Luna also had many locals that considered the club their home base and were there quite often. I would be included in the list of locals that loved Luna and was there regularly during the week checking out new bands.

I first met The Strokes when they were there passing out flyers in front of Luna for their upcoming show at Baby Jupiter, another club around the corner. They had just played their first show at Luna. On any given night, I was handed numerous flyers from bands, so sometimes they just got ignored. However, when The Strokes handed me a flyer, I paid attention to it and put it in my purse. There was something about them that made me interested in what they were about and what their music sounded like. I chatted with them inside and outside the club for awhile. They were young and had a fresh, stylish look, so I went to the show they were promoting on that flyer. It was then, after seeing them perform, that I started working as their promoter and booking agent and started doing various music management things with them. They asked me to book them a better night at Luna, and I did, and that was a very big show. I spent many hours promoting it to anyone and everyone I knew, which included Gordon Raphael and Ryan Gentles.

The Strokes' music had a classic sound with some cool modern twists. They were cute and the girls seem to love them. Their show was packed with many local models. They also were a bit rough around the edges, but given their age, I knew that with practice and the right demo, they could be something really big. This is where Gordon Raphael came in. He was a producer I had met recently who had relocated from Seattle, after the Seattle scene died down, so I invited him to see The Strokes play at Luna. I had listened to some of the music he produced and had a good feeling that he would know just the right direction The Strokes needed to go in to get them noticed.

I knew Ryan from the local music scene too. I recall one of our first few meetings was at Arlene's Grocery where his band, The Seltzers, often performed. He also was a friend of Terri O'Rourke and she introduced him to me a few times. After that, I started seeing him at all the same local clubs around town as it seemed we had a similar taste in music. I started KerriBlack Promotions the year before, in 1999, and Ryan's band also played on bills with some of the bands with whom I had worked. A year or so after that, he became a booker at Mercury Lounge and because of my promotion company, I often promoted new bands to him that he could later book. I asked him to come check The Strokes out at Luna so, after that, he would book them a show at Mercury."

The Strokes had really started to develop a following after their first show at Luna. By the time they performed at the show in which Kerri was helping to promote, in a matter of only several weeks, the band had risen to the top of the scene.

There were a lot of jealous musicians who resented their instant celebrity. I'm sure people were talking some negative nonsense, but not much of it around me. I wouldn't have any of it. The Strokes were a really good band and getting better very fast. That's all there is to it. They were an anomaly on Ludlow Street. If someone resented what was happening, then it was up to that person to become a better musician, to make his band that much better.

A few bands did improve, inspired by the attention that The Strokes were bringing down to the Lower East Side. Some of them should have been signed and given the opportunity to cast their sound out into the world. And, while I do not think comfortably of music and bands as in competition, I have to admit that in this experience, for the most part, many of the other bands were outclassed, out maneuvered, and left behind in the dust.

Steve Schiltz continues the story,

"Ryan Gentiles was a friend of Kerri Sweeney, AKA Kerri Black. Kerri used to go around the East Village at night, always with her little dog in her hands. She knew a lot of bands. One night she brought Ryan to a Longwave show at Luna. After the show he came up to me and said he loved the band, thought we were great. Then he asked me, "How much did you make tonight?" I was shocked that he had the balls to ask. We had

probably made forty dollars. He then told me,
"I've just started booking the Mercury Lounge, around the corner. You should come and play my club, and if you bring this same crowd we can really pay you."

Mercury Lounge had a typical admission charge of around ten dollars from which they could pay the band. Steve continues,
"That was the first step of Longwave moving out of the Luna Lounge. For awhile we played both there and at the Mercury, and then we didn't play at Luna anymore."

The band was growing up, their following was growing and fans were now paying to come see them perform. Steve continues,
"Ryan was also a singer/songwriter at that time. He has since been quiet about that, but since we had become friends, we would occasionally play shows together with him or his band.
One night he opened for Longwave at a place called The Harvest Moon Brewery, in New Brunswick, New Jersey. He brought with him a handful of the coolest looking guys I'd ever seen. They all kind of looked the same, and I remember only Julian, The Strokes' singer. Longwave had an upcoming show at the Bowery Ballroom, a new club that was unreachable for most local bands. Julian said to me,
"I'd love to play there one day."
I had been very proud of this show, which Incidentally, had been booked by Ryan. But for some reason, I was unable to keep this confidence when Julian was asking me

about it. I had a very strong feeling that this guy's band was going to be a real force."

The Bowery Ballroom has a capacity of over five hundred people. It is a true milestone in the career of a New York band to perform at and sell out the venue. Steve continues,
> "Ryan had told me that he was helping The Strokes get some shows. He got them a gig at a club called The Cooler. He also helped them get a deal to put out their three song EP in the UK. I started to hear less from Ryan around this time. One day we were both at 2A, hanging out."

The bar, 2A, is a staple in the East Village. At the corner of Avenue A and East 2nd Street, it is only half a block from the apartment to which I had moved when Dianne and I split up, even closer to where The Strokes recorded with Gordon, a block from Mercury Lounge and only two blocks from Luna Lounge. Steve continues,
> "The Strokes needed him for something and they came by to pick him up in a white van. I got in and went with them for a few blocks and then jumped out at the train. As I said goodbye to those guys and as the door closed, I thought, my friend Ryan is gone. He had been swallowed up.
> The next time I saw all of them was on the last night of a residency The Strokes did at the Mercury. They played every Wednesday night for a month. Ryan had asked Longwave to open this last show, but I was too cocky. Longwave didn't play on a Wednesday! So I went to see The Strokes and the show was sold out, jam packed. They played "Hard To Explain", and I felt like I could see the future of this band.

They were SO good. I have never felt such a combination of jealousy and complete admiration as I did when I saw them perform on that night.

There was a lot of talk about The Strokes around this time, and most of it was from other bands in town who were very jealous. People said a lot of mean things about them, about how good things were happening to them for reasons other than their talent. I remember when I finally saw them, thinking, you have to be deaf and stupid to miss this one. I felt happy just because they EXISTED. The Strokes became the rising tide that lifted all boats among the local New York bands at that time. Ryan did keep in touch off and on, and offered me more shows for Longwave opening for The Strokes. Longwave was very happy to play with these guys, since they were good and things were happening for them. It was no coincidence that Longwave signed with RCA and started working with half of their team of people. Longwave had been banging our heads against the wall for over two years by this point. I can't imagine what would have happened to our band if those guys hadn't come along."

In a very short time to come, The Strokes would play and sell out The Bowery Ballroom. Most bands could be around for years and never play that venue. Now, still without an American recording contract, The Strokes were bringing in hundreds of people to their shows. They certainly were not going to play at Luna Lounge anymore. From where I was standing, I thought of The Doppler Effect, the sound something makes as it passes you by. I'm lucky I was there, if only for a moment in their lives.

The Strokes with Longwave poster

Julian Casablancas of The Strokes – 2001

Gordon Raphael
(Two Thousand Light Years From Home)

Gordon Raphael used to come to Luna Lounge to check out the new bands. His studio was on the same block where I lived. Gordon tells his story,

"Live music was a tricky issue, in my view, at that time. The cultural music climate, seemingly in the US and England, was that guitar driven rock, and even all music played on instruments was a dying art, out of fashion and rare to come across. Brits, that came to my recording studio, first on Ludlow Street and Grand Street (Chateau Relaxo, with Scott Clark), and then the Transporterraum NYC on 2nd Street and Avenue A, with my partner Jimmy Goodman, told me that live venues were shutting down in droves in London, and it was fucking hard to find gigs. In Manhattan, I saw so much deejay action, and guys with big gold chains and backwards baseball hats spinning dance music while the crowds practically worshipped them, it kind of made me sick! Also, the few bands that were trying to do something, often had these professional muso-guys fleshing out their lineup, and you could actually see these bass players and sax players checking their watches while onstage, to see if they were gonna be late for their next gig! The romance that bands were all for one and

Gordon Raphael

one for all, and tightly knit, was for the most part non- existent!

So, the nightly route was Kush, an Arabian styled bar with kind of Eastern trance music spinning, or real Moroccan music, then to Luna Lounge to check out what bands would be playing. Usually, they had three or four per night, and though I didn't see tons of bands that I loved there, occasionally there'd be a gem! Then, across the street was the Pink Pony, which had a really cool decor and vibe before it got new owners (or a development deal!) and went from a down-lo cool coffee shop to a highbrow chi-chi dining place with pretty good, but expensive food. Next door was Max Fish, which was already going from cool local hangout with a pool table, to kind of an after-work hours congregation of yuppies, loudly talking about quite boring things and wearing generic sporty clothes. Around the corner on Stanton Street was Arlene's Grocery, a place that you actually had to pay to get in, like its neighbor four doors down, Baby Jupiter. So, though we went to many shows at these two, you really had to know who was playing, and that you'd like them, before investing the four or five bucks to get in. It was this little circle of cool clubs that made NYC livable after dark for this period of time.

I have to say that during these years, I was not into drugs or drinking at all, so in a weird way, even among my own peer group, I was always in a slightly different state of mind than they were, and was looking for other kinds of experiences from going out at night.

Both of my studios were located within a few blocks of this area, and so I would regularly go to see bands and music artists, hoping not just for inspiration and enlightenment (which I have always gotten from good music) but also to hustle music players and writers to come work with me in my basement studios.

Luna Lounge was the one club I'd check in with most frequently. I knew some of the bar staff, and even got to know Rob, the main man. Even though I never ordered a beer, unless I was buying for a friend, they never gave me funny looks when I ordered water, and it was always pretty damned friendly there. I could always peek in and check out a band, and if I wasn't into them, go on the rounds in the neighborhood in time to get back to Luna for the second, third, and often, fourth act.

Many of the bands I recorded, including The Astrojet, Melomane, and Longwave, were often onstage at Luna Lounge, though that's not how I met them. However, I did have one rather life changing encounter with a band called The Strokes.

There was a young music promoter/manager I had heard of called Kerri Black. I was interested in working with her because my band Absinthee really needed some guidance in our career, and booking gigs. She invited me to witness a night that she was putting on at Luna Lounge, circa early September 2000. I was eager to see if she could get a good crowd assembled there, a trick/skill I've never mastered, really! She told me about this night she was promoting at Luna Lounge, and that there would be two bands, one of which The Strokes, she told me would be looking do to some recording. I might be able to see if they wanted to try me out as a producer. So with two winning possibilities, a gig producing, and a way to get help with my own band, I went to the club that night.

The first band I saw was called, Come On, and honestly, I was smitten with them, it was really Beatles-ey to me, with great songs and vocals and harmonies. I loved their show, and diplomatically approached some of the band members with my big line at the time,

"Hey, I really liked your show! If you want to do some recording, I have a studio two blocks from here and some really cool gear, and can give you some very good quality results for a really low price..."

"How much?" they'd ask and I'd say,

"Three songs in three days, two hundred dollars per song!"

Next up were The Strokes, the band Kerri had brought me to see. They took the stage and had a very noticeable aura of cool style. They looked really fresh and a bit 1980's new wave, in a way, and were very young. The music started up, and if I may be honest, something about the singer's attitude, and the way the guitarist, Nick, held himself onstage, I just felt there was a lot of great pride being demonstrated, but the music didn't really move me. I remember that the other guitarist was wearing a suit, mmm, not really my style either! There was one thing that I was really focusing on throughout their entire short show, which was their drummer, who seemed to be hitting his snare so hard, on each beat, using his whole back and neck to snap down on it. I was sure he was going to kill himself by snapping his spine in half during that show, and I couldn't look away! In my small hustler style, I went up to the band afterwards and gave them the three days, three songs for six hundred dollar deal. I didn't exactly tell them I liked their show, but I was trying to be friendly and useful. What do you know... Come On never got back to me, but three days later I get a call from Albert Hammond Jr.. He, and one of his band mates, wanted to come check out my Transporterraum NYC recording studio, and showed up right on time.

 My place was really nicely decorated and designed with music and artists in mind. Me and my partner, Jimmy Goodman, and Anna Mercedes helped decorate it, along with Joe and Manny Hadlock who lent their great music studio designing skills. They own and operate the gorgeous Bear Creek Studios, in Woodinville, Washington, where artists including Eric Clapton, Ginger Baker, Alice in Chains, Soundgarden, Foo Fighters, The Gossip, Elvin Jones, Blonde Redhead, and Soko have spent time making great music. Our studio had red and purple glitter walls, leopard print and silver sound baffles and an old fashioned window from a farmhouse, peering from the control room into the live playing area. There was also a lamp made from a thrift shop Barbie Doll, wearing a scary looking dress, and lots of cool amps and guitars around. Apparently we passed the inspection, and a date was made to do the proverbial three song demo deal.

 I think, The Strokes were looking for a decent representation of their band to get more gigs in the city, and informed me straight away that they generally had had pretty miserable recording attempts at other, more corporate studios, but were willing to give me a chance. I was happy to get this gig. I needed that exact amount of money, six hundred dollars, for a trip back to Seattle on October 1st, to celebrate the official end of Sky Cries Mary, my old pals and former band mates. (They have re-formed since!).

Once we were hard at work, I saw and heard in The Strokes a lot that I didn't perceive when I saw them live. First and foremost, I heard what I could only understand as a great influence from classic underground rock bands, which I grew up memorizing and listening to thousands of times. But, it really struck me, how could these young guys living in a Prodigy, acid jazz, hip hop and techno-rave world, have even heard these great bands, let alone dare to open themselves to their influence. So, of course, I got great ideas about using high energy aggressive methods of recording their music based on these reference points that I quickly visualized when I got to start with them in the studio.

They actually asked me to produce a sound that was like 'nothing being recorded today'! I instantly realized that by playing music together, as a band in a studio all together, making a joyous, loud-ass din, and trying to get that recorded while it was hot, this would be a method that was seemingly anti-everything that was going on in those days. Click tracks, sequences, sampled layers of kick drums, highly edited digital music was the latest thing. And, here were these young guys agreeing to take a chance to jump in and just rock, as they always did, and have me press the red button, hoping for something useable and interesting. I learned that The Strokes were all very aware and communicative musicians, and had many strong ideas and abilities to contribute while we were recording. They brought in their trusted comrade, JP (the Guru), who I did not understand at first, but as history bears out, we made a very powerful team with our different methods of interpreting sounds and working together. This little demo was called *The Modern Age*, and Albert was often seen handing a few self pressed copies to Kim's Video on St. Marks.

No one was more shocked than me, when he told me one day in passing, that Rough Trade in London, had signed that EP and released it 'as is', and that they were getting a tremendous response from it.

I wound up moving to London, and then to Berlin, where I still do music and production things, but I am forever grateful for that one night at Luna Lounge, that still has repercussions for me almost every day!

Without Luna Lounge, the history of rock would have changed. I may never have met The Strokes. And, the number one album of the decade may never have existed at all."

Those songs on that three song demo, along with the other songs which were subsequently recorded with Gordon and appeared on The Strokes' first album, *Is This It*, was chosen by N.M.E. magazine as the most important record of the decade. Rolling Stone called it the second most important record of the decade. There are a lot of albums that come out over a ten-year period. I feel fortunate to have had some effect on that list.

The Strokes (part two)
(Is This It)

Sometime in May of 2001, a few months before The Strokes' full length album was released in England and about five months before it was released in America, I was invited to see Longwave and The Strokes perform at a small club down in Philadelphia.

Jody Porter and I got in my old 1980 Chevy Malibu sedan and made the trip down Interstate 95, otherwise known as the New Jersey Turnpike, together in true Fountains Of Wayne style.

When we got to the club, I noticed that there were only a few tables. It was a pretty small place. One of the tables had a sign that said, "Reserved". I looked at Jody and said,

"They must have known we were coming." We sat down at the reserved table and thought nothing more about it. Longwave performed their set and then The Strokes played to the crowd that had filled this small club.

At the end of The Strokes' set, some guys came in and approached our table. It was the band, Oasis. They had performed with The Black Crows earlier that night in Philadelphia. They came to the club wanting to see The Strokes perform but had narrowly missed their set. That table wasn't reserved for us, afterall.

What surprised and impressed me most that night was that the Gallagher brothers immediately recognized Jody and were completely surprised and excited at seeing him in the club. There were only about twenty people left when Oasis walked into the bar. Mostly young girls, they had those disposable cameras that were so popular before the digital age. Jody and I made room for Oasis at their table while the girls took photos from two or three feet away. The Strokes casually joined us. I'm not sure if they had ever met Oasis before that night, as they seemed very surprised and bemused at their coming. I remember connecting directly with Julian who truly seemed in awe of this transcending moment.

I recall watching the guys in Longwave who were packing up gear only a few feet away to my left, as they observed the table at which I was sitting with this bevy of heavyweight rock stars. Shannon and I smiled at each other, knowing that this night was something to be remembered.

Jody and I had had a blast down in Philadelphia and when we got back in my 1980 Chevy Malibu and made the drive back up to New York, we both agreed that the night had been one for the books.

Steve Schiltz continues,
"Lots of incredible stuff was happening around that time. Ryan was still working at The Mercury. He would try to book bands into the club, but The Strokes began to demand more of his time. Later on I heard him tell people that he had to quit the job because people were starting to call him more for The Strokes than for the club.
I have several memories of Ryan around that time, out late at night, on his cell phone, sitting on the sidewalk outside bars, talking about business when his friends were drinking inside. The Strokes brought the entire music industry to Ryan, all at once, and he worked his ass off for a few years there. I saw it."

Later that year, at the end of November 2001, I was invited once again to see Longwave and The Strokes perform on stage. This time it was at The Stone Pony, in Asbury Park, New Jersey. Before the show, the club deejay played songs from the Kitty In The Tree album that I had co-produced and released on LunaSea Records. That was a complete surprise to me and it made me feel very good.

Longwave had a particularly good set that night and Julian paid tribute to them from the stage. Steve continues,
"Opening for The Strokes at The Stone Pony in Asbury Park, New Jersey, this was the first show we had played together since things had really started to happen for them. When they played, I watched as Julian leaned over the barricade and put his hand on the head of a girl in the front. He propped himself up on her head, and looked over the crowd, singing with his eyes wide. I thought, this girl is going to hit him. Then I saw her face, and she was just in ecstasy. I thought, these guys were BORN to do this."

It would be the last time that I would ever see both bands perform together but they would go on tour together in America and on a magnificent tour in Great Britain.

These were heady days. It was a twenty-first century version of Beatlemania. There were screaming teenage girls everywhere. The UK press was everywhere. Shows were sold out. The Strokes album was all over the radio and Longwave were as close to the action as anyone could get.

Our close friend and artist, Jason Oliva, went over with Longwave and documented that tour with a high definition video camera. He took over thirty hours of video footage. He edited some of it down to about thirty minutes and showed it to me just after the bands returned from England. It was filled with action, backstage scenes, a Longwave soundcheck performing the Guns n' Roses classic, "Sweet Child O' Mine" with Nick Valensi of The Strokes joining Steve on lead guitar. It looked like great fun. Steve continues the story,

"A show we did together in Glasgow, at Barrowlands. This was a little bit later. The Strokes record was out, and things were full on for them. We had done a tour with them in the US that had ended badly. The last show of that tour, Julian had lost his voice and I sang two songs [at the end of their set]. There was partying going on. I thought, this is where the wheels come off for them. All the Longwave guys thought that. When we rejoined them in Glasgow, we were curious to see what had happened. We played, and I thought we did OK. Everyone was patting each other on the back. Then, The Strokes came out and played, and they were on fire. The crowd was rabid, it was like a surge of electricity went through the room when they came on. I had to smile, it was so perfect."

Our Bartenders
And
J. Mascis, Stephen Malkmus, Kevin Shields
(Freak Scene)

A bar is only as good as the people who work there and for the most part, the bartenders represent that energy.

Our primary bartenders were Harri Kupiainen, who some will also know as the exciting guitarist from the bands Piss Factory, Emma Peel, and Dead Combo. Also, Paul Widdowson, who we called English Paul on account that he originally came from Sheffield, in England. Paul Alves, who we called Little Paul, was shorter than English Paul. Laura Rogers, was a bartender at Luna who some will know as the beatific drummer in Ruby Falls and The Rogers Sisters. Eric Jakobssen, who we all knew as Eric J. Toast, was the singer in Honky Toast and then in the very awesome band, Pisser. Robyn Calloway, originally a coat check person at Mission, became a bartender at Luna too.

Gillian Murphy worked many of the same nights as me and lived with our resident hedonist genius, J.C. of the band Individual Fruit Pie, but eventually married the video artist and composer Kurt Ralske, who some may remember from his project band, Ultra Vivid Scene. Sean Shertell, the person from whom we originally bought our first speakers when he had moved to the West Coast, returned to work for three or four years at the bar. Sean developed our website and internet radio station.

John Brattin, a filmmaker, painter, and installation artist, is a good friend with J. Mascis, guitarist and singer in Dinosaur Jr. J. would often come by and hang out with John at the bar. I also recall making a momentary stop into the bar one night when I was not working. It was a busy night and John was behind the bar. At the moment that I got John's attention, he said to the guy standing next to me,

"There's Rob now. Why don't you just give it to him?" At that, the guy with whom John had been talking, turned to me and asked,

"If I give you my album, would you put it into the jukebox?" I looked down at the CD and was surprised to see that it was the first solo recording from Stephen Malkmus, of Pavement. Stephen was personally giving me a copy of his album for the bar. I looked up at him and said,

"Of course, but I want to take it home first and listen to it tonight." What an honor, I felt. John knew a lot of cool people.

Jimi Shields was a bartender at Luna Lounge. His brother, Kevin Shields, is the genius behind My Bloody

Valentine. The MBV album, *Loveless*, is one of my favorite recordings.

One year, for my birthday, Kevin came into Luna with a package for me. It was two autographed copies of My Bloody Valentine albums. I'm not one to collect autographs, in fact, I have no others in my collection. But, my signed copy of *Loveless* reads "Happy Birthday Rob, From Kevin Shields". Nice...

We sat at a booth up front in the bar and talked about music and recording techniques for awhile. Sharing an hour in conversation with Kevin was a very nice birthday gift from Jimmy.

Interpol
(Turn On The Bright Lights)

Eric Altesleban was a bartender at Luna Lounge. He was also the keyboard player in Interpol on their live tours supporting their brilliant first album, *Turn On The Bright Lights*. N.M.E Magazine, in a critic's poll, ranked this recording as the ninth most important album of the entire decade. Eric would go out on the road and play in front of thousands of people, then come home and resume bartending at Luna.

One of the first bands to emerge out of the post modern revival, Interpol created a new sound inviting obvious comparisons to darkwave bands of the past. They made beautiful music. Deep water and dark grey days, sunrise on a winter's morning, space, a single moment absolutely captured in time; for me, these are images conjured up in the sound that Interpol create.

We all start out from someplace and the same is true for a band. It was on a Wednesday night in 1997 when thirty-eight people saw Interpol's first performance at Luna

Lounge. From that point on, the band spent almost five years developing their sound and their songs, finally releasing their debut, *Turn On The Bright Lights*, in 2002, to massive commercial success and critical artistic acclaim. But, nothing happens overnight. It takes time to develop the songs, to know what is working and to know what should be left behind. The early days found the group working with influences and working at finding a balance between the various players in the band.

Interpol played their last show at Luna in 2002, after the recording of their debut album but just before its release on Matador Records, in celebration of their first upcoming tour. Now, they were a gigantic buzz band on The Lower East Side. The club was so packed that I could not get into the back room to see them perform. Literally, it was impossible to move and I was grateful that no one died in the press of the crowd. I had to content myself with watching the show in the front room from behind the bar on our closed circuit TV. Still, I could clearly hear and enjoy their set.

Five years later, I went to Coachella, the giant music and art festival held in the California desert near Indio, California. It was my birthday, the twenty-seventh day in April. Backstage, I had run into Ratatat, a band whose members were once in a band called Pony Express, another favorite of mine at Luna. Fountains Of Wayne had played on that day too.

Later that night, Interpol went on stage as the next to last band, just after The Jesus and Mary Chain and just before Bjork. As I stood out there under the desert evening stars, I couldn't help but think back to the days at Mission when we hosted parties for The Jesus And Mary Chain and The Sugarcubes. Now, all three bands were on the same stage, on the same day, in front of sixty five thousand people. I was grateful to have connected, if only for a moment, and it seemed like I had touched upon something truly significant in my life.

Paul Banks and Carlos D of Interpol at Luna Lounge.

Brian Wilson
(You Still Believe In Me)

It was in the summer of 2005 when I received a phone call one afternoon from Jody Porter. He wanted to know if I would like to go out to Jones Beach on Long Island and see Brian Wilson perform later that evening. Brian had just received a lifetime achievement award from one of the performing rights associations that administer his publishing royalties. The association, Broadcast Music Inc, had asked Brian to attend the event and had asked him to suggest a few bands that Brian would like to hear perform his music that night. One of the bands that Brian Wilson requested was Fountains Of Wayne and they performed "Be True To Your School". At the BMI presentation, Jody met Brian and the members of his band. They struck up a friendship and when Brian came to the New York area, they contacted Jody and asked him to come out and see them in concert. Jody called me and we got back in my old Chevy sedan, back on the highway and we headed for the beach out on Long Island.

When we got to Jones Beach, we discovered that the facility is alcohol free and there was no beer to be purchased anywhere in the venue. We made our way to the backstage area where Brian Wilson, his wife, Melinda, Jody, myself, and three or four members of Brian's band where hanging out, standing in a small circle together about twenty minutes before the start of the show. The backstage area at Jones Beach has no roof and it is open to the elements except for a few small dressing rooms. I looked up and saw a thousand stars in a beautiful clear summer night sky. Jody looked down and noticed that some of the band members were holding bottles of beer. He mentioned that we could not find any to buy. They told us that the beer that they were drinking was the last of what they had consumed in their dressing rooms. Melinda interjected at that moment,

"We have beer in Brian's room. I'll go get it for you." While she was away in Brian's dressing room, Brian looked up at the sky and said aloud with a sigh,

"I always have beer in my room but I can't drink it anymore." Then he added, with his voice trailing off by the end of his sentence,

"You know, the medication and all." It was a moment in which he didn't have to say anything; no explanation to us was required. Not by what he said, but by what he did not say, Brian let us know that he wished to have been able to be 'one of the boys' and drink beer like the rest of us, that he had once been able to do that, and that he was no longer able to partake. He seemed a man filled with quiet dignity and in his sigh he expressed a childlike honesty and vulnerability. No one said anything in reply; an awkward silence for a brief time filled the air until Melinda returned, carrying the bottles of cold beer for us. That was a small, but genuine act of kindness for which I will always remember her.

Of course, Brian Wilson had made records that changed the course of history. If Brian Wilson had died in 1970, our collective memory of him would be as that of Jimi Hendrix or Janis Joplin, glorious as it was frozen somewhere in the past. Brian's own personal history, checkered and strained as it was, had become his overwhelming burden. Choosing to abstain from recording, he quietly checked out for decades. But, he had taken a huge chunk out of his life when he stopped making music. In addition, he witnessed the deaths of his brothers with whom he had shared his success. If Brian thought about returning to the process of recording, he would have had to contend with critical and commercial comparison in regard to his own musical pedigree. But, for now, recording new music would not be the issue. Instead, it would be his performing the music that he had previously created back in the 1960s when he was at his cutting edge.

Brian Wilson and his band, on this night, were going to perform the symphonic avant-garde album, *Smile*, which was created, but remained unfinished in 1966 and 1967.

At the time, there was dissension among The Beach Boys who had complained that Brian's music was becoming abstract and increasingly difficult to perform on stage. In addition, executives at Capitol Records were apprehensive about releasing the album, unable to hear the strength of any radio single. Without a strong single, the album would not sell. This was 1967 and radio was virtually the only means that people had in which to hear new music.

Perhaps, this was the catalyst for Brian's retreat from making music. Or, maybe it was only one of many issues with which he had to contend. In any event, on this night more than thirty five years after its creation, Brian was finally going to perform the album for an audience that had come, not only to hear what was familiar and beloved, but what was for Brian, a musical triumph that he had until recently never performed in public. It took courage to put a new band together and say,

"Yes, I can do this again, it will be good, and it's going to be fun."

Brian looked up at the stars as the rest of the band stood around making small talk with Jody. Brian seemed to be getting just a bit nervous; I wondered if stage fright had begun set in on the man. Brian stopped talking and seemed to lose focus on the people around him. He continued to look up at the stars but it seemed as though he was emotionally leaving the circle of musicians in which he was standing.

Melinda took Brian's hand and led him away from us. They went up on the stage but were away from the notice of the audience in a back area behind a large curtain. I was curious as to what they were doing and without invading their privacy I quietly walked over in their direction. I observed Brian sitting on a chair. Melinda was standing behind him. They had their backs to me. She was massaging his neck and shoulders. It was an intimate moment and another act of kindness from Melinda. I thought, it might have taken a long time to find her, but how fortunate Brian was to have Melinda in his life. I'm sure that she is the predominate reason why he has found his own personal resurrection and why he is making music once again. She seemed to have a deep capacity within herself to be able to give loving energy to other people.

The tour manager came over to the band and told them it was time to start the show. They joined Brian at the back of the stage and all made their entrance together to the cheers of more than five thousand people. I heard Brian say,

"We're gonna play some jukebox music and then we're gonna perform the album, *Smile*, for you." The crowd roared their approval, and at that, the band went directly into one of my favorite songs from The Beach Boys, "Do It Again".

Jody and I stood in that backstage area for a moment taking it all in. We looked at each other in silence. And, then looking back at the stage, Jody said,

"He's an icon, that Brian Wilson." It was a glorious understatement.

Totally Blind Drunk Drivers
(We Are The Men)

I got a phone call from someone who wanted a band from Estonia to perform at Luna Lounge. They were called Totally Blind Drunk Drivers. They were coming to New York to perform for an Estonian music and art festival and according to the voice on the other end of the receiver, were the biggest band in their country. I had no idea of what to expect. I had not heard their music. I thought that they could come in with a couple of accordions and a trumpet. I had no idea. But, they were a very good indie rock band and I was very impressed. What a surprise to me. I didn't even know that people in Estonia listened to that kind of music. It was my own ignorance; the crowd knew all the words to every song. These guys were superstars in their country. At the end of their performance, they closed with a cover song from The Jesus and Mary Chain.

We hung out at the bar for the rest of the night and I learned a great deal about their part of the world. They told me about Estonian beer and we agreed to release their album on LunaSea Records in America. It's a very good record and I still listen to it today. And, I still drink Estonian beer.

Totally Blind Drunk Drivers came back to New York to perform twice in 2001. The first time was during the middle of April. It happened to coincide with the death of Joey Ramone. The Ramones meant a lot to these guys. They witnessed the outpouring of love for Joey which manifested itself in a street memorial in front of CBGBs. On the sidewalk next to the entrance to the club, New Yorkers had placed candles, photographs, album covers, anything that they could find to express their connection to Joey and his music. The Estonians were visibly moved by the moment and I was happy to know that, in a small way, I was part of the reason that they were here in New York at that time. I told them that I had known Joey and that I thought that he would have enjoyed their band had he had the opportunity to hear them perform.

The next time that Totally Blind Drunk Drivers returned to New York, was to perform at Luna Lounge during the CMJ Music Festival of 2001, which was scheduled to start on Wednesday, September 12th.

The band arrived a couple of days early and we spent some time together on the evening of Monday, September 10th. Then, the following morning, they awoke to the news that shocked the world. They were here in New York and bore witness to the events of September 11th. More than that, the band members became the eyes and ears of their nation since all airline flights were cancelled after the terrorist attacks. They received phone calls from their national media and reported back to the people of Estonia, in their native language, as to what was happening in New York.

Although they were visibly shaken, the band members soldiered on like the rest of us. When flights finally resumed several days later, they returned to their country where they were interviewed extensively on Estonian national TV.

In a small way, I had helped to facilitate, through this band of musicians, the story of what it was like to be in New York City on September 11th, 2001.

Radio-Indie-Pop
(Do You Remember Rock-n-Roll Radio)

I listened to demo tapes and CDs from more than twelve thousand different artists and booked around five thousand different bands to perform at Luna Lounge over a ten year period. Of the five thousand artists that played at least once, about two thousand were invited back again to perform. There was a great deal of competition for the available time slots at Luna Lounge. An artist had about a one in six chance of establishing a longterm relationship with the club.

Almost none of the bands that were playing at the club were receiving any radio airplay, although a number of them had well recorded albums. I decided to do something about that when I established an early internet radio station, Radio-Indie-Pop.Com, in which I programmed music from many of the artists who were performing at Luna Lounge.

In order to raise the profile of these bands, I mixed in well-known indie rock artists who had established careers and had albums out on various indie and major labels. You could hear the Ton Ups music between Jon Spencer & The Blues Explosion and White Stripes. You could hear Skywriter between Bright Eyes and Joseph Arthur.

I was pleased with the formula and received letters from hundreds of people from all over the world in support of the station. To someone listening in India, Japan, or New Zealand, the distinction between a well-known band and an obscure artist in the United States was often blurred and not very important. They usually reacted to a good song and Radio-Indie-Pop was filled with good songs from artists who performed at Luna Lounge.

The radio station had thirteen different programs, one for each day of the week and five specialty channels. The station was completely automated and each channel had twenty-four hours of continuous music that the listener's computer would sequence in random patterns. You could listen for twenty-four hours and not hear one song repeat.

I would play quieter music on Monday and Tuesday and melodic alternative indie rock on Wednesday and Thursday. I would play loud indie rock on Friday and Saturday. I would spin eclectic, free form on Sunday, with an emphasis on trip hop, electronic, and instrumental tracks.

Since we were heard all over the world and people's native languages were varied, I purposely preferred to not have a deejay speaking words, the station was one hundred percent music. Listener's computer screens would show the name of the artist, the song title, and the artist's website address.

Among the specialty channels, there was a channel devoted to a brand new album of the month, an alt-country program, an eighties new wave and post punk program, and an all Ramones radio channel, possibly the only one in the world.

The 'album of the month' channel was particularly successful and brought a lot of new listeners to our site. I usually tried to spotlight a well-known artist on that channel as I thought that there was a greater interest in their music. Perhaps listeners would click on to one of the other available channels once they had checked out the new album of the month. I felt particularly good when I had The Strokes and Interpol albums up as our album of the month, as both of those very successful bands had started their careers at Luna Lounge.

I played around with the remaining channels and changed their focus a few times. One of the channels was devoted to the unknown artist. It was a spotlight on a worthy band that I was pretty sure most of the world had not yet discovered. I received great satisfaction from hearing from those artists when they told me that they had gotten letters from listeners who discovered them through the radio station.

I thought about playing nothing but live music, alternative stand up comedy, or interviews with musicians on the last remaining channel, but I never settled on a particular idea. I continued to offer Radio-Indie-Pop to the world, free of charge, for several years.

The station had no advertising. I thought about soliciting donations but ultimately decided that that was more work than was worth the effort. My gut instinct told me that no matter how much people enjoyed using the service, they would not spend money for radio on the internet.

Eventually, the bandwidth usage went through the roof. It costs a lot more to provide music than it does to simply offer printed words. The more people who came to the station, the more debt I incurred. I was spending almost three hundred dollars every month to pay for the website. I was willing to do the work as long as I could afford it. It was something I truly loved. Eventually, when I could no longer afford the expense, I had to turn off the radio station. My heart died a little bit on that day. Someday, I would very much like to do it again.

Real Estate Killed The Video Star
(Money Changes Everything)

So much had changed over the decade that we were in New York. The peace and security brought about by Mayor Giuliani's quality of life initiatives had created a city in which more and more people had wanted to live. This pleased real estate holders to no end and it directly led to astronomical increases in rent and building values. We estimated that had we been offered an opportunity to stay in our building, our rent would have soared from five thousand dollars to seventeen thousand dollars each month.

I was sure that the landlord must have had a buyer for the building. That was why he had tried to evict us. The city was crawling with real estate developers in the late 1990s and into the mid 2000s. There was a boom going on and the cannon was aimed at us.

I looked at dozens of buildings but none of them was appropriate for the use of a nightclub. We needed to be in a low-rise building. But, every one or two story building was being sold for demolition to make way for a high-rise apartment. It is very difficult to put a nightclub on the ground floor of an apartment house. It rarely works out well. Eventually, the residents get together and pressure the city to close down the club for noise violations. The political process in New York City is completely designed against the interests of the club and its patrons even though many thousands may enjoy and support it, in favor of the residents who live in, or nearby the building. People would laugh at me if I suggested that apartment owners should be required to have soundproof windows. The bar business is a very important part of the nightlife in New York City. The slogan is "The Big Apple: The City That Never Sleeps!" However,

I felt that it was unwise to look for trouble. It was a battle in which we could not win.

I looked around for where I could find an appropriate building for the next incarnation of Luna Lounge. I continued looking for more than five years. I really wanted to stay in Manhattan, but eventually I discovered that no landlord would talk to us. If they had an empty one or two story building, it would be 'in development'. It was not available for rent. Anything else was inappropriate for our needs.

I started looking around in the Williamsburg section of Brooklyn, just one subway stop on the other side of the East River. Some people were aghast at the idea of Luna Lounge relocating to Williamsburg. They would never go to Brooklyn. I had to ignore their reactions. There were no other options. Well, there was one, I could keep the money I had made and call it a day in New York.

But, Williamsburg had a vibrant music scene of its own. There were plenty of industrial and commercial one and two story buildings there. I looked seriously at a dozen buildings over a two-year period. I discovered that the city building department was creating a new zoning plan for Williamsburg and the building owners there did not want to write leases on their commercial property. They were hoping that the new zoning changes would allow them to develop their low-rise commercial buildings into high-rise apartment houses, as was already happening in Manhattan.

I was reminded of The Buggles' song at the dawn of MTV in the early 1980s, "Video Killed The Radio Star", except that I changed the words in my mind, to "Real Estate Killed The Video Star."

Eventually, time ran out. Our lease ended. We stayed a few additional months, but I knew that the day would soon come when I had to close the doors one last time and call it an end to one very important part of my life. We had had more than we could ever have imagined within those walls.

We had met all kinds of wonderful human beings, many of whom had had an opportunity to perform in front of friends and fans at the club. Luna was a unique experience and no other place like it seemed likely to fill the space that Luna had been in New York.

A good nightclub is about more than just selling beer. It's not about velvet ropes or guest lists. It's about providing something for the artistic expression of the citizenry. It's the young people that make a club special. Luna Lounge was a place where people came and met each other, many of whom would create lifelong relationships. Luna was a family. It was a large family with many diverse personalities.

Some people came for comedy, some people came for the music, and some people came for foosball in the front room. Some people came for the bartenders, some people came to meet friends, and some people came to just sit at the bar, content to be taking it all in for a night.

Despite all of the good will, all of that now behind us; the time had finally come to move on. It was time to give up our success and give up our keys to the club. We had had a very good run. Many great clubs have come and gone; their legends live on through the years. We received expressions of love and sympathy when the news got out that the doors to the club would close. People wrote letters, newspaper articles appeared in the press; many people wanted us to somehow find a way go on. I am grateful for what we accomplished. When Luna ended, it seemed to me that many people felt that a piece of their lives had certainly ended too, and that a piece of Ludlow Street had suddenly died in their arms.

I thought of The Strokes. I wondered if in their heady days of success and stardom if Luna Lounge meant anything to them any longer. Did we have resonance? I thought of Interpol and of watching Paul Banks with his friends in the club. I thought of Longwave and how far they had come as a band. I thought of Elliott Smith, knowing that he had discovered a new home in New York, and a new home in his seat at the bar. I thought of all the other bands: The National, The Bravery, stellastarr*, and the many thousands of musicians who found a place running with a kindred spirit, and the good times that had finally come to an end. I thought of Janeane Garofalo and Louis C.K. and Marc Maron and Todd Barry. I thought of the other comedians. I thought of how the musicians had given Luna a heart and how the comedians had given Luna its brain.

    I watched the wrecking ball fall against the walls on the last day of the Luna Lounge almost ten years from the day that we opened; a bright beautiful summer day that should have been filled with uplifting joy and promise. One blow after another took piece by piece of it down, until finally, without fanfare, and alone, the building in which Luna Lounge was located at 171 Ludlow Street was simply a pile of broken and tattered bricks; its time now consigned to the past.

Meeting The Girl That I Married
(Baby's Got Her Own Ideas)

    When I had first started booking bands at the bar, I had stayed away from having 'out of town' bands perform at Luna Lounge. They either needed to be paid as they had much greater expenses in getting to New York or they had no following yet developed in the city. Since we were a free music venue and we collected no money on their behalf, we could not afford to pay those groups more than a token amount. Also, if they had no following, the club would not have folks buying anything at the bar and the venue could be empty during their show. Over time, once the club was firmly established I received more and more requests from 'out of town' bands and I would book some of them from time to time. Eventually, we developed some wonderful relationships with bands from other cities.

We did many shows with Helicopter Helicopter and Fooled By April, who both hailed from Boston. We had shows with Skywave, from Washington DC, whose former members would eventually split into two bands, Ceremony and A Place To Bury Strangers. We did shows with bands from South Africa, Estonia, France, Japan, Germany, and from other places in America. This all started with my decision to book The Mayflies USA, from Chapel Hill, North Carolina. They reminded me of a southern American version of Teenage Fanclub, with additional influences from Big Star, two bands I had always appreciated. They had not yet performed in New York but I didn't care. I really wanted to see them and it was easier for me to have them come up than it was for me to go down to North Carolina. They understood that Luna Lounge was a free music venue and were willing to finance their trip. They were one of the bigger new bands in Chapel Hill and they were ready to expand their fan base. They had some friends with whom they could stay nearby in the neighborhood.

They arrived the night before they were scheduled to play at the club. As so often happens with inexperienced bands in New York for the first time, they left their equipment overnight in their van. Someone broke into it and stole much of their gear. They were an unhappy bunch of guys when they arrived at Luna on the next night. Fortunately, they were able to borrow equipment from one of the other bands on the bill. I was the sound engineer at the show that night. Even without their own gear, The Mayflies USA proved to be a very capable group. They had great songs and a real spirit I thoroughly enjoyed. They had good vocals and an occasional well-placed harmony. They were loud and they rocked quite well.

I first noticed the woman who I would eventually marry

when she came to see The Mayflies USA. Her older brother, Matt McMichaels, was a guitarist and vocalist in the band. She and I did not speak to each other on that first night. That was months later, when the band came back up to the city and performed at Brownies. I went there to see them and I stood behind her in the small crowd. She turned around a few times during the show and glanced in my direction. After their set, she came up to me and told me that the band was having an after show party at a friend's apartment and she gave me the address. The band had already told me about it but it was very nice to receive her personal invitation. Her name was Susan.

I stopped by Luna first and ran into my friend, Pete Min. I told him about the party and he decided to join me, as it was only a couple of blocks away. When we arrived, I noticed that Susan was there with another guy so I observed her from a distance but made no attempt to engage her in conversation. Eventually, that guy left the party and Susan left shortly thereafter. I decided to follow her downstairs where we met at the bottom of the landing. She had just called for a car to come pick her up. We made a bit of small talk and I asked if she would like me to wait until her car service arrived. She told me that it would not be necessary. I said goodbye and made my way home in the early morning sunlight. A few days later, I called Susan's brother, Matt, and asked for Susan's phone number which he provided for me in order to invite her to my birthday party which was happening at Luna Lounge the following week. She already had plans but she was able to come by for a short while and we were able to speak to each other again.

We had a few more conversations at the bar and on one occasion I met one of her girlfriends who she knew from back down in North Carolina. I was sure that I was being sized up with a second opinion. There were eighteen years between Susan and myself. I figured that could be a problem but Susan seemed to become more interested each time we were together. By the time we had our first official date, we had already hung out together several times.

That was a wonderful year for me. Dianne and I were no longer angry at each other and we had settled into a reasonably comfortable friendship. The bar was doing well and we were finally making a profit. I had set up LunaSea Records and was producing an album with Kitty In The Tree. I had a nice friendship with Elliott Smith and had recently met Marty Willson-Piper. I was compiling the twenty-three songs that would be on *A Tribute To Big Star*. I had met Steve Schiltz and was very excited about working with Longwave. The comedy show we presented was doing better than ever. Apart from some meager concern over the Y2K scare, 1999 was a high water mark in my life.

Unfortunately, although there were some absolutely wonderful moments in the following years to come, my personal life would suffer as I would struggle with Susan to be understood, respected and loved. When I look around and observe couples at play in a bar, I can't help but wonder what it is in each other they currently think that they see. Perhaps, too much is made about this business of falling in love. How many times do we grasp at what we believe will bring joy, only to fall short within the shadows of our disappointing, or disappointed lover? For how long, and how many times will we keep trying? Is heartache an investment in sadness from which we draw no dividends but the interest we earn from experience?

I believe that I wish to never hear another woman make a pronouncement of the condition of her heart for me and that I never indulge in the same, for there is nothing in the reality of that moment that is everlasting. It is better to appreciate the moment for what it is and never diminish and degrade it again with a declaration of spoken words. Susan and I did love each other but what does that really mean? Words from an imaginary love song:

"We argued more time defining the wrong that was driving us further apart, and while we tried to believe in the love we could see, we were losing it right from the start." That was the truth of it. Still, we hung in there, trying always to mend what was broken: square peg, round hole...

Luna Lounge In Williamsburg (Starting Over)

I found a building in Williamsburg, at 361 Metropolitan Avenue. It was in between the first and second stop on the L line in Brooklyn, not far from either station and easily reached from Manhattan on a main road used by commercial trucks and buses.

The building had been a warehouse, an auto body shop, and an indoor parking garage at various times. Once owned by Al Capone; he made bootleg gin in the building next door. It was a large building as compared to my old Ludlow Street spot, more than twice the size of that room. It had high ceilings and no support columns to obstruct the view to the stage. But, the space was in need of repair. The ceiling would have to come down and the roof was rotten in spots. The plumbing would need to be upgraded and the electrical state was a mess. And, that was the work that was needed before we built a new club.

Then, we would have to install a sprinkler system to meet NYC fire codes, a fire and smoke monitoring station, install a new floor, build a stage, a bar, two backstage dressing rooms, new toilets for men, women, handicapped, and toilets for backstage too. We had to buy all the equipment for a bar: ice machine, soda system, walk in refrigerator and a draft beer system. Then, we installed the stage monitors, house PA speakers, soundboard and all the wires and cables that made the connections.

At first, I thought that we would run a wall down the middle of the building, sublet one side and put the new Luna

Lounge on the other. Looking back, that is exactly what I should have done but I got another idea in my head at the time. Williamsburg was filled with musicians; many of whom had been forced out of the Lower East Side. I wanted to build a world-class venue for the neighborhood, working with national acts, and have Brooklyn bands open the shows as support.

Susan, who had insisted on becoming a full partner in the new corporation, was doing everything possible to keep us financially afloat. She had secured the second and third mortgages on our two small apartments which we had used to finance the building of the club. She made the rounds of the banks trying to find us more credit. During the course of demolition and construction, we had maxed out all of our credit cards and had used every available credit line. She worked on every possible angle, desperately trying to finance the project.

Dianne, who had declined to be a part of the new Luna Lounge, took out a twenty five thousand dollar loan on her credit card for our use. Susan's mom lent us forty thousand dollars. We were in debt for almost two million dollars. The building would take more than a year to develop and cost overruns continued throughout the entire project. It took all of our savings, our apartments, and our complete borrowing capacity. We put everything into the venue for Williamsburg. I believed that once we opened, people would come for the talent who would come to the club and perform. I believed we could make it happen and I believed in the music to come.

The Debacle Of Rob
(Damn This Foolish Heart)

I was completely naive. I didn't know the live end of the music business beyond the 'baby' bands with whom I had worked on Ludlow Street. I could not talk directly with the national acts.

There are about twenty agents that are the middle people between the bands and the clubs and they book nearly all of the indie rock artists in the country. They already had working relationships with another company in New York that has quite a bit of a vertical monopoly. They own or exclusively book at least five live music clubs of varying sizes. Most agents book at least several bands. Some book twenty or more artists. By having clubs at different sizes, that organization has locked the agents into their venues. The agents have some bands that will play the small rooms, some will play the medium rooms, and some will play the larger rooms. Agents had no incentive to run the risk of booking their artists outside of this organization and possibly not getting back into those rooms. I heard that some agents were presented a flow chart at a meeting in the office of this organization with the names of certain agents who booked shows at other venues. If that was true, the intimidation was apparent, if unnecessary. Most agents had no care or concern for Luna Lounge.

There were a few exceptions and I will always appreciate their support. With the help of Sam Kinken, and his lovely assistant Jenn Stamm, who were at a competing entertainment company, we received some very good opportunities to have some national acts perform at the club. We were able to present concerts with The Black Angels, The Meat Puppets, The Pipettes, Rob Dickinson (of Catherine Wheel), The Knitters (an off shoot of the seminal Los Angeles punk rock band 'X'), Witch (a heavy metal band in which J Mascis of Dinosaur Jr. played drums), Kate Nash, The Horrors, Dean and Britta (of Luna), Shonen Knife, Witchcraft, And You Will Know Us By The Trail Of Dead, White Rabbits, Steve Forbert, The Slackers, O'Death, Roger Miret (of Agnostic Front), The Warlocks, The Constantines, The Melvins, Wheatus, Dub Trio, Northern State, and stellastarr*. And, of course, Longwave returned to Luna Lounge too for a sold out show.

Sam believed in my vision and did all that he could do to book national acts for us. But, even he and the company for which he worked could not get more than a handful of agents to book their artists at the new club. Also, the company at which Sam worked soon opened a venue in Manhattan of similar size to the new Luna Lounge which further syphoned off our available opportunities. They were now competing directly with us for bookings.

Then, Sam left that company. After Sam was gone, we were told that we were not going to receive the services of that company any longer. They were going to focus all of their energy on booking their own venue in Manhattan. We had a meeting up at their office with someone new that was running the company who had only recently arrived from Los Angeles. He told us to consider turning Luna Lounge into a catering hall. We could book weddings and bar mitzvahs. I walked out of that meeting feeling absolutely sure that that man had no idea of what Luna Lounge had meant to New York. It was a debacle, the Hindenburg disaster of my life. Because the agents would not book their bands with me, I could not get bands that were big enough to fill up the room. I booked local unsigned bands to play at the club but they were unable to bring in enough people to make the club any profit. Eventually, we fell further and further behind in paying the rent and the landlord gave us an ultimatum. He would give us three months to find a buyer for the club, otherwise, we were going to be evicted.

The Knitting Factory is another nightclub in New York. They started out as a small neighborhood bar in the East Village that presented eclectic folk, modern jazz, acoustic music, and semi electric rock music in the early 1990s. They left that small space and expanded into a larger nightclub location in Tribeca in the mid 1990s. Eventually, new well-heeled residents moved into Tribeca who no longer wanted a nightclub in their community. The owners of The Knitting Factory were informed that their lease would not be renewed. They starting looking for a new space and came to the same determination to which I had come in regard to the problems in opening a live music venue in Manhattan.

When I heard that they had started to look for a building in Williamsburg, I called them and suggested that they might be interested in the building in which I was operating the new Luna Lounge. I wanted to sell them my lease and find some way out of my difficult situation.

They came and took a good look at the club. They were impressed and they asked me why I was selling my lease. I told them about my problems in getting agents to book their bands. They understood. They had the same problems too. But for them, the situation was not as difficult. They owned three other nightclubs in three different cities. Two of their clubs earned them a great deal of profit as they had almost no competition in those other two markets and I was told that they use the profits from those other clubs to finance the existence of their flagship club in New York. All they wanted to do in New York was break even. I had no such luxury. We quickly agreed upon terms which were quite reasonable for both interested parties.

There was quite a great deal of stress in my life. It was my first financial failure and it was colossal. I had worked endlessly at trying to bring shows to the club but my dream of making the new Luna Lounge a success was a catastrophe in the most desperate sense of the word.

My marriage was destroyed in the course of my financial demise. My wife, disappointed, fearful and angry, was no longer coming home two or three nights each week. I had no idea where she was, who she was with, and what she was supposedly doing. But, there was no point in confronting her now. I had no spirit left for that fight. Whatever she'd say would never have made any difference. She was my wife but her loving connection was gone. I thought about our wedding vows and how I really meant those words, "for better or worse". But, I felt like I had let down all of our friends and family who had come to our wedding and gave us their love and support. Humiliated, she blamed me for our failure which lead to her financial collapse. Now, instead of her owning fifty percent of the company, she owned fifty percent of the debt. My wife found a place of her own. She ran away, taking Gus, our beloved golden retriever. A yellow cab pulled to the curb and she got in the backseat with our dog. She never looked up to see me in the window. And, she never looked back again.

Alone, in the late night silence, I sat at my bedroom window and watched the traffic lights go though their cycles for hours. An occasional car would pass through the scene while the empty early morning buses came and went on their way. She served me papers for our legal divorce. And, she told me that she would not agree to the sale of our company lease unless I agreed to the terms of her divorce. She owned half of the corporation; we both needed to be in agreement in order to sell our lease. The divorce settlement stipulated that although we had used the credit cards to finance the business in which we were equal partners, that I would be responsible for the credit cards that were in my name. That came to around eighty percent of the credit card debt. It hardly seemed fair. She had a very good day job in corporate America and she earned a decent income too. I had no income. Whatever I had earned I made through the profits of my bar. Now, I had no profits, I had no bar, and my credit was shot to hell. I consulted with an attorney. He told me that I could sue her for alimony. He told me that she was legally responsible for half of the debt. But, I had a broken heart. My confidence was shattered. I was under pressure to make the deal or be evicted. I sadly agreed to her terms.

In front of the executives of the Knitting Factory, at the very same meeting before we signed the contract agreeing to the sale of our lease, my wife forced me to sign her divorce settlement. The Knitting Factory executives were looking at me. I could feel their hearts silently reach out from across the conference table. Perhaps, this was her way of emasculating me. I had to reach inside and find my own inner strength. You could say this was a low point in my life.

I came home to an empty apartment. It was early evening on a beautiful day and I opened a beer on my roof. The sound of laughter floated up in the breeze from the courtyard of the bar next door. It made me think that somewhere in the world, the day was turning out good. I turned off my phone as the daylight receded; twilight preceding the night. My senses were heightened, I was experiencing the world for what felt like the very last time. I was in a comfortable chair and I could lie back and see a great big slice of the sky. One by one, the stars began to appear. It really was the end of one hell of a beautiful day. I thought about the light I could see and how far it could be from the place of those distant worlds. I remembered that the light left from those stars many thousands, if not millions of years ago. And as I looked up and out from myself, I began to wonder aloud, if I was looking at you, could someone be looking at me?

I could see precious moments passing before me like someone had turned on a flood. And in that bright light that shined, I slowly slipped back in time. I was in the hospital to see Elliott when he was soon to be leaving this world. I saw him take a sip from a container of apple juice. I saw him really taste it and appreciate the flavor, all without saying a word. I was on the altar; it was my wedding day. I had just turned around, my friends and family had so much good feeling for me. I felt loved like I never knew I could be. Then, I remembered that my wife had just recently told me that she regretted our wedding day. I saw her take her wedding ring off and give it back to me, no longer my wife, no longer my love. I gave it back to her and told her that when I gave her that ring, it was forever and I had not changed my mind. She could do what she wanted with it but her offer of return was declined.

Somewhere, a neighbor was listening to The Beatles. "I'm Fixing A Hole When The Rain Gets In" and "She's Leaving Home" were in the air, *Sgt. Pepper's Lonely Hearts Club Band*, a soundtrack for this day. I thought about a release from the pain. I could see my mother, my father, my brother and sister and I knew I would be breaking their hearts. I was sending a message of sadness like a rocket sent out to the stars. Then, somewhere from out there in the sky, someone from out in the black, was paying attention; somehow letting me know that the love I put out in the world would somehow find its way back. I can't tell you for sure how I knew this for I never heard the words conceived, but somehow I knew that the message they sent, was that message that I had received.

I fell asleep under those stars. I stayed there for quite awhile and when I awoke the lively voices were gone from the bar next door. It was quiet, and apparently much later in the night. I was stiff from being out in the cool spring air. I sat up and thought of walking Gus. But, Gus wasn't there. He would never be there again. And then I cried. I cried from the deepest part of my heart and soul. I cried for the love of the message I had received earlier that evening and I cried for the thought of me wanting to leave this world. I cried for what I had gone through and what I knew I had lost. I cried for every conceivable pain ever suffered by anyone else in the world.

I came in from the roof and sat by myself for sometime. Shadows moved back and forth on the wall. People walked by my window; pieces of detached conversation floated up like Ambien dreams in the air. I turned my phone back on. No one in this world had called. I took a sleeping pill, showered, and crawled into my bed for the night.

Early, the next morning, I got a phone call from Dianne. She told me that she had just had a dream in which she was walking down a street. She came upon a stoop where Elliott Smith was sitting. He looked up and said,

"Say hello to Rob for me." Dianne told me that she awoke feeling disappointed that Elliott had not asked how she was doing and that she felt that he had ignored her somehow. But, I knew that Dianne was Elliott's conduit. By letting me know that he was there, he was sending me his message of love and goodwill, using Dianne as his personal amplifier. I was not alone in the world. I was appreciated. I was connected to something beyond the scope of my own logic. Perhaps, it was Elliott, whose presence the night before I could lovingly feel on my roof.

Later that morning, I got a phone call from Steve Schiltz. He wanted to know if I would meet him for breakfast somewhere in the neighborhood. He gave me a bit of advice on that day. He said that when a relationship ends with someone you love, you mourn not for the loss of that person, but for the love from her, or him, that you had never before received. I will always remember those words and those eggs will forever taste like friendship...

Steve Schiltz

This Year
Music and Lyrics By
Steve Schiltz
Performed By Hurricane Bells

Black tar full on India ink, dressed up like a crash
But don't know where you're going
Tonight I'm so alone, I'm gonna stay at home
I ain't going out at all
Until everything is alright,
Alright, alright

If I had a boat I'd drift to Mexico, well, there's a place I could go
I'd get swept away
End up in some other place, when the current changed
I'd just get swept away
On the back of your wave
Smashing all to pieces
When it breaks

On another day
On another day

This year is the year
It's going to be really something
I've got all my friends
In case it comes to nothing
You can always walk away
If you see me coming
I don't think about you
I don't think about you

It's been a long, long year
And it's hard to remember
It's been a long, long year
But it's getting better
All the time

It's been a long, long year
And it's hard to remember
It's been a long, long year
But it's getting better

You Have To Take Care Of Yourself
(Won't Get Fooled Again)

We paid back my wife's mother and the loan from Dianne with some of the money we had received from the sale of our lease. We paid the landlord's back rent. We paid back some other bills too. After all the good years at Luna Lounge on Ludlow Street, the Mission, and Sanctuary, almost all that I had ever earned was gone. My wife's last words to me, on the day she walked out, were in my ear,

"You have to take care of yourself."

I had a bit of survival money, enough to eat and pay some rent for three or four months. I had a little bit reserved for a new neighborhood bar if I found a location and if I could find someone with whom I could partner. I was going to stay in Williamsburg. I had a couple of weeks to pack my things, put them in storage, and find a new place to live. We had been living on a second floor above the front part of the club. Soon, the Knitting Factory would take over this space, bring their staff over to Brooklyn, and use my former apartment for their new office location.

It seemed to me that I had no employable skills. I had been a bar and nightclub owner for more than twenty-five years. I was too old to bartend and too worn out to even give it a try.

I decided to drive a cab and registered at Master Cabbie Taxi Academy. My dad had driven a cab for twelve years when I was a little boy. He owned his own medallion and our family car was that Checker Cab for a few years. I remember being in his taxi on days when my father would babysit while he drove through the city. Sometimes, he would pull the cab over and we would have lunch in an interesting working class restaurant in some faraway part of our town. We would drive across 42nd Street in the days before porn and I would see more than a dozen movie houses with their marquees all ablaze promoting the films that were running inside those theaters. It was all great fun and quite an adventure for a four or five year old boy. My dad was now eighty years old. His life was nearing its completion and I was thinking that I would like to share the experience of having driven a cab like he had done so many years ago at the start of my life. He had always made a good living. He had bought a house and raised three kids. We always seemed comfortable on the living he had earned. I wanted to connect with him and I figured that I could earn a decent living for awhile until I found a better opportunity.

    Going to cab driving school was a real awakening. I was the only guy born and raised in New York in my class. Everyone else was from South Asia or from the Caribbean. Almost no one spoke English as a native language.
    The classes were not difficult but you did have to apply yourself and study. The hardest part was learning the geography of the city. You had to know where the airports, hospitals, certain hotels, and the major tourist attractions were located. It was important to know the main roads and highways as well as secondary routes to certain destinations. I also had to learn the rules and regulations of the New York Taxi And Limousine Commission (TLC). The course took three weeks.
    I had great fun in taking that class. I would come in early and do some free tutoring for some of my classmates who were having trouble understanding the language. I passed the TLC exam with a grade of ninety-six; the highest grade in the class. I started calling the garages, looking for a cab I

could drive, and found it a bit of a challenge. Most of the garages had waiting lists for drivers. Eventually, I did find an opportunity to drive and started my cab driving days in August of 2008.

In the meantime, I had found a sublet and had moved out of the apartment that my wife and I had shared. I was on my own and I was taking care of myself.

I asked my father for advice about driving. He told me to go straight out to the airport everyday after picking up the cab at 5AM. He said that the redeye flights would be arriving at 6AM and that I could be first in line, before the rush hour, to pick up fares going back into the city. I tried that on my first day.

When I got out to the airport, the line was three hours long already. I did not pick up my first passenger until eight thirty, which put me right into the middle of rush hour. It was bumper to bumper all the way into the city and it took an hour and a half to get there. I had now been working for five hours and I had earned fifty dollars towards paying for the cab for the day. I still had to earn another sixty dollars to break even, which took me a good part of the rest of the day. When it was all said and done, I earned less than ten dollars an hour for myself for that day's excessively stressful work.

I hoped that I would do better as I gained more experience but it never got much better. I always averaged around the same amount. Driving a taxicab in New York was a miserable experience. The shifts were twelve hours long. It was dehumanizing. The city has set up a system to exploit people who are immigrants; making them work twelve hours each day, preventing them from forming a union, and setting the rates that they can charge customers while doing nothing to keep the rates from going up that garages charged the drivers for the cabs. Whatever happened to the eight-hour workday? Whatever happened to the forty-hour workweek? What ever happened to overtime for work beyond forty hours? I wish a civil rights attorney would challenge the system and bring the whole exploitive thing down.

Lucky for me, a nearby storefront had become available for rent. Dave Ellis, the contractor who had built the new Luna Lounge, agreed to be my new partner. I was now lucky twice. Perhaps, the year would end on a rising note.

I continued driving taxi cabs while Dave built the new bar. Meanwhile, State Liquor Authority officials were holding up a number of applications while letting others process exceptionally fast. I was up at their Manhattan office three times demanding to know what was taking so long. On the day before I finally got my license, the SLA office was raided by law enforcement officials who carted a bunch of SLA cronies off to jail, with bribery charges.

Finally, in mid April of 2009, after more than six months in the processing of my liquor license application, I was back in the bar business in my little place called The Satellite Lounge.

Field Of Mars
Written by Steve Kilbey
Performed by The Church

It's a long way home from the Field of Mars
Distant, alone, beneath the platinum stars
And I turn to look, but I'm never any closer
Only just the rain makes the skin feel colder

All my life seems so far away
The air is soft in the Field of Mars
Tears and loss feed the overgrown grass
And I have to leave, but I never seem to go
Only more sad clouds where autumn winds will blow

All my dreams seem so long ago
Oh, Field of Mars

Time is past in the Field of Mars
Grief won't last in the departing cars
And I call her name, but she never, ever hears
And I call again to the cruelty of the years
Oh my love she's so far away
Oh, Field of Mars

A New Beginning
(Hanging On A Star)

The smell of something familiar, the smell of something absent; today is the anniversary of the first year of The Satellite Lounge.

I am sitting at the bar, early afternoon, and I am waiting for a liquor delivery. Only four or five bottles are coming; I used to order several cases at a time when Luna was on Ludlow Street. Business here is not what it once was when I lived through the glory days, or should I say glory daze, on the Lower East Side.

Still, I have some new friends and know some new bands that hang out here and I am grateful to be relevant in their lives. Lance Rautzhan is an artist. He says anarchy is the quiet monkey in the room. Lance bartends here. Stephan Cherkashin is from Belarus. He's a guitarist and has great taste in music. Stephan is a bartender too. They help me to stay interested in my story. The Vandelles, Telltale, The Morning After Girls, and Cruel Black Dove; friends who hang at the bar keep me connected to that thread of musical creation with which I've sewn my life.

Thinking about last night; saw The Church perform an acoustic show in celebration of their thirtieth anniversary. Thirty years have passed since I first saw their video for "Unguarded Moment" at the Sanctuary; thirty years have passed since Dianne and I met that very same month. I did finally talk with Steve Kilbey for the very first time; vocalist, bass player, and songwriter in The Church, in the backstage basement after the show, although it was just to ask him if he knew where Marty was. He did, and he helped me to find my friend who had come back up to the stage in the main room which was now filled with bright light and staff in the middle of their closing procedures.

Felt very good to see Marty and have a few moments to speak with him, but there's never enough time to reconnect when a band is just passing through town; miss him very much today.

Tomorrow is my birthday. Fifty-four years have passed through my life; fifty-four years since Elvis created the first rock 'n' roll album to ever make it to the top of the pop charts and the first rock 'n' roll album to sell more than a million records. In a few days it will be the fifty-fourth anniversary of his first number one single. Fifty-four years of music; the one constant upon which I have set the course of my life, still here with me after all the joy and disappointment, after the lovers who have come and gone, and after my friends who are now departed.

I never lost faith but how have I arrived at this place, exiled on Havemeyer Street, disconnected from the joy my dreams brought so long ago? If I had the money, I would do it again. I would open another Luna Lounge and it would have free shows. It is the best way to entice the public to come and discover new bands, and there are always new bands in New York. Bought a lottery ticket today.

Yesterday has slipped into the past, disappeared within the haze and the fog that lingers within the space between the notes. Today seems vague, empty, and strangely sad. That sums up my life right now. Need to be a Buddah, be at peace with myself; I can't change what has happened and accept that at the moment I am hardly working with music.

Maybe, next year my life will change. Maybe not, but I am working at being at peace with wherever I am right now. It's a good time for me to figure this out. I have struggled and railed against this for too long, always looking for something just beyond my reach and never satisfied with the balance of my life. Time to relax, to let go, and to let the river take me wherever that river may flow.

  I do not believe that I have ever met anyone who knew both Joey Ramone and Elliott Smith. They occupied different worlds and for the most part their music may have appealed to vastly different people. Still, they were artists who used music to define their lives. Music kept them alive; giving them a purpose for as long as they could stay connected to this living world. Each man was unique. They both lived with an inner sadness and had great difficulty in finding and keeping long term intimate relationships. They both were children whose fathers left their mothers when they were very, very young. They both had half-siblings in their lives. They were gentle human beings and both suffered years of isolation before gaining, to some degree, recognition from the greater world.

I once mentioned to Elliott that I had been friendly with Joey Ramone. Elliott seemed to be greatly interested in how that had come to be and what kind of person was Joey. He seemed in awe of my experience which somewhat surprised me a bit. But, even for Elliott Smith, Joey Ramone was certainly an iconic figure. It is sad that Joey and Elliott never met.

Joey Ramone was in one of the world's loudest and fastest playing bands. He once said to me,

"Rob, you know our set used to be sixty minutes in 1978. That set now, we play in thirty eight minutes." He told me that in 1992. He was quite proud that The Ramones could play faster and harder, even fifteen years up the road, than they could when they were younger.

Although Elliott was not a loud rocker, I think Joey

would have appreciated Elliott's sense of melody and the dark nature of his lyrics. They both loved The Beatles. Joey reached beyond the world of punk rock in his musical tastes. We used to have friendly debates about music. He would ask what I thought of Iggy Pop and I would answer,

"*Raw Power* is a great album." Then I would counter with a request for his opinion of The Jesus And Mary Chain. He answered,

"Well, *Psychocandy* is a fuckin' great record." It was fun. It would have been fun to include Elliott in a round of these debates. I wonder what Elliott would have said in his opinion to Joey, what would be his 'must have' record at home. Maybe, they would have both agreed on John Lennon's, *Imagine*, or Bruce Springsteen's, *Nebraska*. It's only speculation but it's the kind of game that was fun to play.

Both, Joey and Elliott were revered by their fans and are now larger after death than they were when they were alive. Both have a mystique and a mythology around their lives. Both, are now gone long enough so that the first generation of young people who were children at the time of their passing have grown up and are now old enough to be in bands of their own. Without doubt, Joey Ramone's and Elliott Smith's music will survive for many generations to come.

Too many people whom I have known have died too young in their lives. And, with every passing from this Earth, a little bit of myself has passed with them too. Yes, new people, new friends, have come into my life and they bring new revitalizing energy but no human being can ever truly be replaced. I miss them and I wish they were here. I can still access their spirit and talk with them anytime but I cannot touch them; cannot see them grow old. They are forever left and seen in my mind's eye as they were at the age of their passing. That disappoints me. To see how they would have changed as they would have continued to add on the years would be a gift I would truly appreciate. But, that cannot be and I have had to make my peace with that idea a long time ago.

Music was the conduit through which my friends, my generation and I had passed, and it was the bond from which we were united together before we moved on to explore other issues of friendship, camaraderie, fraternity, loyalty, and desire. Music was the starting point, the location where our personalities would meet and greet each other and then proceed to a place where we could engage; helping each other to more fully comprehend our reason for being here on this Earth. When someone dies young I can't help feeling that that process has been forever altered; I can no longer help them grow or have any effect on their being, no matter how close we may have been at any previous time in the world.

I am sitting here at the bar; The Flaming Lips', "Waiting For Superman", is in my head and I'm thinking about all the people waiting for something to turn up or turn on in their life. We try and hold on but some things are just too heavy for even a superhero to lift. I am holding on.

Steve Schiltz just called to wish me a happy birthday. He's on tour somewhere in Texas today, somewhere out there bringing his music to fans now just discovering Hurricane Bells, the new album he has created this year; his first post Longwave album to be released. His career is doing better than ever, the public just now beginning to catch up and discover the talent that I was fortunate enough to meet almost a dozen years ago, this year.

So, what have I learned in this life? I came into this world with a prescribed disposition; a secluded old soul at the wheel. I have lived the life that I have wanted to live; to be a musician, to be near the music, and to share it with you, who love music too.

There is nothing more important than pursuing the song that comes directly from your heart, for it will be in the twilight of your life when you take stock of who you are and from where you have come that you will know the joy of having had that song to sing. Take care of yourself; take care of your friends. Take care of your family. Life owes nothing to our endeavors; there is no guarantee that any of us will be here tomorrow. I have made mistakes and I have some regret but who can honestly say that all went right in their days? It's not what I do; it's what I feel that counts, it's the message in the bottle conveyed. To feel good comes directly from what I give of myself, and what I am willing to share each day; giving in a spirit of friendship is to give myself what I crave.

Everything I ever was, was wrapped up in Sanctuary, Mission, and Luna Lounge; three clubs and thirty years of my life. The clubs were an expression of my love for myself. The people, who came in return, were expressing their desire to connect with each other and to share in their lives among friends. I was expressing myself through the canvas of the club and leaving just a little mark in time, but it was the people who were there inside the rooms who really know, that the clubs were really yours, not mine.

Rob

Postcards From Paradise
(Wish You Were Here)

"Luna was the last rock-n-roll club where I felt that I belonged. There were always people to talk to who shared the same dreams of success. The bands supported one another and would socialize at the club together. My embarrassing moment was being asked by Kurt Ralske (Ultra Vivid Scene, producer) did I like The Red House Painters as I sat down to join him and four gentlemen, all dressed alike in red shirts,
"Not really, why?"
"Oh, because these are the guys I'm producing." Each minute felt like an hour!"

Ed Rogers
Sparkle Lane

"I was a regular at The Mission towards the end of their run on East 5th Street. It was the one bar that you could go to in which you always felt welcomed. They played really great music (Echo & The Bunnymen, Stiff Little Fingers, The Mission UK, Ramones, Clash, The Sisters Of Mercy). It was a place where famous musicians could go and hang out without being bothered. It kind of replaced the Ritz for that quality to some extent.
When Rob and Dianne opened up Luna Lounge, Ludlow Street was still pretty much no man's land.

I remember going to the opening night party and thinking, this is not the Mission, but a step in a new musical and cultural direction. The indie rock scene was growing in lower Manhattan and Luna was a place you could rely on for booking great up and coming bands. I can't tell you how many Scout, Longwave, and Travis Pickle shows I saw there, not to mention the countless great bands I would see and then walk away a fan. I played Luna Lounge many times with my own band, Shelby.

    I spent quite a lot of time there. I attended a wedding reception there once and think there might have even been a wake or two there. The place had a great family vibe to it. The jukebox was great, and the bartenders were all very cool. There was never a hint of attitude in the place.

    When Rob told me that they were closing the place, I knew that it was the end of an era. CBGB had become a tourist hang out, Brownies had stopped booking shows and had become a regular jukebox bar, and the Mercury Lounge was never a place to hang out. Rob and Dianne's contribution to the music culture in lower Manhattan is undeniable. Luna Lounge paved the way for the Lower East Side to become the hot bed of activity that it has been over the last ten years, for good or for bad. Rob and Dianne should be very proud of what they built up, their contribution to the New York indie rock scene, and the legacy that remains."

Phil Schuster

"In around 2001, I was just starting to try to get my band off the ground in New York. With the recent rock hysteria coming out of this city with the success of The Strokes, Interpol and The Yeah Yeah Yeahs, New York City was suddenly a hot spot again for artists looking to get some attention. Websites, like MySpace and Pitchfork, hadn't yet become the monsters they are now, and overnight success stories were few and far between. Playing live gigs was still really the only way to garner a following and gain attention from critics.

    Luna Lounge became the place for these bands to prove to the world that they were worth your time. And, what better way than to offer this showcase to your friends and patrons of the bar, for absolutely no charge. This was your band's ticket into performing consistent gigs in the upcoming hip area that is, and some may argue, that was the Lower East Side.

    Rob prided himself on handpicking the bands that would grace the stage. Drop off your demo at the bar and cross your fingers. In addition, this was your band's chance to socialize with other new up and coming acts and meet some really great people. Stellastarr* and Aerial Love Feed were two of the bands we tended to bill with and with whom we traded stories. Tracy Thompkins, from ALF, had Rob throw us on as an opener for our first coveted Friday night slot. From that point on, we became regulars at Luna.

    Rob's initial reaction to the band was its name, Sportfuck. We thought that the public could handle this cute and edgy Fight Club reference, especially with a girl fronted act. Rob's response was something like,

    "I can't put that name on the board outside my place." We wanted to play. We wanted people to know about us. After this, and a few other similar reactions, we decided to evolve the name into something I would have to repeat over and over again, syllable by syllable, and describe the meaning to people - Asobi Seksu.

Everyone was talking about a so-called New York rock revival. Stellastarr* was in the midst of a buzz frenzy. Major labels were knocking on their door and their fans wanted to answer, as much as they did. Just before signing to RCA, they had themselves a jam packed showcase at Luna. I don't think I ever saw that place as crowded as it was on that night. Luna was the perfect size at this level, to be able to completely pack the place out, or if you were just starting, to have a healthy looking audience.

The Strokes blew up out of nowhere, everyone wanted to move to New York and follow in their footsteps. Of course, with their thoroughbred, was a tough act to follow. One night, we had a gig and I was hanging out at the bar with my bassist at the time, Steve G. We were going on in about twenty minutes. Somebody just popped "Last Nite" on the jukebox and ten seconds later, in came Albert Hammond Jr. and Fabrizio Moretti, of The Strokes. It was almost like a TV show, the way the timing of that worked out. These guys "made it". They were rock stars and here they were hanging out at my show at Luna Lounge. Of course, they weren't there to see us, but I had to pass on a demo in typical fashion. As we kissed their asses, they reminisced their times at Luna. We played our gig and I was excited to find out later that they were rocking to our tunes from the bar."

Keith Hopkin
Asobi Seksu drummer (2000 - 2005)

"There was a sense that if you were looking for a bassist, guitarist or drummer, the Luna Lounge might be a place to check out. Many musicians were in multiple bands, bouncing from one to another, hoping to find the one that would launch them to the next level. And because of this, the world of indie rockers became smaller and smaller, morphing into different amalgamations until they had the right line-up. Half the audiences at Luna were in bands themselves, and they all kinda knew who each other were.

After the World Trade Center, I was laid off and had no money. Subsequently, I was inspired by a street artist on Spring Street who painted faces on newspapers. I asked Dianne if I could hang up some paintings to sell at Luna. She took a look at my portfolio and said 'yes'. At the time, I remember art on the walls of Luna being a transient thing. Sometimes there was artwork, and sometimes there wasn't. I think after my show and Jason Oliva's show, it became more of a regular thing. The third time I showed my work there, I remember having to wait two months for two shows ahead of me. That's when I knew Luna's rep for having artwork on the walls had really caught on. I showed my work at other rock clubs and galleries in the area, but always sold the most at Luna Lounge, and was able to live off it for a year before signing with RCA.

I recall seeing the Strokes at the Luna Lounge in October of 2001, in front of maybe 20 people. Later, I found out that was the same show that Gordon Raphael had attended, before he recorded their first demo (and first record). Their energy was unparalleled, hopping around the stage like firecrackers ready to explode. I had befriended Albert at the time, and told him I thought they were going to be huge. A year later, it happened. I had never really experienced people I knew becoming stars like that, until then. It was surreal. They were my favorite NYC band we had played with, and still my favorite to this day."

Shawn Christensen
stellastarr*

"While back in the 90's heyday of Luna Lounge on Ludlow Street, I was playing in a NYC rock band on Futurist records called Supple. We later did a well received 2007 reunion show at the new location in Williamsburg. We still have the little black Luna Lounge drink tokens somewhere. Many of my friends' bands were regulars at the early Luna, and I was a regular attendee for shows by my friends' band Girlfriend, among others.

One of my favorite experiences was one night when I happened to drop in after seeing Lush at Irving Plaza, and there they were, sitting in the second booth! I was majorly obsessed with the band at the time (like all things 4AD) and was especially smitten with Miki Berenyi. I took a risk and made an ass out of myself to say hello to them all and tell them what a great show it was. Sadly the band later ended with the tragic loss of their drummer, but that memory remains one of my favorites.

These days, I'm still playing music in a new band called Automatic Children, also out of New York City, with Rob McCulloch, of Supple, producing."

Adam Lippman
Supple/Automatic Children

"The first time I met Elliott Smith in Luna was when I just happened to stop by to say hello to Harri and have a beer before heading back to my apartment on 14th Street. Was kind of early, the bar was probably just open for a hour or so, when I came in. Harri was talking to Elliott at the end of the bar, close to the door where the bartenders enter, by the jukebox. I came in and sat somewhere in the middle of the bar. There were only a few other people and it seemed there might have been a couple more milling around in the back live room. When Harri saw me he said,

"Hey Joooohhhnnnny", in his Finish-American accent and called me over. He introduced me,

"Hey this is my friend, Johnny. He is a singer songwriter as well. John, this is Elliott". So, I sat on that end of the bar.

Elliott was very nice, very shy in a way, spoke very softly with his trucker hat on and bangs hanging down almost covering his eyes. To be honest, I did not know of him or who he was at that time and only later that week, or so, realized he was the guy from Heatmiser. I had heard about the band but had never seen a picture of the musicians.

We chatted for a while about songs that where coming on the stereo in the bar, and about guitars. I told him I just bought an old Guild acoustic, from the late 60`s, and was so proud of it. I asked him if he had played in the bar and he said once in a while, doing acoustic sets. He told me he really liked to play in Luna Lounge, to try out new songs and such. I told him that I agreed, that the venue was the perfect size stage and place to be with the crowd while you play. I said I would come and check him out next time he played. A few months later, I saw him on television doing a song live, from the Goodwill Hunting soundtrack, to some surprise!

A few weeks after that, I bumped into Elliott in Luna Lounge again, when it was very crowded. He told me he had just finished a solo acoustic set, and I told him that I was sorry I missed it. I just got off of work. We chatted a bit more about music and I told him that I had his latest album and really liked his other band, Heatmiser, as well. He seemed to crack a little smile which was nice to see.

After that, I was able to make, what I think was one of his last shows in Luna Lounge, before his heading out to L.A. to live. As a songwriter myself, I really appreciated his lyrics and the brief chance of meeting and talking to him. I could understand a bit of his personality in the songs. Very nice fellow.

Later, hearing of his death, it shocked me just a bit, but not to the bone. Through the years, a lot of my friends were lost by way of drugs or other self inflicted means. It is interesting to know that being a part of the Luna Lounge scene meant you could meet people of all types and enjoy music together. Luna was almost always my first and last stop on our night out on Ludlow Street."

John Tirado
The Nash

"We spent so much time at Luna and were so comfortable, it felt like we were at a house party. I remember, Rob [my boyfriend and drummer in Lotion, and now, husband] and I were going through a bloody mary stage, and there was never any tomato juice at Luna, so we started bringing our own. Every time we did that, inevitably someone else would see us drinking them and order one. Harri would tell the patron that we brought our own juice and might point the person out to us if we were nearby. We'd consider the person, and if we deemed him or her worthy, we'd let them have a bloody, using our juice."

Kim Youngberg

"I had a memorable meeting at Luna in 1999. At the time, my band Junk Male, just finished our set and were hanging out by the bar when I noticed Elliott Smith sitting quietly by the bar sipping a beer. By chance, I was speaking with one of his crew and he asked if I'd like to say hi to him. I walked over, introduced myself, and praised his latest album, *XO*, telling him I heard the George Harrison influences in some of his songs. He thanked me and when I asked what he was up to next, he casually said he was going to be on Saturday Night Live and then off to tour Europe. I was struck by his humility and unaffected way he dealt with his sudden pseudo-stardom. I'm still saddened that he's no longer with us. In my opinion, he was one of the all-time greats."

Larry May

"I miss those times, to me it feels like things really changed after Luna closed. The whole neighborhood went down hill!
I still miss the Ramones like crazy and I still have a hard time believing I got to tour with them around Europe, a band I had loved since I was six years old, even stranger that they are all dead, apart

from the drummers.

You gave me my first ever job in N.Y.C., at Luna Lounge, and it was as a bar-back, of some sort. It felt a little odd seeing a lot of the music industry folk that I had just a few years previously worked with, drinking and partying at the bar, and here I was, just a few short years later, cutting limes for their gin and tonics! I enjoyed it. I have never forgotten how cool you and Dianne were to me.

Also, I think [my previous band] Birdland had an after show party at the Mission. It was the first time me and Monica got together, after first meeting at Birdland's show in New Jersey. We had limo's outside and my dad was hanging out. Monica took me home to her little place around the corner from the Mission on Avenue B, after the party. I remember the tramps in the middle of the street sitting round a fire outside her apartment. So, of course, I was suitably impressed enough to begin a relationship that would bring me back to stay here for the next fourteen years, without ever going back to the U.K..

Actually, I just got my green card two weeks ago, I still can't believe I'm free now. I still don't want to go back."

Lizzy Lee Vincent

"Living two blocks away from the Luna the whole time it was open was special to me. I sure spent enough time there drinking and watching bands."

Jack Rabid
The Big Take Over

"My old band, pOp*stAr*kiDs, played our first Luna Lounge show in February or March of 2001, and over the course of our six-year tenure, we made Luna a regular stop. Right from the get-go, our fans always had a great time at those shows, and I'm convinced that the reason for this was that Rob, Dianne, and the staff were good people who cared about what they were doing, and this vibe invariably trickles down in a rock club. The bands are happier, the audiences are happier.

One Luna show that I'll never forget took place on Sept 21st, 2001, just ten days after the terror attacks of 9/11. After the Trade Center went down, there was a somber pall over all of NYC for a long time afterward. As the twenty first approached, I wasn't even sure if we should do the show, would our brand of mischievous, joyful electro-rock seem disrespectful so soon after this horrific event? Would people be ready to rock again? There were songs that I knew we most definitely could NOT play: "Jumbo Jet", "Do the Crash". Everything just seemed so *inappropriate.* After a band meeting, though, we decided to do the show. After all, canceling would have been tantamount to letting the terrorists win, right?

On the night of the twenty first, Luna Lounge was packed, and there was a bristling energy in the air. To our surprise and relief, the place went bananas for us that night. It seemed like everyone wanted a break from mourning, and the show was an explosive catharsis. After, a good friend told me, "You guys vanquished demons tonight!" It was a very emotional, very joyful, electric night and one of the best gigs I've ever played.

Luna Lounge was the kind of place where people felt loose and comfortable as soon as they walked through the door, and it's hard to imagine a show like this going off so well at any other venue. Thanks, Rob, for all the support, and for caring about what you do."

andee blacksugar
Vocals and guitars

"Luna Lounge was the place. Hands down – best room in New York City. The closing of Luna Lounge was a huge blow in the East Village and was also the end of an era. Not only for a massive group of folks that partied there and joined up every weekend but also for my band, pOp*stAr*kiDs. It was the end of an era. We played there on a monthly basis and when we weren't playing, we were hanging out. It was our home base. The room itself was not an ass kickin' sounding room to play and the monitoring and the pa system were not totally ass kicking. But, the vibe was so thick in the back room, and by the time you got up to play your set and the audience gathered around you like a tiny encapsulated bubble, that shit was incredible. Magical. You forgot about the shotty sound system and monitors that you couldn't hear. You just played your set and blasted off into another world. That's what made Luna Lounge so special for me.

Dianne and Rob became big fans of the band. On any given night, when you stopped in for a beer, our music was playing in the juke box. I mean, these guys were totally all about the independent scene. They lived it and they walked it like they talked it, totally committed to the local band scene. It was a genuinely supportive scene, which if you've ever played in a band, you will rarely get to experience.

We used to get dressed in the basement of the club because there was no green room. Rob would open the doors for us and let us just hang out downstairs with the inventory of beer and kegs littered around the basement. We were so amped up to play and just ready to explode. When the club was really packed it was just insane. It was so packed you could barely move and get your equipment up on stage. Those moments, hanging out with Andee, JB and Clancy, just moments away from live musical destruction, that was the rush of blood to my head to which I always looked forward. I miss it. I miss that club. It was pure magic."

Glenn Schloss
Keyboard / Tambourines / Back Flips / Samples

"Wheatus didn't fit in on The Lower East Side. I would kid myself that we were CheapTrick-ish enough to pull it off, but we weren't. Then, Rob gave us a show at the Luna Lounge and we were suddenly cool enough to play down there. Which we did, about a dozen times from 1997-1999 when we signed to Columbia Records. Wheatus would never have gotten a show anywhere south of Houston Street had Rob not given us our Luna show. He actually opened up other clubs for us.
Luna was a simple place. It was more like Rob's house than a club. It felt like he'd opened his home to the music he liked. I think people respected Luna more than other clubs because of that.
 Anyway, we started with our friends and family and we promoted hard. I was terrified of letting him down, but it grew to include people we didn't know after a short time. Rob did the sound and that was unique because he was very good at it. He was there for soundcheck. Jesus, who the hell cares

that much? Are you kidding?

Rob also had the best staff in the city. Valentino kinda ran the front room. He did the door as well. He once said to me,

"Every time you guys play here I get my ass kicked, so you must be doing something right." I felt bad.

It was a privilege to play there because there was no competition in it. No contest. If you brought a crowd you had the place for the night. All the people who came could stay and hang out after the show. There was no cover charge so fancy guest list arguments never happened. I don't think Rob ever did the whole 'crowd gets kicked out after the first set of bands' thing either. I think the reason he was able to do that was because he could pick great bands. I can't ever remember disliking any of the other acts we played with there. No filler at Luna Lounge, never ever.

When we had our hit overseas [Teenage Dirtbag] I knew we had to go back and hit Luna again. In the fall of 2004 Rob gave us a residence of four Saturdays in October-November. They were the best shows I can remember. The last night was the best. The following morning it was eighty degrees and sunny. We'd gotten in at five am from the show and I was in no shape to ride but I decided to head out on my BMX bike anyway. It was to be the perfect conclusion to four perfect weeks. I broke my collar bone that day doing dirt jumps. I wrote a song about it. I cannot perform the song properly unless I imagine myself on the stage at Luna.

Luna moved to Brooklyn right around the time that I did. We had a farewell show for my sister Liz there in 2007. I thought we had it made and that Luna would would be our hometown show place forever. Alas, it was not to be.

For so many reasons Luna is the setting for

imaginary performances. I dream that place all the time, red paint, easy lights. It is now and always will be the backdrop of my musical life. Thanks Rob."

brendan b brown
Wheatus

"During it's tenure, Luna Lunge became the L.E.S. epicenter for indie bands. There hasn't really been a venue in that neighborhood that has stepped up to take its place. Luna Lounge was great at booking up-and-coming talent. The sound was good on stage, and in the audience, and you could tell the engineers took special care of the equipment.

There was a mutual respect between bands. This probably came about because the venue had a musician centric vibe which I think attracted a certain caliber of artists. Also, the venue did a nice job of booking bands from the same ilk. I remember during soundcheck, we saw another band load in with the same Korg analog synth we use and we instantly became buds! We looked forward to meeting the other artists and sometimes that would lead to a connection. I became friends with some of the other bands I met playing at Luna (The Vita-men, The Supertones.) Also, as an up and coming band,it was cool to be listed on the Luna website alongside bands like Interpol and The Strokes. Maybe it "stroked" our egos, but I think we performed better because of it."

David Oromaner
Drums
Changing Modes/Marianne Pillsbury

"Luna seemed to sense if a band was serious or honest and had talent and wasn't trying to make you feel like shit for simply existing. It was a stage for fuck's sake and I wanted to play on it and people wanted to see what was on it. That was a big factor at the time.
A weird thing about my band is every time we played someone in the band got laid. Luna was particularly good for that. Plus people went there for the music and would line up to see it. And the soundman had hearing. Weird."

Dylan Nirvana

"Luna' closing down was when I knew the Lower East Side was a place in which I had no future. It just was a sign that a new, less friendly community culture had basically swallowed up the neighborhood.
I have lived on Stanton Street for almost three decades and was often at Luna. Surprisingly, I never played there because I thought my music was, well, not so fun for a walk-in crowd. A little somber... But, I loved going there; to just walk in and hear something magical and feel spontaneous energy in a real music obsessed crowd. Often, I went to see my bandmates' group, Barbez, among others, but I would also go to meld with the crowd. The bartenders were always nice. I was otherwise a hermit so it was good to have a place to head. I had gone to Ludlow Cafe fifteen years earlier, on the block, with my electric typewriter, to sit and write poetry in the corner and have vegetarian chili."

Rebecca Moore

"An early incarnation of The Compulsions played Luna Lounge a few times back when it was on Ludlow Street. We always had a great time there. My most vivid Luna Lounge memory was when a guy rushed up to me after a Compulsions show to say how much he loved us. He also said he recognized my lady friend from the gym. Evidently, he and some other guys at Crunch would position themselves behind her on the Stairmaster so they could stare at her ass. He then got all embarrassed and apologized for being out of line. It was an awkward moment. I said,
"Don't worry about it. If I went to the gym, I'd work out behind her too."

Rob Carlyle
The Compulsions

"If your band was any good, the soundman would not have been eating a sandwich during your set." Rob Sacher to Tyson Lewis (now of Hopewell) - 2002

"Thinking back, you made a pretty strong argument. I must have taken it to heart, as I've never seen anyone eat a sandwich during a Hopewell set! Some seriously funny shit, though..."

Tyson Lewis

"Once we played Luna a few times, we started getting shows at other places much easier. Luna was really accommodating to the bands, and that was especially important for the unproven bands that were trying to get something going. You could walk in any night and discover bands without the inhibitor of a cover charge. It was great for the listeners and the bands. Luna had good line-ups in there..."

Chris Brocco
The ios

"One cool memory I have of playing Luna was on a Sunday afternoon which was one of our first gigs there, and I think we went on at 6 or 7. And although not many people were there, Elliott Smith sat in and watched most of our set which was a thrill for us. I gave him a copy of our CD, *A Knock Out in Slow Motion*, and he said he loved the title."

Christian Edwards
Locket

"We first learned of the Luna Lounge on a Friday night in 2003. While in New York, we stopped by to see Cordalene, another Philadelphia band. We had wanted to set-up a show with them in Philadelphia for a long time, and we were grateful to get a chance to catch the end of their set and meet them. The room was packed as we worked our way through the crowd to get to the front of the stage. We were blown away by the incredible energy from the band and the audience. In short, we first entered the Luna Lounge as fans. We returned to Luna for a few incredible shows ourselves. Somehow, our draw always exceeded our expectations. Hanging out with our friends from New York and reconnecting with some high school crushes we hadn't seen since puberty, made those Luna Lounge shows priceless. And, all that reconnecting, breaking margarita glasses, spotting James Iha, from the Smashing Pumpkins, outside the door of our show, definitely incorporated good energy into our performance.

Joel Blecher
The Perfectionists

"It was the right venue at the right time, a perfect size room to squeeze in your crowd and create a lot of excitement. The acoustics of the space were lively and you had to play with lots of dynamics. The sound engineers and bartenders were cool, friendly and low key. There was also an amazing jukebox that played great music including some local artists.

Luna had an underlying punk rock sensibility, like CBGB's, it was OK to be quirky, to play loud, to be yourself. The room was usually low lit and it just had this incredible vibe. When you played a gig at Luna you just felt like you were part of something special, a collective musical community. Luna was the place you went to check in with that community.

Luna embodied the spirit of rock and roll in a very unpretentious way. Few music clubs are able to balance all these elements but Luna did it with grace and ease."

Brandon Wild
Thisway

"I was the lead singer and drummer for the band, Mold, from 1993-1999. Rob took a shining to us and booked us regularly at Luna. Rob suggested that I step out in front of my drum set and just concentrate on singing for some or all of our set. I took his advice, at the right time too because I was pregnant with my daughter, Stella, and didn't have the desire to lug my drums around at that time. Luna was a great place to see music. I saw Elliott Smith, Longwave, and so many other great bands there.

Probably in about 2007, I ran into Rob outside his new Luna Lounge location which was in Williamsburg. We were standing outside before a Dean & Britta show (Dean Wareham of Galaxie 500 and Luna, and Britta of Belltower and Luna.) It was then Rob told me that the name for Luna Lounge was inspired by the band, Luna (one of my favorite bands of all time.) I miss Luna Lounge. The community, the vibe, and playing there.

Christy Davis

"FIRST IMPRESSIONS ARE LASTING. Eighteen years ago, I attempted to hand deliver to Rob a demo tape of my band, Sweet Little Roxana. Trying to become rock stars, we had high hopes of playing at Luna Lounge. As he headed toward the door of the club, I cornered him and began my spiel. Having freshly arrived from super polite Canada, I fully expected to be greeted with open arms. I was shocked when my advance was not received that way.

"Can you mail your demo to me?" Rob asked as he tried to escape.

"But it's right here. I can hand it to you. We're both right here." Turning back as he walked into

the night, he simply replied,
"It'll be better if you just mail it to me."
Needless to say, years later, we finally played...
Fast forward, present day: Rob and I are now partners in a new club called Satellite Lounge. The other day, as we sat at the bar, he asked me for the phone number of an insurance broker. I replied,
"Sure." I wrote the number down and tried handing it to him.
"Could you email that to me?" he asked straight faced. Some things never change..."

Dave Ellis

"Luna was, hands down, my favorite place to play. I loved that it was free for people to watch music, which made it feel like it was all about the MUSIC. I loved the laid-back feel. And I loved how everyone always hung around up front after a show to chat and mingle at the long bar. Since Luna closed I haven't found a venue to replace it. I was heartbroken the day I found out it closed and will continue to miss it like a sweet childhood memory that brings me a mix of joy and pain (pain because it's over) every time I think of it.
Thanks for making Luna!"

Jodi Jett

"We fell in love with Luna Lounge not just because of the foosball table, but because it was a very relaxed atmosphere, almost like you were at a college party but with fantastic music. Even when we weren't playing a gig, we would hang out and see bands that we didn't know.

Performing on New Year's Eve, Dec.31, 2004, and especially on the final night of Luna lounge on June 11th, 2005, felt like we were part of something big."

Eric Butler, Jim Connolly, and John Vitelli
Motel Creeps

"After the Motel Creeps performed on June 11, 2005 I found a seat on one of the couches in the front of the bar. From across the room, I saw Kerri Black, who I thought was an interesting person because I had seen her once or twice before at other gigs and venues around the city. I think it was her birthday that evening because I saw people giving her well wishes and hugs.

Meanwhile, two random female fans of Motel Creeps sat down beside me and we chatted. After a few minutes or so, one of them began licking my ear. I looked over to see where Kerri Black was because I wanted to introduce myself before she left. Eric, the guitar player for Motel Creeps, gave me the signal that I needed to help load equipment, the amps, drums, and guitars into our van, and I sadly excused myself from the two very interesting girls.

A short while later, coming back in from packing up the van, I approached Kerri to briefly introduce myself and I wished her a happy birthday. I left a few moments, afterward, with the band. That was officially the first time I met the woman who would become my wife, Kerri."

Greg Welch
Motel Creeps

"It seemed like a time for a hopeful resurgence in the music scene in NYC in 1997. Newly moved, and settling in, I was trying to become accustomed to the scene and see where I fit in. Ludlow Street was the place to be at night. Everyone had a local favorite, Max Fish (known for its punk history), Pink Pony, and Route 66. Amongst those, was a place called Luna Lounge, the place everyone would go to start off their evening, and meet friends. There was Valentino, the doorman, the inviting bar, the couches, the foosball table, and the magical back room that hosted at least three or four bands a night. Luna was a dive-y club where you could witness someone possibly on the verge of greatness.

My band, AERIAL LOVE FEED, was trying to resurrect the 90's era shoegaze sound, since this was especially lacking in NYC. One of our first shows took place at Luna Lounge, and we continued to play Luna for years. There were all sorts of mixes of people who would frequent Luna, and the way the sound emerged from the back room and into the bar was a great way to introduce your sound to fellow scenesters.

The best show I was a part of was, ALF, Skywave, [with members evolving into A Place To Bury Strangers and Ceremony], and Apollo Heights, all on one bill. A friend of mine recently commented, "Remember that bill? That was insane!" I was proud to see our upcoming show posters plastered on the huge front windows facing Ludlow Street. I saw Interpol in their early stages here, as well as The Strokes. It was an exciting time, and I will remember it forever.

At one point, my bassist moved into an apartment down the street from Luna. I recall some pre-show parties at his place, and would walk down the street and party all night at Luna, then sometimes invite the entire party, from Luna, back to his apartment. It was a wonderful, exciting, and energetic feeling that radiated from the Luna Lounge. "

Wade Settle

"The Inevitable Breakups was scheduled to play Luna Lounge for the CMJ Music Marathon 2001, which unfortunately coincided with Sept. 11th. My brother, and bassist, and I lived downtown in Chinatown but had to re-locate to the folks' house in New Jersey, since the police had cordoned off our street, with no access, for several days. Rob emailed us, and asked us if we'd still like to play the show, even though CMJ was to be rescheduled for dates in October. He felt people might want or need an escape after a traumatizing week. I could have probably used that escape, as up until that point I had remained on the sofa, watching the news for three days straight. We regretted not being able to play that show, but fortunately some bands did, and it was a case of New Yorkers trying to help and contribute something positive in any way possible. I heard that it was greatly appreciated by those who came out.

Later, Rob asked us to play New Years Eve on Dec. 31, 2001. NYC was a surreal place at that time. After 9/11, people were on edge with anthrax scares and worry about any type of suspicious activity. There was a lot of news about New Year's Eve security in the media. I've always thought that the best way to spend New Years Eve is to be playing a show. We played at 11PM, ending just prior to midnight.

The TVs at Luna were showing the ball drop from Times Square. Plastic horns, noisemakers, tappers, and champagne were passed around. After our set, we somehow found a spot amongst friends in the crowded front room. You could feel a sense of nervousness about what to expect as the minutes ticked down to midnight. I consoled myself by realizing that no matter what happened, I was there with my brother, my girlfriend and friends. Then, "Three, two, one, Happy New Year!" The cheers sounded like any other New Years Eve, but it felt like it was so much more. A weight was lifted when everything went to plan, the toasts, kisses, and hugs. I looked at the TV, almost in astonishment, seeing the confetti in Times Square and all the people celebrating. Best New Year's Eve ever.

I remember asking Rob to put us on a bill with Orange Park, a local band that featured brothers Jeff and Justin Moore on shared lead guitar/lead vocal duties, cousin Jeff Moore on drums, and Harv on bass (that's it, just "Harv"). They always put on a great show and we were fans.

When rehearsing for the upcoming gig, we were having a little fun and ended one of our songs by going into the same D, A, G progression used in one of Orange Park's songs. We kept playing and then added the "ooh, ooh, ooh's" making the cover now complete, or at least as much of it as we could remember from seeing their shows. The progression was actually ripped off from an old Who song, but it's been used in countless rock songs. As a joke, we decided we would play our little tribute at the show by starting our last song, "Tonight", with the "O.P. Intro" as we called it. First the drums and big chord hits (D, A, G), and then the "oohs". When the "O.P. Intro" was complete, we launched straight into "Tonight" and finished off our set.

After the show, I ran into Justin at the bar, who told me he was sitting there when he heard us playing D, A, G with the same drum hits and his first thought was, "oh they ripped off that song too". Then came the "oohs, oohs, oohs" and it hit him, "wait, they're playing OUR song". I think they were honored but also a little bit freaked out, so mission accomplished. They knew our joke was in good spirits. Fifteen minutes later, they rocked their own version.

Several gigs later, we repeated the joke with the Orange Park song, "Are You High Now?" This time, we knocked out the whole song. But, we did it at our soundcheck, just after OP had completed their soundcheck. It would have been too cruel a joke to play the song at the show. You don't usually expect a joke to work twice, but it did, as again they seemed a bit confused, but honored. Justin told me it was cool hearing his song from out in the room, instead of from onstage. I guess I never really thought about it, but it would be cool to hear someone cover your song."

Daniel Stampfel

Seeing as we were a band who initially formed with the sole intention of playing in New York City and then disbanding (the 9/11 attacks pretty much thwarted this aim!), the Luna Lounge was always a special place for us, as it was where we made our Big Apple debut back in April '02. Don't remember very much about that actual show, though, as we all accepted the bar staff's generous offer of free tequila shots before we went onstage – and it turned out that NY tequila shots were nothing like the feeble offerings we were used to back in the UK! (this all made our bassist Chris, pogo during the set, which was more than he ever moved during the entire rest of the band's existence.)

We played Luna again in November '03, only this time with a stand-in drummer, who played with a jazz grip, which disconcerted us all. The incident I remember most clearly from this visit was witnessing a fellow visitor to the bathroom attempt to snort what was left of his coke after dropping it all over the sink (which was covered in grime, dust and pubes). It was then that I realized I definitely wasn't a 'cocaine' guy."

Mauro Venegas
The Rocks

"On a very January morning in 2003, I awoke at a friend's place in the East Village, unusually so. At the time, I had been living on Staten Island, and to make this Wednesday work-commute easier I stayed with my friend. Leaving her apartment early, I walked out into the cold and made a right, but realized I needed to go left. I turned and nearly walked into a stumbling old friend of mine, Elliott Smith.

In 1996, we had worked together on his songs at Waterfront Studios in Hoboken, NJ, where I had been a recording engineer at the time. Since then, we would bump into each other randomly. Once, across the F train platform whereby Elliott transmitted his phone number to me via fingers. Another at Lakeside Lounge on Avenue B, and yet again at a recording session I was working on with

Guided By Voices, at Loho Studios, on Clinton Street. This time on East 6th was different. Elliott was not wearing his jacket. He was cold, not very together, and was just as shocked as I that we were looking at each other in the dead morning cold of New York City. At the time, Elliott was living in Los Angeles but was returning that morning from playing bass on a session with Jon Spencer Blues Explosion. After handing me a CD of rough mixes for his next release, *From A Basement On A Hill*, I helped him hail a cab to his hotel.

Fast forward to that afternoon, I received a call from Elliott. He was doing a "surprise" show at Lit Lounge, on 2nd Avenue, blocks from where we met that morning. This was to be the first musical performance at the venue. A sound system was being purchased by the club and installed that day and Elliott felt more confidant if I was there doing sound for his solo acoustic set. We met at my late-afternoon-happy-hour-bar, St. Dymphnas, on St. Mark's Place. At the bar, he was rested and warm, and having finished my workday, I was glad to be of service. He was not only a friend but also one of the greatest songwriters of our times.

That night, the show was packed and Elliott was in true intimate form, reflecting where he was during this period of his life, just him on a chair with an acoustic guitar and a big bottle of venue-supplied whiskey nearby. It was crowded, celebrity-infused, and raw. After the show, Elliott and I split to hang out at Loho Studios. We enjoyed the rest of the night together inside, comfortable, and awake until another cold dawn greeted us.

Elliott Smith died in October, just ten months later. The show at Lit Lounge, incidentally, was his last performance in New York City. This had always troubled me as a friend and as a fan. "Last performance" just seems not right. The only consolation is that we got to share it together. [Greg performed at Luna Lounge in two bands, Speedsters & Dopers and Sounds Of Greg D.]"

Greg Di Gesu

"I was a regular on Ludlow Street, since Max Fish opened sometime in 1990 or so. We all would meet up there, have drinks; get loose with friends when we were not on tour. A lot of us were in bands. My main band was Railroad Jerk. Some other bands of our friends and Ludlow Street crew included, Unsane, Surgery, Jon Spencer Blues Explosion, Chrome Cranks, Jim Thirlwell, Jonathan Fireeater, and the list goes on and on. We definitely had a great time on Ludlow.

Soon, after Luna opened, I got talking to Rob one night, sitting at his bar, and we realized we had a lot of music in common. I had also been to his old spot, the Mission. We soon became fast friends, at one point we also started doing music together, as well. Harri, a bartender at Luna, and I would go on to make music together too. He lived on Ludlow so we could just go there after the bar closed.

I met Elliott Smith at the bar, some time before he was nominated for that award. We would sit and drink and write or draw on a napkin, passing back and forth.

The back live room was such a good spot to see music, the system was always on point, plus I loved the stage so much. It had an almost cabaret feel and was very kind of cozy and intimate. At some point, Railroad Jerk needed a spot to film our promo video for our fourth album and Luna was the obvious choice. Actually, the concept was partially built with the back room in mind."

Tony Lee

"Luna Lounge was home-base in my twenties. My band, Youngster, must have played there one hundred times or more. Rob and Dianne put a real personal touch on the place and they were the center of a great musical community.
 Of all the Youngster shows at Luna, the last one was probably the most memorable. The room was packed. Rob did the sound, as he usually did, the crowd energy was phenomenal and their response was magical. We had announced that show as our last show with the intention of disbanding. Even though we kept playing occasional shows after that, Luna's closing really marked the end of Youngster's heyday.
 A real community of rock bands sprouted at Luna, it was fertile ground where bands could blossom into their potential. There hasn't been anything like it since.
 I'm still playing drums in a band, with Jody Porter & The Black Swans, but Luna's absence is felt very strongly."

Jared Nissim

"The thing about performance, even if it's only an illusion, is that it is a celebration of the fact that we do contain within ourselves, infinite possibilities." Sydney Smith (1771-1845)

"This quote from the late sixteenth century perfectly sums up the spirit of the Luna Lounge in the late twentieth century. Luna Lounge was all about performance and possibilities: infinite possibilities. There was always the sense that something big was about to happen here. I never saw a band at Luna that didn't have potential and potential in many ways is what makes artists exciting. Potential is Rock and Roll.

I had a marvelous time playing the Luna Lounge about a dozen times between 1997 and the year 2000 in the band, Probe. I also had the great experience of co-producing Kitty in the Tree with Rob for the Luna Lounge label, LunaSea Records. I'm sure I am biased but looking back on the experience, I still believe that both Probe and Kitty had a lot of potential....."

Bob O'Gureck aka Robert Greene aka Buzz Mercury

On Ludlow Street
Faces are changing on Ludlow Street
Yuppies invading on Ludlow Street
Nightlife is raging on Ludlow Street
History's fading
And it's hard... to just move along.

Julian Casablancas

"A musician is never poor; a musician is always rich."
Quote from a Pakistani deli cashier.

Index

1000 Homo DJs, 109
2A, 258
4AD, 95, 111, 331
A Place To Bury Strangers, 289, 348
Aaron Minter, 8
Absinthee, 212, 213, 264
ACE, 148
Ace Frehley, 29
Adam Green, 10, 167
Adam Lippman, 7, 332
Adam Schlesinger, 215
Aerial Love Feed, 226, 328
agents, 146, 186, 294, 295, 296
Al Jourgensen, 6, 106, 108
Al Lewis, 115
Alan Bezozi, 212
Albany, 145, 146
Albert Hammond Jr, 1, 7, 245, 251, 253, 266
Albert Zampino, 112, 127
album of the decade, 1, 20, 163, 268, 274, 283, 284
Alex Coletti, 87, 163
Amanda Schatz, 7, 176
Amsterdam, 151, 153
And You Will Know Us By The Trail Of Dead, 295

andee blacksugar, 7, 337
Andy Blitz, 182
Anna Mercedes, 212, 213, 266
Apollo Heights, 348
Apples In Stereo, 133
Arlene's Grocery, 255, 263
Art Stock's Playpen, 48
Asbury Park, 271
Ashen Keilyn, 240
Asobi Seksu, 226, 329, 330
Avenue A, 65, 66, 77, 79, 114, 147, 193, 212, 258, 261
Avenue B, 77, 82, 96, 104, 193, 335, 353
B.B. King, 164
Baby Jupiter, 254, 263
Bachus, 62
Barbez, 341
Barrowlands, 272
Barry Goldstein, 111
basement, 6, 159, 160, 168, 199, 217, 218, 220, 221, 223, 228, 235, 236, 249, 264, 321, 338
beach party, 59
Bear Creek Studios, 266
Ben Lurie, 105
Berlin, 268
Beth, 35, 38
Big Pink, 6, 72
Big Star, 39, 230, 247, 289, 291
Bill Burr, 178
Billionaire Boys Club, 218
Birdland, 335
Bjork, 6, 75, 92, 94, 95, 275
Black Box Recorder, 15, 99
Blondie, 53, 55, 133, 210
Blondie Chaplin, 53
Blue October, 245
Bob Dylan, 26, 53, 70, 163
Bob Fitzsimmons, 176
Bob O'Gureck, 229
Bob O'Gureck, 7, 356

Boss Hog, 225
Boulevard Tavern, 87, 147
Bowery Ballroom, 214, 257, 258, 259
Brandon Wild, 7, 344
Brian Wilson, 11, 15, 29, 277, 278, 280
Bright Eyes, 283
Brooklyn, 4, 18, 24, 27, 30, 31, 33, 42, 43, 63, 77, 87, 120, 124, 125, 139, 143, 144, 147, 174, 214, 225, 247, 286, 292, 293, 303, 339
Brownies, 202, 290, 327
Bryan Mechutan, 86
Bryce Goggin, 133
Bush Tetras, 50
Byrds, 30, 53
Byron Guthrie, 95
Camper Van Beethoven, 11, 15, 221
Cardinal Woolsey, 214
Carl Perkins, 164
Carla Capretto, 6, 7, 227, 229
Carlos D, 6, 276
CBGBs, 65, 117, 118, 125, 126, 281
Ceremony, 289, 348
Certain Distant Suns, 226
Chapel Hill, 202, 289
Charles Brown, 75
Charlie Papaceno, 62
Cheap Trick, 48
Chelsea, 115, 131, 142, 154, 176, 193
Chicago, 82, 142, 170, 171, 172
Chris Brocco, 7, 343
Chris Connelly, 6, 7, 82, 107, 171
Chris Morik, 188
Chris Randall, 142
Chris Rock, 178, 179
Christian Edwards, 7, 343

Christian Finnegan, 182
Christy Davis, 7, 345
Chuck Beardsly, 101
Cibo Mato, 219
Cindi Lauper, 113
CJ, 122, 132
Clara Venus, 226
Clem Burke, 210
CMJ, 218, 243, 244, 245, 247, 281, 349
Coachella, 275
Cocteau Twins, 105, 111, 150
Colin Quinn, 182, 184
Come On, 265, 266
Concert, 56, 66
Coochie's, 62
Cooky's, 24, 25
Creation Records, 100
Cruel Black Dove, 320
Crush, 88, 126
Crush Management, 88
Dan Grigsby, 91, 247
Dana Locatell, 112
Dana Distortion, 189
Dana Gould, 178
Daniel Stampfel, 7, 351
Dave 'Taif' Ball, 151
Dave Attell, 178, 182
Dave Becky, 176, 178
Dave Ellis, 7, 306, 346
Dave Gahan, 113
Dave Kendall, 7, 82, 83
Dave Marchese, 237
Dave Pirner, 218
David Cross, 178, 182, 184
David Oromaner, 7, 341
David Rockefeller, 10, 136, 137, 138, 139, 141, 142
Dead Combo, 272
Dean and Britta, 295
Debbie Harry, 9, 49, 50, 133
Dee Dee, 122, 123
Demetri Martin, 182, 185
Dennis Diken, 210

Depeche Mode, 75, 94, 95, 113
Dianne, 9, 10, 67, 68, 69, 70, 77, 91, 93, 94, 95, 112, 114, 126, 127, 129, 134, 137, 138, 139, 140, 142, 143, 144, 145, 146, 147, 148, 149, 150, 151, 152, 153, 154, 155, 157, 159, 162, 170, 184, 188, 189, 191, 192, 193, 199, 218, 220, 223, 227, 228, 233, 247, 248, 258, 291, 293, 300, 303, 321, 327, 330, 335, 336, 337, 355
Dick James Music, 40, 41, 42
Dick Manitoba, 127, 128
Dinosaur Jr, 273, 295
Dirty On Purpose, 226
DL Hughley, 178
Donna, 8, 23, 33, 34
Doppler effect, 259
Dresden, 151, 152
Dublin, 14
Dudley Gaffin, 188
Dylan Nirvana, 7, 341
East Village, 6, 9, 65, 66, 67, 77, 78, 79, 80, 81, 83, 86, 95, 97, 119, 140, 142, 148, 154, 155, 156, 179, 193, 194, 202, 212, 213, 228, 256, 258, 296, 337, 352
Eating It, 10, 176, 177, 178, 181, 186, 188
Ed Helms, 183
Ed Rogers, 7, 326
Eddie Pepitone, 182
El Duce, 134, 135
Electric Angels, 88, 100
Electric Lady Studios, 39
Electric Light Orchestra, 29
Elliott Lloyd, 6, 9, 73, 74, 76
Elliott Smith, 6, 10, 15, 195, 196, 198, 200, 201, 202, 203, 206, 207, 208, 247,
288, 291, 300, 322, 323, 332, 334, 343, 345, 352, 354
Elvis Presley, 20, 21, 56, 164
Elysian Fields, 171
Emma Peel, 272
Endsongs, 237, 243
England, 27, 89, 99, 113, 148, 150, 243, 261, 269, 271, 273
Eric Altesleban, 274
Eric Butler, 7, 347
Eric J. Toast, 273
Estonia, 280, 282, 289
Eugene Mirman, 182, 188
Falcon, 218, 237, 249
father, 8, 17, 19, 21, 23, 33, 34, 38, 108, 139, 140, 147, 153, 176, 219, 220, 299, 303, 305
Fez, 199
Foetus, 170, 171
Fooled By April, 218, 224, 226, 230, 289
Foosball, 163, 190
Fort Lauderdale, 48
Fountains Of Wayne, 15, 214, 215, 269, 275, 277
Fred, 111, 112, 113, 126, 127, 129
Fredric Schreck, 111
French Kicks, 15, 222
Front 242, 108
Front Line Assembly, 82, 108
Galaxy 500, 99
Gang Of Four, 50
Gary Hardy, 165
Geoff Green, 112, 127
George Wallace, 20
Germany, 151, 153, 289
Gerry Gerrard, 103
Glasgow, 13, 105, 272
Glenn Schloss, 7, 338
Glenwood Housing Projects, 29
Gordon Raphael, 1, 6, 7, 11, 80, 212, 251, 255, 261, 262
Gordon Wright, 224

Government Mule, 143
Green Apple Quick Step, 39, 40
Greenwich Village, 81
Greg Di Gesu, 7, 354
Greg Fitzsimmons, 7, 176, 179, 182
Greg Welch, 7, 348
Guns n' Roses, 272
Gus, 5, 200, 297, 299
Gus Van Sant, 200
Guy Chadwick, 149
Halcion, 213
Harold Kramer, 7, 86
Harri Kupiainen, 272
Harry Chapin, 6, 9, 34, 35, 36, 39
Heatmiser, 206, 332, 333
Heavy Trash, 225
Helicopter Helicopter, 218, 224, 226, 289
Henry Kissinger, 138
Highspire, 226
Holiday Bar, 66
Honky Toast, 273
House Of Love, 150
Howie Gertzman, 125
Howlin' Wolf, 164
Hula, 226
Human Drama, 226
Hurrah, 50
Hurricane Bells, 8, 301, 324
Iggy Pop, 79, 323
Individual Fruit Pie, 226, 273
industrial rock, 82, 101, 107, 108, 109, 138, 142, 143
Interpol, 11, 15, 218, 274, 275, 276, 284, 288, 328, 340, 348
Iowa, 127, 128, 129, 130
Ira Eliott, 210
Iron Butterfly, 39
Is This It, 11, 268, 269
J. Mascis, 11, 272, 273
J.C., 273

Jack Rabid, 7, 335
Jackson Browne, 39
Jaleel Bunton, 210
James, 40, 41, 42, 73, 95, 137, 138, 140, 141, 164, 344
James Brown, 73, 95
Janeane Garofalo, 178, 182, 185
Jared Nissim, 7, 355
Jason Oliva, 8, 242, 271, 330
Jeff Garlin, 178, 182
Jeff Moore, 8, 222, 350
Jeff Singer, 186, 188
Jeff Zimmerman, 62
Jeffrey Ross, 178
Jenn Stamm, 295
Jennifer Charles, 171
Jeremy Greene, 237
Jerry Jaffe, 9, 97, 99, 100, 103
Jerry Lee Lewis, 164
Jesse Malin, 133
Jim Connolly, 7, 347
Jim Ferguson, 162
Jim Norton, 178, 182, 184
Jim Reid, 1, 6, 7, 102
Jim Thirlwell, 10, 15, 169, 174, 354
Jimi Hendrix, 39
Jimi Shields, 273
Jodi Jett, 7, 346
Jody, 6, 8, 10, 15, 59, 60, 61, 62, 214, 215, 216, 218, 219, 269, 270, 277, 279, 280, 355
Jody Porter, 6, 7, 8, 10, 15, 179, 181, 182, 185, 201, 214, 216, 269, 277, 288
Joe Cocker, 29
Joe McGinty, 6, 7, 10, 15, 91, 112, 113, 130, 131, 162, 163
Joel Blecher, 7, 344
Joey Ramone, 6, 10, 15, 52, 57, 86, 112, 114, 116, 117, 120, 126, 128, 131, 133, 228, 281, 322, 323

John Ashton, 91
John Brattin, 273
John Cage, 133
John Carruthers, 113
John Lennon, 29, 117, 219, 233, 323
John Moore, 6, 9, 15, 95, 96, 97, 98, 103, 148
John Tirado, 7, 333
John Travolta, 125
John Vitelli, 7, 347
Johnny Cash, 164
Johnny Depp, 9, 47, 49
Johnny Lydon, 10, 155, 156
Johnny Maestro, 42
Jon Groff, 181
Jon Spencer, 11, 15, 192, 225, 283, 353, 354
Jon Stewart, 10, 183, 186
Jonathan Daniel, 7, 87, 100
Jones Beach, 277
Joseph Arthur, 283
Joy Division, 111
Joy Zipper, 202, 203, 226
Joyce Bowden, 114
JP (the Guru), 267
Judy Gold, 182, 185
Julian Casablancas, 251, 252, 260, 358
Julie Chadwick, 224
Kate Nash, 295
Keith Hopkin, 7, 330
Kerri Black, 7, 250, 253, 254, 256, 264, 347
Kevin Hart, 178
Kevin Shields, 11, 272, 273, 274
Killing Joke, 15, 83, 94, 103, 105, 108, 113, 117, 151
Kim Youngberg, 7, 334
Kim's Video, 268
Kiss, 29
Kitty In The Tree, 218, 226, 228, 229, 230, 271, 291

KMFDM, 108
Knox Chandler, 113
Kristen Schaal, 182
Kurt Ralske, 95, 273, 326
Kush, 263
Lach, 167
Lake Awosting, 62
Lake Minnewaska, 62
Lance Rautzhan, 7, 320
Lard, 109
Larry May, 7, 334
Laura Rogers, 273
Leonard Nimoy, 154
Leshko's, 66
Levon Helm, 6, 72
Lewis Black, 182, 184
Limelight, 83, 142
Liquid Liquid, 50
Little Elliott, 73
Little Elliott Lloyd, 73
Little Feat, 39
Liz Frasier, 6, 150
Lizzy Lee Vincent, 7, 335
Lloyd Cole, 151
London, 10, 13, 99, 147, 148, 150, 261, 268
Long Island, 35, 37, 39, 40, 41, 50, 52, 277
Longwave, 11, 13, 14, 15, 218, 223, 230, 231, 232, 233, 234, 237, 238, 239, 240, 241, 243, 244, 245, 246, 256, 257, 258, 259, 260, 264, 269, 270, 271, 272, 288, 291, 295, 324, 327, 345
Lori, 31
Los Angeles, 148, 186, 200, 203, 204, 205, 206, 207, 295, 353
Lotion, 10, 15, 162, 163, 164, 220, 221, 229, 333
Louis CK, 178, 182
Love And Rockets, 111

Lower East Side, 10, 132, 156,
    161, 163, 164, 169, 176,
    177, 178, 183, 195, 212,
    256, 275, 293, 320, 327,
    328, 338
Ludlow Street, 157, 163, 166,
    177, 191, 212, 213, 221,
    225, 226, 256, 261, 287,
    288, 292, 294, 303, 320,
    331, 333, 342, 348, 354, 358
Lulu, 149
Luna Lounge, 1, 3, 4, 6, 7, 10,
    11, 67, 68, 143, 144, 157,
    158, 159, 161, 163, 164,
    165, 166, 167, 168, 169,
    174, 175, 177, 181, 182,
    184, 185, 186, 189, 191,
    195, 201, 202, 203, 205,
    206, 208, 209, 210, 211,
    212, 213, 214, 215, 217,
    220, 221, 222, 223, 225,
    226, 228, 230, 234, 239,
    240, 241, 243, 244, 248,
    249, 250, 251, 254, 257,
    258, 259, 261, 263, 264,
    268, 273, 274, 275, 276,
    280, 281, 282, 283, 284,
    286, 287, 288, 289, 291,
    292, 293, 294, 295, 296,
    297, 303, 306, 321, 325,
    327, 328, 329, 330, 331,
    332, 333, 336, 337, 338,
    340, 342, 343, 344, 345,
    347, 348, 349, 351, 354,
    355, 356
LunaSea Records, 11, 226, 227,
    229, 231, 234, 247, 271,
    281, 291, 356
Lush, 105, 111, 331
Lydia Lunch, 10, 174
Madder Rose, 225
Madison Square Garden, 124, 216
Magazine, 50, 58, 66, 215, 274

Main Drag Music, 237
Manhattan, 10, 29, 50, 65, 77,
    80, 93, 140, 146, 153, 163,
    212, 213, 254, 261, 286,
    292, 295, 296, 306, 327
Marc Maron, 6, 181
Marc Philppe Eskenazi, 8
Margaret Cho, 182
Maria Montessori, 25
Marty Willson-Piper, 6, 8, 11,
    15, 230, 241, 243, 244, 248,
    291
Master Cabbie Taxi Academy, 303
Masterdisk Studios, 237
Matt Long, 6, 8, 202, 242
Matt McMichaels, 290
Matt Verta-Ray, 225
Max Fish, 169, 201, 205, 263,
    348, 354
Max's, 65
Mayor Koch, 81
Mayumi Nashida, 8, 240
MC 900 Foot Jesus, 108
McCarren Pool, 143
Meat Beat Manifesto, 82
Melinda, 277, 278, 279
Melomane, 264
Memphis, 164, 165
Mercury Lounge, 255, 257, 258, 327
Mercury Rev, 163, 223
Michael Hilf, 7, 83, 134
Michael Jackson, 40, 43
Michael O'Brien, 176
Michael Portnoy, 181
Michael Showalter, 182
Mike Birbiglia, 178
Mike Daly, 226
Miki Berenyi, 331
Millie's, 26, 28
Mini King, 226
Ministry, 10, 15, 82, 83, 107,
    108, 109, 138, 171, 172

Mission, 6, 7, 9, 10, 67, 68, 77, 81, 82, 83, 85, 86, 87, 88, 91, 93, 94, 95, 96, 99, 100, 101, 103, 104, 105, 107, 108, 110, 111, 113, 117, 127, 131, 137, 138, 142, 144, 146, 147, 149, 150, 151, 161, 163, 167, 170, 188, 191, 273, 275, 303, 325, 326, 327, 335, 354
Moldy Peaches, 167
Molotov Cocktail, 214
Mondo Bizarro, 130
Moonrats, 226
Morgan Visconti, 127
Motel Creeps, 226, 347, 348
Motel Girl, 226
mother, 8, 17, 19, 22, 23, 24, 25, 33, 34, 38, 49, 64, 145, 299, 303
Moths, 226, 231
Motorhead, 100
Mrs. Edelson, 32
MTV, 75, 82, 83, 87, 93, 99, 101, 109, 163, 176, 286
My Bloody Valentine, 111, 150, 274
My Life With The Thrill Kill Cult, 82, 107, 108
my sister, 8, 33, 34, 339
Nada Surf, 15, 133, 210, 218, 230
Naiomi Steinberg, 186
Nancy, 63
Nebraska, 323
Neil Diamond, 29
Neil Rosen, 237, 249
Nettwerk, 82
New Jersey, 51, 63, 214, 257, 269, 271, 335, 349
New Paltz, 43, 47, 49, 53, 55, 57, 62, 65, 73, 144, 145, 146
New Riders Of The Purple Sage, 29

New York, 3, 4, 10, 14, 15, 17, 19, 25, 29, 30, 39, 41, 43, 47, 49, 50, 56, 58, 59, 67, 77, 87, 88, 89, 90, 93, 96, 100, 103, 105, 107, 108, 110, 113, 119, 120, 123, 124, 133, 138, 139, 144, 145, 146, 149, 152, 153, 154, 156, 165, 166, 172, 175, 176, 177, 186, 195, 196, 199, 202, 203, 204, 205, 206, 212, 213, 214, 215, 218, 221, 229, 230, 231, 235, 237, 243, 244, 245, 247, 251, 258, 259, 270, 277, 280, 281, 282, 285, 286, 288, 289, 290, 294, 295, 296, 304, 305, 321, 327, 328, 329, 331, 337, 343, 344, 351, 353, 354
Nick Swardson, 179
Nick Valensi, 272
Nine Inch Nails, 10, 15, 86, 99, 100, 101, 103, 108, 109
NME, 215, 274
Northern State, 226, 295
Oasis, 15, 100, 269, 270
Odessa, 79
older brother, 22, 29, 33, 57, 124, 290
Olivia Tremor Control, 15, 218
Orange Park, 218, 222, 226, 350, 351
Oren Bloedow, 171
Our Daughter's Wedding, 50
P&Gs, 62
Patrick Borelli, 182
Paul Alves, 273
Paul Banks, 276, 288
Paul Dillon, 223
Paul Ferguson, 94, 112, 113, 117
Paul Widdowson, 272
Pavement, 133, 163, 273

Pee Wee Ellis, 73
Penny's, 27
Pete Min, 227, 229, 231, 290
Pete Seeger, 26
Peter Jennings, 154, 155
Peter Kember, 218
pharmaceutical, 207
Phil Schuster, 7, 327
Phillip Boa And The Voodoo Club., 151
Phono, 214
Pia, 152
Pigface, 82, 107, 108
Pink Pony, 263, 348
Piss Factory, 272
Pisser, 273
Pleasure Unit, 226
Pleasurehead, 113, 126
Polyrock, 50
Pony Express, 226, 275
Pop Star Kids, 226
Portland, 195, 196, 200, 204, 206
Probe, 226, 356
Psychedelic Furs, 9, 89, 105, 117
Psychic TV, 108
Psychocandy, 323
Pussy Galore, 225
PYLON, 50
Pyramid Club, 66
Quasi, 206
Queens, 61, 111, 120, 122, 147, 153
Radio-Indie-Pop, 11, 282, 283, 284
Railroad Jerk, 15, 218, 354, 355
Rainer Maria, 15
Ralph Avenue, 28
Randy Staley, 229
Ratatat, 275
Raw Power, 323
Ray Davies, 6, 9, 43, 44, 46

Ray Manzarek, 130, 132
Rebecca Moore, 7, 342
Reverend Jen, 182, 189
Revolting Cocks, 109
Richard Butler, 90
Richard Manuel, 70, 71
Richard Thompson, 100
Rick Danko, 6, 9, 52, 53, 54
Rick Shapiro, 182
Ricky Fataar, 53
Ritzer's Bungalow Colony, 30
Rob Carlyle, 7, 342
Rob Corrdry, 182
Rob Dickinson, 295
Rob Lorenzo, 7, 65
Robbie Robertson, 69
Robert Klein, 113, 178, 356
Robin Danar, 249
Robin Williams, 200
Robyn Calloway, 273
Rochester, 231, 232, 233
Roger Lian, 237
Roger Miret, 295
Rolling Stone, 134, 268
Ronnie Spector, 133
Roseanne Barr, 178, 183
Roy Orbinson, 164
Roy Orbison, 27
Ruby Falls, 273
Rudolph Giuliani, 81
Ryan Gentles, 255
Sam Kinken, 295
Sam Philips, 165
Sanctuary, 7, 9, 55, 56, 57, 58, 59, 61, 62, 63, 65, 67, 68, 73, 76, 88, 191, 303, 321, 325
Sarah Silverman, 6, 178, 180, 182, 184
Satellite Lounge, 306, 320, 346
Scout, 226, 231, 232, 233, 236, 237, 240, 327
Sea Ray, 226
Sean Lennon, 10, 15, 218, 219

Sean Schertell, 8, 166
Seattle, 80, 108, 212, 213, 255, 266
Semi Gloss, 226
Sex Pistols, 26, 56
Sgt. Pepper's Lonely Hearts Club Band, 299
Shannon Ferguson, 7, 235, 242
Shawn Christensen, 7, 249, 331
Sheffield, 273
Shirelles, 22, 25
Shonen Knife, 295
Shoot The Doctor, 111
Sicky Wife Beater, 135
Sigtryggur (Siggi) Baldursson, 94
Silver Rockets, 223
Simone Lester, 9, 61, 64
Sin-e, 228
Siouxsie And The Banshees, 105, 113, 117
Sister Machine Gun, 10, 142
Sisters of Mercy, 105
Skinny Puppy, 108, 109
Sky Cries Mary, 212, 267
Skywave, 289, 348
Smashing Pumpkins, 82
Smile, 279, 280
Smithereens, 210
Smitty's, 62
SNL, 178
Snug Harbor, 62
Sonny and Cher, 31
Soul Asylum, 218
sound engineer, 44, 166, 209, 211, 245, 246, 249, 251, 290
Spaceland, 205, 206
Spacemen 3, 218
Spectrum, 218
Speedball Baby, 225
Speedies, 50
St. Marks, 268
Stanley Demeski, 210
Stanton Street, 263, 341

Stefanie Haynes, 144
Stellastarr*, 15, 218, 288, 295, 331
Stephan Cherkashin, 7, 320
Stephen Malkmus, 11, 272, 273
Steve Brockway, 190
Steve Kilbey, 8, 318, 321
Steve Rubell, 124
Steve Schiltz, 6, 7, 8, 13, 231, 238, 239, 240, 244, 256, 270, 291, 300, 301, 324
Steve Wickins, 227
Steve Young, 41, 42, 66
Steven Schirripa, 182, 185
Studio 54, 50, 124, 125, 126
Stupid, 226
Sun Studio, 10, 164, 165
Susan Collins, 29, 30
Sydney Smith, 356
Tabitha Tindale, 7, 202
Tammy Faye Starlight, 182
Tampa, 17, 19, 21
Taoist, 196, 208
Teardrop Explodes, 50
Teddy Thompson, 245
Teenage Fanclub, 289
Telltale, 320
Terri O'Rourke, 254
Texas, 107, 229, 324
The Ancients, 10, 110, 112, 113, 114, 115, 117, 126, 127, 131, 226
The Astrojet, 218, 226
The Band, 9, 52, 53, 69, 70, 71
The Beach Boys, 53, 279, 280
The Beatles, 27, 28, 40, 41, 44, 117, 121, 220, 299, 323
The Belltower, 15, 215
The Black Angels, 295
The Black Crows, 269
The Brains, 50
The Bravery, 15, 288
The Buggles, 286
The Chance, 77

The Church, 8, 68, 243, 244, 245, 246, 247, 249, 318, 320
The Clash, 26, 56, 58
The Coasters, 27
The Cogs, 226, 231
The Comas, 226
The Compulsions, 226, 342
The Constantines, 295
The Cooler, 258
The Cure, 50, 113, 138
The Damned, 117
The Doors, 130
The Feelies, 210
The Flames, 53
The Flaming Lips, 324
The Fleshtones, 50
The Funhouse Hotel, 119
The Go Gos, 50
The Grass Roots, 41
The Harvest Moon Brewery, 257
The Hold Steady, 15, 226
The Hong Kong, 226
The Horrors, 295
The Inevitable Break Ups, 218, 226
The Irreversible Slacks, 226
The Jesus And Mary Chain, 1, 10, 15, 96, 99, 100, 102, 103, 104, 275, 323
The Kids, 48, 49
The Kinks, 43, 44, 45
The Knitters, 295
The Knitting Factory, 296, 298
The Libertines, 13
The Library, 202
The Lonely Souls, 31
The Mayflies USA, 202, 226, 242, 289, 290
The Meat Puppets, 15, 295
The Melvins, 295
The Mentors, 10, 134, 135
The Moony Suzuki, 15
The Morning After Girls, 320

The National, 15, 139, 288
The Pipettes, 295
The Pixies, 100
The Pretenders, 9, 47, 48, 49
The Psychedelic Furs, 15, 89, 90, 91, 113, 131
The Ramones, 26, 61, 118, 121, 124, 126, 127, 130, 252, 281, 322
The Realistics, 226
The Red House, 326
the Ritz, 65, 101, 103, 131, 327
The Rogers Sisters, 273
The Scrap Bar, 166
The Seltzers, 255
The Shangri-Las', 39
The Soft Explosions,, 226
The Spinanes, 206
The Stone Pony, 271
The Strokes, 1, 11, 13, 14, 15, 80, 226, 237, 245, 250, 251, 252, 253, 254, 255, 256, 257, 258, 259, 260, 264, 265, 266, 267, 268, 269, 270, 271, 272, 284, 287, 328, 329, 348
The Sugarcubes, 9, 15, 75, 92, 93, 94, 275
The Turtles, 31
The Twenty Twos,, 226
The Vandelles, 320
The Warlocks, 295
The World, 65, 83
Thesis, 62
They Might Be Giants, 237
Thurston Moore, 79
Tim Butler, 91
Timberlake, 40
Timo, 219
Tish and Snooky's, 81
Todd Barry, 181, 182, 184, 288
Todd Rundgren, 29
Tom Tom Club, 114

Tommy, 8, 23, 29, 57, 124, 126, 178
Ton Ups, 190, 226, 283
Tony Visconti, 88, 127
Toss, 226
Totally Blind Drunk Drivers, 11, 280, 281
Tracy Morgan, 178
Transporterraum, 261, 266
Travis Pickle, 218, 224, 226, 227, 228, 229, 230, 231, 327
Trent Reznor, 103, 105, 109, 111
Tribeca, 296
Turn On The Bright Lights, 11, 274, 275
TV On The Radio, 210
TVT Records, 86, 101
Tyson Lewis, 7, 342
UCB, 178, 179
Ultra Vivid Scene,, 95
Ultrasonic Sound Studios, 39, 230
Valentino, 10, 162, 166, 339, 348
Vanilla Fudge, 39
VH1, 176
Vietnam, 31, 33
Wade Settle, 7, 349
Waitresses, 50, 100
Wanda Sykes, 179, 183
Warren Haynes, 10, 15, 142, 143, 144
WDST, 57, 58
We Are Scientists, 226
Wheatus, 226, 295, 338, 340
Whiskeytown, 226
White Rabbits, 295
William Tucker, 6, 10, 15, 82, 84, 107, 169, 170, 171
Williamsburg, 11, 225, 235, 236, 237, 286, 292, 293, 294, 296, 303, 331, 345
Winston Churchill, 118
Witch, 295
Witchcraft, 295
WLIR-FM, 39
WMCA-AM, 28
Woodstock, 29, 53, 57, 69, 72
Woody Guthrie, 26
WPDH-FM, 48
WPIX-FM, 47
Yanni Naslas, 7, 228
Yianni Naslas, 227
Youngster, 355
Zack Galifianakis, 178, 179
Zee, 160, 189

Made in the USA
Charleston, SC
21 March 2012